TRAVELER
OF THE
CROSSROADS

Traveler of the Crossroads

A Biography of Adventurer Nicol Smith

An authorized Biography

by Sharon E. Karr

Log Cabin Manuscripts
Dorrington, California

Cover: Portrait of Nicol Smith by Barnaby Conrad. Reproduced with permission.
Burma Road photograph from Nicol Smith's private collection. Map from the inside cover of *Burma Road*. Reproduced with permission.

Karr, Sharon E.
    Traveler of the crossroads : the biography of adventurer Nicol Smith / by Sharon E. Karr.
    p. cm.
    Includes bibliographical references and index.
    Preassigned LCCN: 94-077271.
    ISBN 0-9639864-1-4

    1. Smith, Francis Nicol. 2. Adventure and adventurers--United States--Biography. I. Title.

CT9971.S65K37 1994   904.092
                                        QBI94-1557

First Edition
10 9 8 7 6 5 4 3 2 1

Cover layout by Imagecraft, Dorrington, California
Printed by Griffin Printing, Sacramento, California

Published by Log Cabin Manuscripts
Post Office Box 4341
Dorrington, California 95223

To
my dear sister
Kathryn Ann Karr Manuel

CONTENTS

CONTENTS

ACKNOWLEDGMENTS

For a biographer, the many surviving letters, diaries, manuscripts, published and unpublished works written by Nicol Smith are an endless treasure. His unqualified permission to search Lashio Lodge and use anything I found was the blossoming of this biography.

Foremost, I must thank Nicol Smith for his help during the interviews he granted to me over a two-year period. His fortitude during a time of declining health made completion of his biography possible.

For more than three years I researched the life of Nicol Smith. Along the way many people willingly assisted me and my gratitude to them is profound.

First of all, I would like to acknowledge the invaluable aid of Mike Macon, who lived with me and this book during the years it was in progress. His all-around good advice made this project flow more smoothly.

Secondly, my sister Kathryn Karr Manuel assisted me in every way possible as the work moved forward. She encouraged, cajoled and empathized with each success and disappointment. She used her vacation to join me in Washington, D.C., to conduct research at the National Archives, drove me to interviews where she occupied cantankerous head maids while I pried information from interviewees and joined me in clandestine searches of ramshackle houses. Her numerous contacts helped me find willing assistants for transcribing, graphics and editing. To my sister I owe a thousand thanks for her support from beginning to end.

I particularly want to thank Nicol's family and friends who gave significant time to meet with me, above all, his cousin Elizabeth Smith Knauer and her daughter Helen "Skeeter" Little in Thorndale, Pennsylvania. Their insights and knowledge of the

Smith family and their hospitality during my visit made our weekend together a special occasion.

Art and Virginia Hall unfailingly provided information, sagacity, shared stories and experiences with me. Art's story-telling ability moved us back in time to the places where the unfolding events had occurred. Virginia's personal interest, telephone calls and assistance when researching Calaveras and Tuolumne County history were indefatigable. I also want to thank their daughter Pat Koehn for her interest and support.

I will be forever grateful for the weekend at Foxlease Farm in Upperville, Virginia, and the forthrightness of the late John D. Archbold. He provided hours of interviews concerning the Archbold family and volumes of letters from Nicol Smith to himself and his mother, Anne Archbold. It was a weekend that will remain a fond memory for my sister and me. We experienced a grand lifestyle at Foxlease that we had only read about or seen in movies. John's style gave me an opportunity to interpret information without his revealing long-standing family secrets. His wisdom allowed me to develop informed opinions about Moira Archbold that otherwise would not have been available.

I treasure my weekend visit with Rebecca "Bex" McBride. She is a lovely person who will remain a friend. Nicol aptly described Bex to me as "the dearest person in my life" before I departed for her home in Arlington, Virginia. Her words painted a picture of Moira that was truthful yet tender. Bex visited her friend Moira every Saturday after her return to Georgetown in 1952 and until her death in 1990. In Moira's later years Bex pushed her wheelchair up and down the long drive at her little log cabin. A true friend always, she made Moira come alive for me. Her son Howard Nicol McBride willingly contributed his childhood memories of Moira. I appreciate his candor and speculation on the woman he knew as dearly as an aunt.

I would like to thank each person who took the time to grant me an interview. Regardless of whether I met them personally or we spoke by telephone, each one was extremely helpful: Flo and the late Andy Anderson, Judy Board, Barbara Bogden, Jane Child, Blake Clark, Lois Clauhsen, Colonel Devlin, Frank Gleason, Bunny Kamen-Longe, Leopold Karwaski, Joseph Lazarsky, Douglas MacArthur II, Nini Martin, Frank and Jean Nicol, Dave Ratto, Joan Rizzo, Elsie Schwarz, Isabelle Taylor and John Timossi.

ACKNOWLEDGMENTS

I received a wealth of letters from people who saved Nicol's correspondence from years gone by, which was a tremendous help. I also thank those that I did not have the opportunity to meet. They preserved Nicol's letters and shared them with me: Flo and the late Andy Anderson, Dr. F. Tremaine Billings Jr., Hugh and Margery Birch of Sydney, Australia and the late John Archbold.

John Taylor of the National Archives in Washington, D.C., provided excellent guidance and suggestion as I researched World War II. His discerning manner and incredible memory sparked new ideas and helped me explore volumes of historical military documents. Through his network he introduced me to history professor Bruce Reynolds at San Jose State University, San Jose, California. Professor Reynolds generously shared research he had conducted and enhanced my knowledge of conditions in Thailand during World War II.

The following historical societies and historians provided information and assisted my research: Calaveras County Archives, Lorryane Kennedy; Capitola California Historian, Lewis Deasy; Columbia State Park Archives and Cemetery, Sharrin Grout; Cumberland County Historical Society and the Hamilton Library Association, Carlisle, Pennsylvania; San Joaquin County Historical Society, Don Walker; Tuolumne County Historian, Carlo DeFerri; Tuolumne County Historical Society Museum, Sharon Marovich; Tuolumne County Researcher, Joan Garusch.

Many schools and colleges attended by Nicol Smith and his ancestors willingly mailed student records: Choate Rosemary Hall, Susan K. Hepler, Lee Sylvester; Convent of the Sacred Heart, Donna Shephard; Dickinson College, Richard Konkel; Dickinson Law School, Special Collections, Marie Ferre; Heald's College in San Francisco; Menlo College, Carrie Rohlfing, Elizabeth Smith, Anna Troesh; Stanford University, Dennis Fau.

Other institutions and organizations also provided assistance in verifying information and historical facts: Bohemian Club, Andrew Jameson; Central Intelligence Agency, Personnel Files; Fairmont Hotel Special Projects Assistant, Connie Hale; Macmillan Publishing Company, Ann Dewell, Senior Contracts Assistant; McGeorge Law Library, Susan Vensuckle; The State Bar of California, Paula R. Bankett, Librarian/Archivist; Sisters of the Holy Names, Province of California, Sister Mary Petra; University of Southern California School of Cinema-Television, Warner Brothers Archives, Leath Adams; Sonora Union Democrat, Buz Eggleston; Veterans of the OSS, Regional Vice President Peter Karlow.

Numerous libraries provided their services during my research. The libraries I frequented included California State Library, San Jose State University Library, Columbia College Library, Salinas Public Library, San Francisco Public Library and Stockton Public Library. Linn Greely of Columbia College Library, researcher extraordinaire was particularly helpful for verifying historical facts and geographical data.

I appreciate the tireless efforts of the transcribers and editors. Linda Heerwagen spent two and a half years transcribing taped interviews. Terry Hill carefully edited and critiqued my first draft and made valuable suggestions. The members of Writers Unlimited provided insights to specific chapters. Vita Richmond professionally edited the final draft and gave me assurance that the manuscript was worthy of publication. Sylvia Hart poured over each detail prior to delivering the manuscript to the press.

Permission was provided by Herb Caen to quote his newspaper columns and Barnaby Conrad allowed me to reproduce the portrait he drew of Nicol Smith for the cover of this book. Mike Rothwell Photography created the photographs included in this book from old and frequently disintegrating pictures. Julie Nolta drew the superb, historical maps from a conglomerate of outdated sources. Her timeliness is greatly appreciated. My appreciation to Peter Muhs and Judy Wilson of Cooper, White & Cooper, the law firm that represents Nicol Smith's interests for their cooperation.

A warm thanks I extend to my family for their interest in my work. Their support made this effort possible.

If I have forgotten anyone in these acknowledgments, I do regret the oversight.

INTRODUCTION

It is nearly thirty years since Nicol Smith retired from his travel career, one that he molded and nurtured from a youthful desire for adventure. Unprecedented opportunities paraded before the young Smith as his longing for new and unusual experiences matured.

His story is one of a life in the making. The ancestry, the history and the family fortune, so often lost and regained, play an integral part in his life and in his career. Nicol Smith was an intrepid explorer, an adventurer, a reconnoiterer of places.

Nicol matured during an era of great "firsts." Charles Lindbergh and Amelia Earhart were performing the firsts of aviation. The first woman Arctic exploration leader and a San Francisco society woman, Louise Boyd was an acquaintance of Nicol's and he followed her travels with the wonder of a young boy. Admiral Richard E. Byrd's Arctic expeditions fascinated him as he avidly read of the explorer's winter alone in Antarctica. The globe presented new wonders as higher mountains, breath-taking falls, African safaris and rigorous jungle explorations took place. Nicol's childhood curiosity about the world was piqued at the age of five when he explored the pavilions of far-away places at the Panama-Pacific Exposition in San Francisco.

The first four chapters of this biography of Nicol Smith presents the arrival of his ancestors in California. They did not play important roles in the forming of the state, but their diverse roles and involvement in the politics of the times illustrates the intellects that merged two well respected names, Nicol and Smith. The earliest arrivals of the Nicol family settled in California after statehood, during the waning of the Gold Rush. The rigors of wagon trains, passenger ships and crossing the Isthmus of Panama were a few of the perils they encountered in their westward journey. They were a hearty stock and farmed the land. Education became the means to improve the lives of their children.

The Smith family settled in Pennsylvania and donated five and a half acres for the building of a new schoolhouse to further the education of their children. Only one descendant, Robert (R.H.) Smith, traveled west to seek his fortune in California. He arrived in the golden state of California a few months after the dawning of the twentieth century.

Following these introductory chapters, Nicol's early life is presented to show the development of his character. His childhood in San Francisco and Burlingame and the influences of his nanny and governess played important parts in the formation of his character. His education as a society child and the bonds of friendship formed far from home were the next phase of his development—the formative years of his adolescence.

Romance played a minor role in his life. Always a true friend, and a friend of everyone, Nicol rarely pursued the heady stuff of romance. His loving relationship developed from a friendship, taking nine years from the first introduction to matrimony.

Adventure and exploration were foremost in his life. Overcoming parental expectations and venturing to little-known portions of the globe were his real love. Even his responsibilities as an officer in the Office of Strategic Services (OSS) during World War II seems like an adventure story when told by Nicol. He conquered more firsts than most explorers. He accompanied the first American to explore Hainan Island. He was the first American to travel the Burma Road after its completion. He was the third party to reach Angel Falls in Venezuela and the first to take motion pictures there. In World War II he successfully led twenty-one, American-educated, Thai men to contact the underground in Bangkok. Nicol's firsts are real and they are varied. Unlike other explorers he achieved notoriety only among those who wanted adventure. From their homes and the lecture halls across America, Canada and England, they traveled safely yet vicariously with Nicol Smith. Nicol was never a national hero. He was a best-selling author, a decorated officer and a noted explorer and lecturer. His career encompassed a lifetime of diverse achievements.

When I first met Nicol Smith, I read the five books he had written and listened to stories he shared with me. I inquired if he had ever considered writing his autobiography. Of course he had. Time had passed and he was now unable to hold a pen to paper. With trepidation I asked my next question. Would he consider allowing me to write his biography? He warmly consented. Nicol and I met twice a week over a two year period to collect information about his past. Twenty-six friends and relatives were interviewed. Two trips were taken across the country to meet his best friend, the late John Archbold, and Moira's closest friend, Bex McBride. Three weeks were spent among volumes of papers at the National Archives recounting his role in the OSS and meeting each of the "Ski" brothers, his World War II buddies.

While writing this biography, I had to separate the myths surrounding Nicol Smith's life and highlight the essential parts of his story. This book does not include all my research. I could fill volumes with Nicol's childhood, career and personal anecdotes. Fortunately, I uncovered information that had faded from memory with each new adventure and the passing of time. His family, their place in society and Nicol's unique career evolved from the research I collected since our first meeting.

As a biography, this book endeavors to present the facts of Nicol's life. Memories and recollections differed tremendously from person to person. I attempted to present all viewpoints in order to present a complete portrait of Nicol Smith.

BOOK ONE:

ROBERT HAYS SMITH

I believe that within a quarter of a century California will be equal to if not without a peer in the great States of our Union.

California offers the choicest impulses in the glorious scenery, her health giving climate and upon all the elbowroom she allows to the individual man. Hence the dominant note of California is that of personal freedom.

Robert Hays Smith
Letter to the Alumni
Dickinson Class of 1898
Written March 1901

1

SETTLING IN UNCLE SAM'S WESTERN POSSESSION

A young man stepped from the train and set his valise down on the platform. Straightening, he looked in both directions down the small Coalinga train station. A few others had disembarked and were assembling their belongings. Four horses pulling a wagon rolled by on the street, stirring up the dust and leaving a fine brown film on the passengers and their luggage. R.H. removed his hat and brushed off the dust. A whistle shrilled and the train slowly began to pull out of the station.

Picking up his valise, R.H. strode through the station and out to the street, looking for the first decent place to have an evening meal. He was tired, hot and hungry and the dusty street wasn't promising to improve his disposition. The September afternoon heat was stifling. Within a few minutes, R.H. found a tavern advertising home-cooked meals. He entered the noisy establishment and found an empty table in an alcove at the far end of the room. As he made his way across the room he observed the other patrons and while waiting for his meal, R.H. listened to the strangers' conversations. He had learned enough during his travels to fill his diary with useful information he gathered from overheard dialogues.

R.H. Smith had left behind his home, his family and his small legal practice in Pennsylvania in the fall of 1900, to find new opportunities out West. He intended to go as far as China, if necessary. He told family and friends he wished "to acquaint myself with the various portions of Uncle Sam's possessions." In a letter he wrote before leaving the bustle of San Francisco for

Coalinga, he reported, "after wandering around for some time, I finally landed in this city."[1]

During the lengthy train trip that finally brought him to the West Coast, R.H. carefully read the newspapers of each region looking for new opportunities. California oil beckoned him. He had a keen ear for useful advice and listened closely when a brief acquaintance at a San Francisco hotel told him a young lawyer would do well in Coalinga.

R.H. already knew the town had once been a center of coal mining activity, as its name implied. Now "black gold" was flowing freely there. A good lawyer could do well for himself without dirtying his hands. The opportunity, supported by the advice of a man who knew the area, sounded ideal. The next day R.H. bought a ticket and boarded the train. He still was expecting Coalinga to be a temporary stop on his journey. His journey to success that might lead him as far as China. Little did he know it would prove to be the last stop in his wanderings.

As he ate, the conversation in the next booth grew louder. It sounded as if two oil men were having a few nips while discussing their oil land speculations.

As he listened, it became clear that the two strangers in the next booth were oil experts and were after leases in the region. R.H.'s interest was piqued. He continued to eavesdrop to learn some of the lingo and tricks of the oil business.

A potential lease was discussed that particularly interested him. He strained to hear every detail. An older lady living several miles out of town had been away for some time. She was unaware that oil had been struck within forty feet of her property line. They were informed by her housekeeper that she was to return early in the evening and they had an appointment following her arrival home. The buggy was rented and it was only a few miles to her place. They had heard she would accept $1,300 for the lease to her land, including the oil rights.

After the two men left, R.H. signaled the waiter and questioned him about the neighboring diners. The waiter confirmed the two men knew their business and were doing well buying up land leases. Obtaining directions to the livery stable, R.H. paid his bill and left.

As he hastily walked through the small, burgeoning town to the livery stable, R.H. decided to pay a call on this lady. Perhaps she had returned early from her travels and would be willing to sell the lease to him. "My money is as good as the next fellow's," he thought.

He hired a buggy and a driver who was quite sure he knew the way to the lady's place. Leaving town at 5:00 P.M. he knew he had a two hour head start. The oil men had mentioned their plan to leave town was at 7:00 P.M.

The driver had no problem finding the house, and the housekeeper answered R.H.'s knock. The lady of the house had returned from her travels barely ten minutes before his arrival. He waited while the housekeeper notified her the man had arrived to work out the lease to the property.

The lady appeared and confirmed that his $1,300 offer was what she was asking for the lease. While she went to get the papers describing the property boundaries, R.H. drew up a simple lease agreement for each of them to sign. Removing his money belt, he carefully counted $1,300 from his horde of $1,500. As he placed it on the table for the lady to count, apprehension gripped him. It had taken years of summer work to save this considerable sum of money. Now, in one minute, almost all of it would be given to a stranger for oil speculation based on an overheard conversation in an unknown town.

They each signed. R.H.'s remaining money was secure in his money belt. The lady stowed her money in a small box and the two enjoyed a drink to cement the transaction.

The two loose-talking diners, arriving within the hour, were shocked to discover that a stranger had beaten them to the oil lease they thought was theirs for the taking.

Twenty-four hours later, R.H. sold his $1,300 oil lease for $80,000 in cash.[2] China was to remain as remote and mysterious as ever. R.H. was in the speculation business to stay.

↩

Not long before, on June 5, 1900, Robert Hays (R.H.) Smith graduated as valedictorian of Dickinson School of Law in Carlisle, Pennsylvania. He entered the three-year law program when he graduated from Dickinson College in 1898. With the consent of the dean, he was allowed to complete the three-year program in two years and in addition he earned a Master of Arts degree while taking a law degree.

Bob, or R.H. as he now preferred to be called, was a good-looking young man, of slight stature, just five foot, eight inches tall. His fine, brown hair was neatly combed to the side above his high forehead. He had a fine brow line over his discerning gray eyes. His clean-shaven face was attractive but not particularly distinguished. His dress was immaculate. He wore a dark, well-tailored suit and vest with a crisply starched white collar, his tie perfectly knotted, tie pin in place and the corner of a silk hand-kerchief protruding from the breast pocket. R.H. was a fine, mannerly young man with a wholesomeness that his Pennsylvania upbringing had instilled. He did not present the image of a shrewd business opportunist.

R.H. delivered the student address at the law school commencement on a beautiful June day. His address, "The Law and the Lawyer's Sphere," challenged each of his thirty-four classmates to honor their profession. He spoke a "few brief words of grateful acknowledgment and reluctant farewell...."[3] to each professor and dean who had assisted them in their studies. R.H.'s speech was considered one of the best student addresses in the sixty-six year history of the law school.[4] The speech was so well received it was later published in the student newspaper for all to read.

Six years earlier, R.H. entered Dickinson College as Robert Smith, arriving from the small town of Oakville, Pennsylvania, some fifteen miles away. His ancestors settled in Pennsylvania after coming to America in the middle of the seventeenth century. Balthazer Smith, his great-grandfather, settled first in Lancaster County, Pennsylvania, before moving on to Cumberland Valley, the fertile agriculture area which became the site of much action in the Civil War.

Balthazer had suffered religious persecution in Germany and was determined to make a new start in America. He was a hardy and energetic man, homesteading his land, marrying after arriving in the States and raising twelve children.[5] One son, William, married Susan Forehop and they had six healthy offspring. Their son, William Smith, Jr., married Charlotte Matilda Gelvin and they had four children.[6] The family was of true pioneer stock. They were tough and intelligent and they wanted their children educated. The Smith's of Cumberland Valley donated land so a schoolhouse could be built near their home.

Robert, the third child of William and Charlotte, was born on January 13, 1877. He and his older brother, Edward, and his sister, Myrtle, were joined by another younger brother, Billy. The children were raised near the village of Oakville in a rambling house near the train crossing.

R.H. attended Shippensburg Normal School seven miles from his home until he left for Dickinson College in Carlisle, the home of Molly Pitcher, the American heroine of the Revolutionary War. An industrious and intelligent young man with grandiose dreams for his future, including political aspirations, he spent his summers working in Illinois on a cousin's farm and saved every cent he earned for college.[7] He left for Carlisle in the fall of 1894 not knowing how he planned to put his education to use. He lived at Mrs. Hausberger's boarding house while attending Dickinson College. Obtaining the degree of Bachelor of Philosophy, R.H. decided to continue with his studies and enrolled in the Dickinson School of Law.

During this time, he felt the simple name of Robert Smith was not adequate for his auspicious future. Choosing a middle name of Hays, initially spelled as Hayes, he felt gave his name an important sound. His college papers were signed with a flourish—Robert Hayes Smith—penned in his beautiful longhand. A year later, he changed the spelling of his newly acquired middle name and dropped the "e." He continued to use this as his middle name throughout his life. Frequently newspapers, friends and acquaintances misspelled the name, using Hayes instead of his legal name, Hays.

R.H. had an intense interest in the political events in China and greatly respected the policies of Secretary of State John Hay. The family wondered if R.H. chose his new middle name out of respect for John Hay.[8] Although it was spelled differently, he may have based his choice on Hay and modified it to sound pleasant. Robert Hays Smith now became known as R.H. by many of his friends and acquaintances, but for the remainder of his life, he remained Bob to his family in Pennsylvania.

At the conferring of his undergraduate degree in 1898, R.H. delivered the commencement speech titled "Our Debt to Science." It opened with "when people think great thoughts, their intellects grow. To think about great things is the way to become great men."[9] R.H.'s plans for his life were grand and he wanted his education to lay the groundwork of his bright future. He continued the speech with an explanation of the religious beginnings of the universe and the evolution of the scientific theory based on the facts of astronomy. He was fascinated with the melding of science and religion. R.H. had already discovered his interests—his lifelong hobbies of astronomy and religion.

California offered everything the young man had dreamed of during his hard-working summers in Illinois. With the discovery of California's "black gold," the petroleum industry was rapidly developing. Demands for converting California's railroads and steamship companies from coal to oil-burning engines, caused a rush for oil in the fields opened in the San Joaquin Valley. R.H. vowed to himself to become wealthy. He hoped his law degree would give him the background he needed to become a legal advisor and not an ordinary lawyer in a practice. He wanted to be a lawyer's lawyer. He wanted to be a business financier, a speculator, an inventor. He dreamed of fame and riches. Someday he wanted to be involved in politics. Writing home to his family about his good fortune in Coalinga, he hoped to persuade his brothers to join him in the oil fields. The family in Pennsylvania was relieved to hear that his travels had ended in California and hoped R.H.'s aspirations did not outgrow the state and cause him to move on to China. It seemed so far away to the family in Pennsylvania.

R.H. had passed the Pennsylvania state bar exam and started a small law practice before he began his travels,[10] but Pennsylvania had not provided incentives to keep the eager young man there. R.H. wanted excitement. He had his future to consider and was willing to gamble. His future never seemed brighter than it did now in California. He wrote to a friend:

> Immediately upon my graduation from the Dickinson School of Law on June last, I set out to acquaint myself with the various

portions of Uncle Sam's possessions.... Being so favorably impressed both with the climatic condition and immense possibilities of the State [California] I determined upon locating here and will here take up the practice of law.[11]

In his contribution to the circular letter written in 1901, a letter in which each member of the class of 1898 from Dickinson wrote a section that was then routed to the other classmates, he told of his plans and emphasized the greatness of California.

Were you familiar with the immense possibilities of this country—you would no longer shiver through your frozen eastern winters and melt in the hot summers, but would come to this country of almost endless sunshine, mild and pleasant in winter, cool in summer. When we look back over the few years and note the trend of events, it would seem that a higher hand had intervened in the interest of this great State. The Spanish war, the capture of the Philippines, the war in China, all tending to open to us the fields of commerce of the teeming east, and now comes the discovery of crude oil which bids fair to rival the discovery of gold in '49, making it possible to utilize the endless, the numberless good things which the great State contains, and will be the means of building up one of the greatest manufacturing centres in the world....[12]

Immediately after his arrival in Coalinga, R.H. set out to meet people of promise and establish himself in business. His first oil lease set him on the road to that goal. Once the word was out about this stranger who snatched a price from under the noses of two experienced oil men, he became the talk of the town. One of the first men he met was George T. Cameron, who later married Helen Margaret de Young of San Francisco and he became the publisher of the *San Francisco Chronicle*. Cameron was an organizer of the Pacific Oil Transportation Company. He was building a pipeline from Coalinga to Monterey, the beautiful bay city on the Pacific, and from Bakersfield, the important center of the oil fields, to Port Costa,[13] northeast of San Francisco Bay. The pipeline was being built for Associated Oil Company and Cameron needed workers and a man with business savvy. R.H. was available.

As he began to work with Cameron, R.H. took the steps he felt were necessary to establish himself in business. He planned to work for himself once he had accumulated the capital he needed. He sat for the California state bar exam, even though it was not required to practice law in the state. He passed the exam on his first attempt three years after his arrival in California.[14]

Finally, Billy, his younger brother, came west on the train and met R.H. in Coalinga. Billy had relished every detail of what his brother had written home. He worshipped his older brother and dreamed of the life R.H. described in his letters. When Billy arrived in Coalinga, R.H. immediately sent him to Bakersfield to work as a tool dresser. Many of the tools that were used in the fields and in the refining of oil were manufactured there. Billy was not even introduced to any of R.H.'s new friends before he was sent to Bakersfield.

Billy had worked hard saving money to join R.H. in California. He arrived from Pennsylvania with nothing. His savings had been spent to pay for his train fare. From Bakersfield he would travel to wherever his labors were needed in the oil fields. Frequently he and his brother encountered each other in the field. R.H. hurt Billy's feelings by rarely introducing him to his friends, and in the few introductions that did occur, Billy was never introduced as a brother. Billy wrote home about his work in the oil fields and this crushing blow from his older brother. He had hoped to be taken under his brother's wing to be tutored and trained in the ways of business in the West. Saving every cent possible, he longed to return home as soon as he could.

Business went well for R.H. He met influential people and his social standing had moved from a stranger to a businessman of wealth and acumen. In 1904, he became the vice president of the National Bank of Coalinga and three years later he became the youngest president of that institution.[15] He joined the Bohemian Club, the exclusive men's club in San Francisco, during the fall of 1905.[16] Two close business associates, William Humphrey, the president of Associated Oil Company who was also in on building a pipeline to transport oil, and C.S. Matson sponsored his membership. R.H. enjoyed the distinguished membership of artists, authors and presidents and frequented the Bohemian Grove, a summer encampment among the redwoods of northern California. He also joined the Olympic Club, the gentleman's athletic and social organization of San Francisco.

Traveling between the Coalinga-Bakersfield area and San Francisco became a necessity for R.H. Business required him to frequent San Francisco and fulfill his growing social calendar as well.

The great earthquake on April 18, 1906, awoke R.H. at 5:13 A.M. in his room at the Grand Hotel in San Francisco. The shaking and the noise from the two-minute earthquake terrified him and jolted him from his bed. He had left Coalinga the week before with business to attend to in the city. The fire that followed forced the evacuation of much of the city and consumed about a third of San Francisco. By then, R.H. had become a Lieutenant Colonel on the governor's staff and was needed in the devastated city.[17] He was immediately put in charge of refugees in Golden Gate Park when evacuees from the fire began to arrive. Everything was forgotten. Business could not resume until the fires were out in San Francisco and the damage had been assessed. The twin disasters of the fire and earthquake caused losses of $400,000,000[18] in the city alone. His time and energy monopolized by his responsibilities, R.H. was unaware that his brother Billy had arrived across the bay by train on his way East.

From across the San Francisco Bay at the Oakland Mole[19] passenger depot, Billy saw the glow of the fires.[20] He knew there had been an earthquake and was told that it had started the fires. No one knew whether any of the city would be saved. Billy did not know where his brother was, or how R.H. had fared in the great disaster. He boarded the train homeward to Pennsylvania wondering about his brother's welfare. He knew his family would ask. He had no answers to offer them.

≁

2

SAVED AT SANTA CRUZ

R. H.'s enthusiasm for California did not abate, rather it strengthened as he became increasingly aware of the state's numerous opportunities. He was meeting men of influence who were making a name for themselves. He planned also to make a place for himself in California business and politics.

As R.H. became involved with business partners and invested in business ventures, the family in Pennsylvania heard from him less frequently. The trips he had made East to visit family and friends during his first years in California were becoming infrequent. He neglected to write his segment of the circular letter to Dickinson alumni during the years 1903 to 1923, except for one letter in 1908. That year was the ten-year reunion of his graduating class. R.H.'s letter expressed the maturity he had acquired since graduation:

> Ten years, doubtless the best ten years of our lives, have passed since the class of '98 scattered from the historic old walls of Dickinson.

> Ten years of structural work, or the formative period of our business and professional careers. How different our views of life, how changed our perspective. What important factors we then were. Everything was bright and alluring. We had but to act and it was ours.

> Ten years of actuality, dealing with the world as she is, not as we supposed her to be, have given us a chance to get our bearings and know our limitations.[1]

R.H. allowed nothing to limit him, not family, money or social status. After establishing financial security with his early oil lease speculations, he began new business ventures. He acquired the proper business attire, rented an office and traveled regularly among his investments. He purchased his first automobile to reduce travel time when overseeing his spreading concerns.

His initial involvement in California politics began in 1906. Politics had interested R.H. since his years at Dickinson, when he followed politics avidly. California's Republican Convention was held in Santa Cruz in September of 1906. The week R.H. spent at Santa Cruz proved to be fateful. The political maneuvering intrigued him, stirring political ambitions and personal concerns about his future.

The convention found R.H. circulating among the Republicans from San Francisco and with Mayor Eugene Schmitz. R.H. had assisted the mayor after the earthquake the previous April. Prior association with Schmitz had warranted R.H.'s appointment during the earthquake and the ensuing fire. Mayor Schmitz had handled the disaster[2] admirably. R.H. knew the mayor was a possible candidate for governor and secretly hoped Schmitz would be nominated, but Schmitz offered his support to James N. Gillett who won the nomination. Gillett was to become the last of the Southern Pacific[3] governors of California to politically serve the railroad's interests.

R.H. learned Schmitz had spoken words on his behalf to the Republican nominee, Gillett. The political favor was timely. Later Schmitz was charged with accepting bribes, extortion and other corrupt acts following the handling of funds for the earthquake recovery.

In 1907, R.H. accepted an appointment to the staff of the newly elected Governor Gillett. His first responsibility included accompanying Gillett to welcome Navy ships to San Francisco Bay. R.H. was given the honorary title of Lieutenant Colonel. His political aspirations were expressed briefly in a letter he addressed to his fellow alumni:

> It is probable that I will be one of the California delegates to the National Republican Convention at Chicago.[4]

R.H. continued to entertain ambitions of becoming involved in politics.

∽

During the week at Santa Cruz R.H. strolled along the water-front, one of his favorite pastimes. Growing up in Pennsylvania, he had often dreamed of living near the ocean. He watched the breakers rolling in, the people playing in the surf and the stroll-ers. After the convention, he decided to spend an additional night and leave early the following morning. The weather was warm that afternoon and a dip in the ocean was in order. R.H. wasn't much of a swimmer and had not swum in the Pacific Ocean before, but the blue water was inviting. Collecting his swimming suit and a newspaper, he headed to the beach house. He donned his swimming suit and found a place to recline on the sand. After reading and eavesdropping on a group of young ladies next to him, he decided the time had come for a dip in the ocean. The surf was cold as he slowly waded in until the waves were slapping against his chest. He took one more step and a wave caught him off guard, washing over his head and sweeping him off his feet. R.H. panicked. He almost regained his footing when another wave pushed him completely underwater. Again, a third wave knocked him down and now he was bobbing up and down, gasping for air.

A young lady on the beach had been watching and wondered if the man was swimming or in trouble. He had not yelled or called for help. The lady stood up. As her friends chatted, she hurried to the edge of the surf. She thought he had been knocked down by the waves and although she could see his bobbing head, his paddling was not bringing him closer to shore. She waded into the surf and with a few swift strokes she reached his side. He coughed and sputtered from the water he had swallowed. He was paddling furiously for the shore, but each wave pushed him under. The water was barely over his head. It was not difficult for the young woman to pull him closer to shore where he could stand on the sandy bottom.

When R.H.'s footing was secure, she asked if he was able to swim. He replied that he had never spent much time around or in water. No, he did not know much about swimming. Embar-rassed, R.H. thanked the lady but she was not about to leave him standing in chest-deep water. He caught his breath and thanked her again. She asked him to return to the beach with her. She had a drink in the picnic basket that would remedy the salty taste in his mouth. Relieved to leave the ocean behind, R.H. followed the young lady to her group of friends and she handed him a beverage. Returning to his blanket on the beach, he sat down to recover from his ordeal, all the time watching the young ladies as they chatted, swam and ate their picnic lunch.

He hadn't asked his rescuer's name, but felt he had seen her before, possibly in San Francisco when George Cameron took him to social functions. When the group began to pack their belongings to leave the beach, the lady came to claim her beverage container and ask if he were feeling well.

R.H. looked at her with adoration and thanked her for saving his life. He was not venturing into the ocean again. She laughed and replied that his life had not been in jeopardy and she had barely helped him. Introducing herself, she asked his name. She hoped to see him the next day at the beach, but he replied he was leaving Santa Cruz in the early morning. After a brief conversation, she left to rejoin her friends. R.H. gathered his belongings and returned to his hotel.

Before departing the following morning, R.H. stopped at her hotel. Leaving his card and a brief note of thanks, he hoped to see her again if she planned to visit San Francisco.

Returning to her room the evening of the rescue, Sue Nicol changed for dinner and sat down at the dressing table with a few minutes to spare. In her personal book, *Chap Record*, where she recorded the names of the men she met, she made two new entries. On the first page, under the heading "THE TWELVE MOST NOTABLE CHAPS," she wrote, "BEST NAME, Robert Hayes Smith."[5] Turning five pages, she entered in chronological order, Robert Hayes Smith. The place was Santa Cruz. The last line was captioned "Opinion." Sue wrote, "A man's man—great!"[6]

~

R.H. had become a prominent businessman. His knowledge of law and his inroads in banking in Coalinga and later in Oakland and San Francisco helped him make various investments. He managed the affairs of other businessmen, often working deals, managing their money and representing them in legal matters.

Writing from San Francisco to Dr. J.H. Morgan, the president of Dickinson College, R.H. summed up his business interests in the following manner:

> By reason of the legal training acquired at Dickinson School of Law I felt I was best qualified for the business world and for this reason, I have devoted my time and energy principally to corporation law, applied to corporations in which I have been and now am largely interested, leaving practically no time to devote to outside practice.... Soon after leaving college, I became interested in banking and was Vice-President of the National Bank of Coalinga at 27 and President of that institution at 30 years of age. Later on, I became associated with larger institutions in this city and Oakland but had no time to participate actively in the management of these institutions.[7]

His political interests continued but were pursued in his spare time. Acting as the governor's personal representative, R.H. attended events Gillette deemed important. He enjoyed his duties as an appointee and welcomed many ships entering San Francisco Bay, including the California, Tennessee and the Kansas. He hoped to further his political career. He became acquainted with Frank Hitchcock, the Postmaster General, who had initially come into prominence as President Roosevelt's private secretary and later as a member of his cabinet. R.H. and Hitchcock were associated in several business enterprises. They traveled throughout Montana and Wyoming investigating opportunities and fishing in their leisure time. Writing a letter to an acquaintance, R.H. mentions Hitchcock's suggestion that he consider a political career:

> In the event of a Republican administration succeeding the present Democratic administration I should accept a position as an assistant Cabinet Officer. His [Hitchcock's] influence in the party would doubtless control such a position and as I hope to have my business affairs arranged by that time so they will look after themselves, his suggestion rather appeals to me. I have always been interested in governmental affairs and when I can afford it, will be pleased to render my country services in accordance with my capacity, if I have the opportunity.[8]

Lieutenant Colonel to the governor of California became the extent of R.H.'s political career. Possibly Hitchcock did not have the influence required to further R.H.'s political ambitions. R.H.'s affiliation with Mayor Schmitz, however brief, may have done more to tarnish his political goals than to help them. In 1907 Schmitz was removed from office and convicted of bribery.[9] He was sentenced to five years at San Quentin, although the verdict was later overturned by a higher court. A more probable explanation is that R.H. may never have felt his business affairs were adequately settled. The next fifteen years brought unprecedented opportunities to the young man. He pursued each one with fervor.

New ventures brought new people into R.H.'s life. As San Francisco was rebuilding, he decided to set up an office in the city. It was time to establish himself in the City by the Bay. He rented his first office at 609 First National Bank Building. His frequent absences necessitated hiring a secretary to overlook his daily affairs and attend to the mail and phone while he traveled.

Following the earthquake, he became acquainted with Rudolph Spreckels who was involved with managing the money to rebuild the city. At the Bohemian Club, he met the astute patent and litigation lawyer, John Henry Miller. Both men found R.H. industrious and quick to access a business opportunity. Rudolph Spreckels would become an important business associate, an extended family member and, finally, an adversary of R.H.'s during the ensuing years. He was the youngest son of the prominent California family founded by Claus Spreckels. His father, a shrewd businessman, had come to control all of San Francisco's refineries. He had established the state's sugar beet industry after financing cane production in Hawaii.

Rudolph made an independent fortune in the sugar and gas company businesses, over which he fought his father. But he was mainly interested in good city government and became a progressive reformer, spearheading the attacks of corruption on Mayor Schmitz. He later became an investor in radio manufacturing through R.H.'s influence in Kolster's directional systems for radio communication, an upstart company in Palo Alto, California. Rudolph lost his entire fortune during the Depression.[10]

John Henry Miller, a lifelong associate of R.H.'s, was a respected California lawyer. John had been admitted to the California bar in 1879[11] following his education in his home state of Virginia. He had practiced patent law since 1885 in California and in several other states, representing many large corporations.

The paths of these three men, R.H., Rudolph and John, converged in what was one of the largest patent cases of that time. All three men were well established in their careers. Together they had financial power.

R.H. was in his San Francisco office one afternoon when his secretary announced an unusual client had arrived. R.H. had no appointments that afternoon but he declined to see him. The man insisted and the secretary persuaded R.H. to grant a brief visit. The man who walked in was disheveled and thin. He introduced himself as George Campbell Carson and politely thanked R.H. for seeing him. Curious, R.H. already planned to hear him out. Never before had such a character walked in off the street. Mr. Carson began by informing R.H. he held the patent for a copper smelting process using a side-feeding reverberatory furnace. The patent was being violated by the copper companies in the United States. He had taken his case before the courts in Seattle but had suffered defeat. He needed skillful counsel. Opening his briefcase, he offered to share his documents with R.H. if he would represent his case.

Whether the claim had any validity was not clear to R.H., although his interest was piqued. He promised to review the material that evening. He needed time to consult with another lawyer. If Mr. Carson returned the following afternoon, he could possibly make a decision about handling the claim. Carson thanked him and returned to the outer office. Speaking to the secretary, he said he had no money for dinner or lodging. R.H. overheard the man and stepped from his office to hand him enough change for an evening meal and lodging. Grateful Mr. Carson left and promised to return the next day. R.H. left for home with Carson's briefcase. He spent the evening pouring over the documents. He called Rudolph Spreckels and repeated the claim made by the strange man. Spreckels agreed to take a look at Carson's papers. The following day, R.H. waited for Carson to return. Late that afternoon, he arrived and R.H. explained his partner was examining the contents of the briefcase. They both felt he had a valid claim and it was probable that the patent had been violated.

The events of those two days were the beginning of six long years of investigation, evidence gathering and attending trials throughout the United States. Forming the Carson Investment Company, R.H. and Spreckels were the capitalists who provided the financial backing to try the case. Miller was hired to begin working on the case and determine who was violating the patents.

George Campbell Carson had been an experimenter and inventor for many years. Often referred to as the "desert rat"[12] or "sour dough,"[13] he appeared to be a poor miner and inventor. Twenty years before his case, in the early nineteen hundreds, he had been offered a job at five thousand dollars a month for one of his early inventions. He was not interested in the demands of a daily job. He continued to experiment. A few years later, he filed two patents, number 1,149,495, entitled "Improvements in Metallurgical Furnaces" and number 1,302,307, "Improvements in the Construction of Roofs of Open Hearth and Reverberatory Furnaces."[14] The patents solved an existing problem with smelting copper. The difficulty was in protecting the walls of a reverberatory furnace from the destructive heat created by the furnace and the chemical action of the bath used to extract the ore. The method of side-charging as proposed by Carson, rather than center-charging the furnace as was the practice, solved both problems.[15] The Carson process fed ore into the furnace through two hoppers on the top near either end. The ore then piled up against the end walls of the furnace, protecting them from the fierce heat and at the same time giving up its values to the central bath.

Under the old system of center-feeding a secondary ore must be banked against the ends and sides of the furnace to keep them from burning out. The Carson system made the use of the secondary ore unnecessary. The new process made it possible to treat seven hundred tons of ore in a furnace in twenty-four hours. Under the old method only two hundred and forty tons could be treated in the same time period.

The first companies to be brought to trial were the Anaconda Copper Mining Company and American Smelting & Refining Company Initially, Anaconda Copper won the case in District

Court in Montana. The facts were not all before the court and a conclusion in favor of the prosecution could not be reached. The petition to the Supreme Court was denied. The Circuit Court of Appeals handed down its opinion in the Anaconda Case and the decree of the District Court was reversed and sent back to the lower court with instructions for further proceedings. Carson's attorney, Miller, submitted supplemental briefs and the case was back in court. The decree was reversed.

The first trial lasted approximately thirty days. It consisted of testimony from twenty-five witnesses and included depositions from expert metallurgists, patent office information, publications and briefs. The material totaled several thousand pages of printed and typewritten information. In addition, there were maps, models, drawings and photographs.

Much the same testimony was presented in the different cases. Each company in violation of Carson's two patents was tried. Lawyers were hired by Miller to represent the Carson Investment Company and try the case in each geographical location. Throughout the United States many companies had infringed upon the patents. A few of the violators were Montana Ore Purchasing Company, Anaconda Copper Mining Company, Lake Superior Smelting Company, American Smelting & Refining Company, Peyton Chemical Works at Martinez, California, and Consolidated Arizona Smelting Company.[16]

The original contention by many of the copper companies was the existence of previous patents that covered the change from center-charged furnaces to the side-charged as claimed by Carson's patents. Evidence was introduced by the defendants to attempt to prove the invalidity of the Carson patents and that they had been anticipated by other inventors who patented earlier ideas. Prior to 1916, all furnaces were center-charged, but during the years of 1916 to 1926 many companies changed their furnaces to side-charging.

Again, the defendants attempted to protect themselves by claiming that Carson provided false representations of his inventions to the Patent Office. Nothing in the evidence indicated this had occurred. The final argument by the defendants was that the copper industry in general adopted the side-charging structure and process solely because of conditions existing at the individual plants and for advantages apparent but not real.[17]

Now ten years later, certain of these defendants remodeled their furnaces to attempt to demonstrate the ineffectiveness of side-charging to no avail. The Judge of the District Court of Arizona concluded that the difference between Carson's patents and previous methods "may be likened to the difference between success and failure."[18] The conclusion was reached that Carson's patents were valid. They contained original and novel features of invention. Carson's methods presented real advantages over the old method of center-charging. The defendants had infringed upon the patent of the process and the patent of the apparatus as well.[19]

On February 17, 1923 the decision handed down by the United States Circuit Court of Appeals stated that American Smelting and Refining had infringed upon the patent rights of the obscure inventor, George Campbell Carson. Wall Street suffered a small panic. The defendants' stock plunged seven points.[20] Anaconda Copper was the first to settle in 1926. Carson asked for a royalty of ten cents on each ton of ore processed. Each company made an accounting of their processed ore, some for a period as long as thirteen years. In addition, they had to pay for the rights to the future use of the invention. It was estimated that some companies owed as much as ten million dollars.[21] Carson's share was twenty per cent, amounting to twenty million dollars. Seven million went to Miller, while Carson Investment Company reaped the remaining dollars. Carson walked through R.H.'s door in 1922 and the final suit was settled in 1929. The timing was superb. R.H. hoped to receive his share in time to buy Capitola-by-the-Sea when it went on the auction block in August of 1929.

↩

The fateful rescue in the surf at Santa Cruz sparked an interest for R.H. and Sue Nicol. Later that fall, R.H. received a invitation at the Bohemian Club from Dr. Washington and Mrs. Dodge. They requested he attend a small dinner party being given in honor of their niece's upcoming birthday. Sue would be in town for a weekend in November and several of her friends would also be attending the twenty-first birthday dinner. R.H. was pleased to hear about the young lady. Although he had suspected she was older than the invitation said, Sue seemed composed and sophisticated even under the conditions of their Santa Cruz meeting. He gladly replied in the affirmative to the dinner engagement.

From the moment he saw Sue again, he adored her. She was pretty, vivacious and especially witty. The luster of her auburn hair, coifed in the latest fashion, set off her smooth skin and pleasing features. She had an elegant, straight nose and sparkling, all-seeing eyes that could cause any young man to squirm with awkwardness. Of average height, she was well-proportioned, always wearing the latest fashion with an air of hauteur. With her quick sense of humor, she was the center of attention among her guests. She graciously introduced R.H. to each friend and to her aunt and uncle. Not meaning to embarrass him, she spun a witty tale about how she and R.H. had met in the ocean. The story was purely entertaining and R.H. was not at all uncomfortable.

The evening slipped by quickly and Sue slipped out to the front stoop to wish R.H. good-bye and a happy holiday season. She planned to return to San Francisco during the holidays for the round of Christmas parties and New Year's celebrations. Sue hoped to see him again when he had returned from his family Christmas. R.H. did not leave for the holidays but spent them with various friends. Another meeting seemed inevitable as each of their social circles grew. Their meetings though were infrequent during 1907 as R.H. was often away from San Francisco during Sue's visits, but the next Christmas season found R.H. sharing the holidays with the Nicol family in Stockton.

Sue's father, Frank, and R.H. seemed to get along well and enjoyed discussing their legal backgrounds. When Frank learned of the young man's interest in fishing, he invited R.H. to travel with him to his property along the Stanislaus River in the Sierra Nevada. He didn't think better fishing could be found in California. R.H. quickly accepted, hoping to build a friendship with the influential lawyer.

As the winter proceeded, R.H. and Sue began to meet regularly in San Francisco. R.H. became a frequent guest at the Dodges and Sue accompanied R.H. on many outings. She joined him in welcoming the Kansas and the Tennessee Naval ships in the San Francisco Bay. On April 2, 1908, R.H. gave a luncheon in Sue's honor at the Fairmont Hotel. They announced their engagement to their friends. The luncheon lasted most of the afternoon, and George Cameron toasted the couple. Quickly the wedding plans to marry in Stockton in June were under way.

～

BOOK TWO:

SUSAN ALICE NICOL

Miss Sue Nicol has the distinction of being exceedingly popular in a social way in two of the leading cities in the state, her home, in Stockton, and San Francisco.

"Society and the Cuisine"
The San Francisco Call
September 30, 1906

3

TWO JOURNEYS TO COLUMBIA

I t was the summer of 1842[1] when young James Nicol and his
lovely Scottish wife, Margaret Lyle,[2] married and began planning their emigration to America. They lived in Johnston, Scotland, where their eldest daughter, Susan, was born to the young
couple.[3] James was nineteen years old when his daughter was
born, Margaret was twenty and they both had dreams for their
future.

A greater responsibility was imposed upon them during their
early years of marriage. James, the eldest child of his family,
found himself burdened with the family home and a younger
brother and sister when his mother suddenly passed away. He
and Margaret took the two children into their home. James sold
his family home and evenly split the money among his siblings.
His portion was saved toward their passage to America.

According to family legend, the younger brother, Colin
Campbell Nicol, bore the name of the family's heritage. James'
and Colin's mother was the daughter of Colin Campbell, the
Duke of Argyll. Their mother had married a common man with
the surname of Nicol. Her marriage was scandalous to the noble
family of the Duke of Argyll and she was disowned.[4] Her aristo-
cratic legacy was continued only through the name of her youngest
son.

When enough money had been saved, the family left Scotland
and paid for steerage accommodations on a ship bound for New
Orleans. Arriving in America, James secured employment as a
school teacher. He had taught before he began to farm in Scotland

and hoped to resume this livelihood when he obtained land. He decided Missouri was the choicest area and the family started northward, now numbering four since James' younger sister had brought disgrace upon herself and eloped to Cuba with a young man. She was never heard from in the years that followed.

The family settled in Missouri where their second daughter, Alice, was born. James' younger brother, Colin, became restless when he heard about gold in California. Each spring he talked about heading west, but James felt his brother at age fifteen, was not ready for the long journey on his own.

Two sons were born during the following years. First James arrived, named after his father, and two years later in 1854, Colin followed.[5] Shortly after the birth of baby Colin, named for the family legend, they packed and headed west to California. They settled in the small town of Pine Log near Columbia, California.

Colin Campbell Nicol could not wait to start gold prospecting. While James hoped to homestead a farm, his brother Colin began working on a placer mine. Soon their fifth child, Sarah, was born,[6] the first of their growing brood to be a Californian.

Tragedy beset them when young James and Colin, ages five and three respectively, mistakenly ate poisoned berries. The two boys died early in November of 1857[7] leaving their three sisters, Susan, Alice and Margaret. The small cemetery in Columbia is where their heartbroken mother, Margaret, laid her two boys to rest.

Pleading with James to return to Missouri where harsh memories would not haunt her, the family left in late spring for San Francisco and traveled by ship to the Isthmus of Panama. There they crossed land on horseback and boarded another ship to New Orleans. The family traveled up the Mississippi and settled in Alton, Illinois, just across the river from Missouri, the location of their previous home. Brother Colin had no desire to travel East with the family. He stayed behind to continue gold prospecting.

The return trip was long and they arrived just as winter began. In midwinter, a son, Francis David, was born on February 17, 1859.[8] It was a harsh winter for the family. With few supplies for the long winter and no place to call their own, James wanted to return to California. In the spring a letter arrived from Colin telling of his good fortune in gold mining. The letter was filled with favorable comments about California and its climate. His hopes and dreams for his life in California included the rest of the Nicol family joining him. Wouldn't they consider returning? He could help provide for them and perhaps even locate a farm his elder brother could begin to work.

That was all James needed. He wanted to return to California, where the farmland was fertile and crops and fruit grew abundantly in the mild, sunny climate. Convincing the tearful Margaret was not easy. She was devoted to her new son and was concerned about how his health would endure the long journey. James reminded her they had made the trip west when baby Colin was less than one year old and returned to the Midwest when Margaret was an infant.[9] Her protests went unheard. Unwilling to put up a real fight, since they did not have a home or farm in Illinois yet, and hopeful about the news from California, Margaret consented.

They arrived late in the fall of 1859 and found Colin had fulfilled his promise. He helped provide for the family by finding a place for them to live and he had laid in a good supply of provisions. Their eldest daughter Susan was enrolled at the schoolhouse in Columbia, while Alice and the other children, Sarah and the baby Frank were kept at home.[10]

Fall passed uneventfully while James planted an orchard on nearby property. He had located a small farm that could support the growing family and with room for brother Colin too. Thanksgiving passed and Christmas was soon upon them. It was a pleasant holiday for the entire family. Margaret doted on her youngest child and frequently visited the cemetery, tenderly caring for the small plot where her young sons had been laid to rest.

Late on Christmas Day, a neighboring farmer rushed into the yard. He breathlessly informed James he was immediately needed in town. Colin was hurt. James hurried to Pine Log and found his brother had been shot. With help he moved Colin home and Margaret, hoping Colin would regain consciousness, dressed the wound. No one seemed sure of the circumstances leading to the shooting. The next day Colin Campbell Nicol died[11] of the gunshot wound.

The death of Colin overshadowed the entire winter. He was buried next to the two young Nicol boys in the Columbia Cemetery. A man named Patrick Flanigan was booked into the county jail on December 26. The following week charges were filed against him for "the crime of murder." He was found guilty and sentenced to the state prison for nine years.[12] From all records, Colin[13] had been an innocent passerby who was wounded by a stray bullet. A brawl had broken out and Colin was an observer along with several of his friends who later testified as witnesses. Shots were fired and Colin was fatally injured.

On July 6, 1860, the census recorder visited James and Margaret in Pine Log. They listed two daughters, Alice and Sarah, and a son, Frank. They claimed all the personal effects in their possession were worth one hundred dollars and they owned no real property. The census listed their eldest daughter, Susan, age sixteen, had married within the year.[14] Susan had attended school but met and married a young rancher, Dan Johnson, from Canada.

Never interested in mining, James continued to farm. He bought twenty-five acres near the settlement of Springfield and nurtured his orchard. The farm's western boundary was the public road that lead from Columbia to Gold Springs, while the south was partially bounded by the water ditch of Tuolumne Water District.[15] The location suited the Nicol family. The children could walk to Columbia to attend school. James' fruit trees and garden flourished year after year.

When the family moved to the farm, only three of their four children lived with them in the small house. Susan had married. On January 25, 1862, their last child, George Woodburn Nicol, was born. He was their second child to be born in California. The family grew, the orchard produced and James sold produce to local stores and miners. Occasionally, he traveled over the mountains to the eastern Sierra mining regions to sell the remaining harvest of an abundant crop.

Sarah, Frank and George attended school in Columbia, while their older sister, Alice remained at home to help with the responsibilities of the farm. The years flew by quickly and a grandson, Richard, was born to Susan and Dan. Tragedy struck again during January of 1874. Sarah, a beautiful redhead, died of consumption and was buried at the family plot in Columbia alongside her brothers and her uncle.[16]

The youngest, George, continued his education at the Columbia schoolhouse while Frank left to study at Heald's Business College in San Francisco. He graduated in 1877 and returned home to begin an understudy in law. His years as a student of law were spent in Caleb Dorsey's office in the nearby town of Sonora, the seat of Tuolumne County. During the Gold Rush, its very streets uncovered rich diggings. Frank found law practice agreeable and became a partner with Dorsey. The practice changed its name in 1879 to Dorsey & Nicol, Attorneys at Law.

Younger brother George finished his schooling at Columbia and became a teacher at the same school.[17] Under Frank's influence, George began to consider law as a profession. Frank arranged for George to understudy law in his firm with Caleb. George began to make the daily trip from Springfield to Sonora and back home again with his brother.

While Frank practiced on Washington Street, he met Edwin A. "Ned" Rodgers, an attorney located around the corner on Yaney Avenue. Edwin was a graduate of Harvard and had studied law before coming to California. His legal career had brought him prominence in Sonora and Jamestown. During 1881 when he was acting as counsel for the Bonanza Mine owners an assassination attempt had been made on his life. He recovered from the gunshot wound and returned to his practice. He encouraged Frank to excel in the legal profession and suggested other career avenues. It was through Edwin that the young man met Adelaide Louisa Dodge, the daughter of Edwin's sister Eliza, who would soon become Frank's wife.

～

Adelaide's mother, Eliza Lawrence Rodgers, arrived in Jamestown, California, a gold rush settlement just southwest of Sonora in the spring of 1854. She had traveled from Vermont to California to live with her brother, Edwin, who was just beginning his legal practice. Soon after she arrived, her brother was admitted as a member of the rather informal bar association of Tuolumne County.

Eliza had been escorted from her eastern home by the disputatious individual, Judge Leander Quint. He had returned to the East from Tuolumne County in hopes of finding a bride. He was unsuccessful, but agreed to travel with Eliza until she reached the safety of her brother's home. She soon married a prominent Jamestown physician, Mark Tyler Dodge. They had two children, J. Washington and Adelaide Louisa. Within a few years, she was widowed and went to work teaching school to support her small family. Her husband's death was never announced in the local newspapers and the mysterious circumstances surrounding his death were never known. She never remarried.[18]

Frank Nicol's career prospered. He was admitted to the bar in 1880 and began his own law practice. Two years later, at the age of twenty-three, he was elected to the state assembly from Tuolumne County. At that time he was the youngest member of the state's governing body.[19] While serving his two-year term, he and Adelaide were married in Sonora on July 30, 1883.[20]

The following year he ran for re-election and was defeated by William G. Long. Then, in 1886, he became the Democratic candidate for District Attorney of Tuolumne County. He lost to the Republican candidate, F.P. Otis. Meanwhile, his son, Edwin Estel Nicol, was born followed by a daughter, Susan Alice Nicol, on December 8, 1885. Both children were baptized at St. James Church in Sonora where their mother had been baptized years before.[21]

~∽

George was following in his elder brother's footsteps. He flourished as an understudy at Caleb Dorsey's legal practice. After completing his studies with Caleb, he joined his brother's business.

The Nicol brothers were handsome young men. Frank was slim, with dark, penetrating eyes. He always sported a mustache, frequently a handlebar style, accompanied by either a trim beard or long sideburns. George was huskier than his older brother, but was endowed with the same rich, brown hair and mustache. George was clean shaven except for the thick mustache that hid both his upper and lower lip. With pale blue eyes, he could command a discerning gaze in the courtroom. George was the more serious of the two, never wasting his words, taking his responsibilities as a public servant with extreme regard. Frank, on the other hand, was an orator and an actor. He charmed his associates, his clients and his family members with his command of the English language and his flair for public speaking.

At the time the Nicol brothers entered the legal profession, attendance at or a degree from a law school was not required to practice law.[22] Instead, the individual studied under the auspices of a practicing lawyer. Prior to 1927, neither was there a requirement for passing a bar exam, although an exam had been offered for many years prior to this date. There was no a requirement to attend law school either. Without a statewide bar association, many local areas organized their own associations to dictate the criteria under which law could be practiced. Unfortunately these early organizations became devoted to social and local affairs and often dissolved due to much infighting. Several attempts were made to create a statewide bar association. Finally, in 1909, a third and successful association began. George Nicol served on the organizational committee.

With increasing interest, George observed Frank's term with politics. He began to consider a political career for himself.

In 1888 George met a young woman who captured his interest. She was the widow of a well-to-do mine owner and had one small child. Julia C. Mock Clark was a prominent citizen of Sonora. Her late husband of one and a half years had left her with his wealth. She proceeded to build a house at the corner of Stewart and Gold streets in downtown Sonora. Often referred to as "Mrs. Clark's Palace,"[23] her home was compared to the finer residences of exclusive Nob Hill in San Francisco. Her deceased husband also left his mining interests and his shares of Tuolumne Water District, a lucrative investment during the developmental period of public utilities. George courted Julia and they were married at her sister's home in San Francisco in 1888.

George had recently been admitted to the Tuolumne County Bar when, unexpectedly, he was asked by the Jones brothers, owners of the newspaper *The Democratic Banner*,[24] to enter the 1890 race for the position of Superior Court judge. In the 1880's in Tuolumne County, it was generally believed to be controlled by a select group of politicians. The paper had just been established by the Jones brothers and a war was on between the stripling newspaper with a large following of citizens and the supposed "gang" on the other side. George was convinced to run after much urging. He won by a large majority in November and took office in January of 1891 at the age of twenty-eight, without ever having conducted a case or appeared as council before any court.

Frank and George were frequently compared. Frank was the orator who possessed a silver tongue and rated as one of the best attorneys of Tuolumne County. But George's career spoke for him. He served thirty-two years on the bench, winning one election with only five votes totaled against him. His beginnings may have been initiated by a political machine and a newspaper, but his later successes attested to his true abilities.

4

SONORA TO SAN FRANCISCO

The Gold Rush days had seen the blossoming of Sonora. With the decline of the search for gold, business was slowing and Frank Nicol felt there were greater opportunities for him in other areas of California. He had purchased several placer claims, including one along the Stanislaus River, where he hoped to extract gold. Regardless of his prospecting interests, he also hoped to expand his legal practice.

In 1888, he moved his family to Stockton, California, a burgeoning town surrounded by rich agricultural land and a growing commerce dependent upon the waterways and the railroad. Stockton had grown in importance during the Gold Rush as a center of communications and trading for the southern mines. Although Frank had built a prominent practice for himself in Sonora, he felt the move to Stockton would promote his career. Travel to San Francisco, where he was becoming well known in legal circles, would also be more convenient. He set up his legal practice, Nicol & Orr, with a new partner, Melvin H. Orr, in the Simpson & Gray Building. Then he moved the family to a comfortable residence on Poplar Avenue.[1]

The family now numbered six. His mother-in-law, Eliza Dodge, had moved to Stockton with them. His wife, Adelaide, was not a strong person and had difficulty with the birth of each of their children. Her mother lived with them ever since Mrs. Dodge's son, Washington Dodge, had relocated in San Francisco. Eliza handled many of the household affairs for her daughter, especially during her difficult pregnancies. The third child,

51

Lawrence, was born shortly after the move to Stockton. Eliza helped her daughter through this difficult time, caring for the other children. Helen Margaret, their fourth and last child, was born in the early summer of 1892.[2] Having outgrown their residence, the family moved to Beaver Street and a year later to North Madison where the family remained until Frank's death. Ned and Sue began their schooling at Weber School.

Frank's law practice flourished and additional rooms were rented in the Simpson & Gray building to handle the growing business. Within a couple of years, another partner, William B. Nutter, joined the practice. Frank became involved with the election campaign for gubernatorial candidate James Budd. Frank was president of First National Bank and served on the boards of directors of the Stockton Library and Pacific Gas & Electric. His legal responsibilities required him to be in San Francisco on a regular basis. He was meeting with esteemed legal businessmen in the city.

Frank's trips to San Francisco frequently included visits with his brother-in-law, Dr. Washington Dodge. Dr. Dodge had recently married Mrs. Alice Lampson Shepherd.[3] Frank enjoyed their fine residence on Van Ness Avenue and the baited discussions he and Washington exchanged on politics. The doctor had previously practiced medicine in San Francisco but currently was serving as Professor of Therapeutics in the medical department of the University of California. The two frequently shared their political aspirations. The doctor and Frank were Democrats. Both were interested in the modernization of their respective home towns, including the development of electric street cars, waterways and telephone and telegraph services. Their conversations looked toward the future of California.

꙳

Sue was becoming a young woman during those years in Stockton. Much later, after she had graduated from Weber School and was living in San Francisco, the local newspaper ran a picture of her sixth grade class (now known as the first grade). The article was headlined with the title "Everybody Knew Susie...."[4] From the time she entered school, Sue, known as Susie in her early years, attracted attention. Her charming manner endeared her to adults and won her friends. Always known as a bright conversationalist, she had young men on her heels as she matured.

After completing her public education in Stockton, Sue attended Convent of the Sacred Heart in Oakland. Finishing her schooling, she divided her time between her home in Stockton and the Dodges' home in San Francisco. She and her aunt, Ruth Dodge the doctor's second wife, became close. Aunt Ruth was frequently Sue's chaperone to balls, trips to Belvedere, the small island in the bay north of San Francisco that was the site of fine summer homes and even to Santa Cruz, the beach resort town.

Her best friend, Anna Peters of Stockton, frequently traveled with Sue on the excursions to San Francisco. It was Anna who gave Sue the gift of a small book for recording all the men she met, the *Chap Record,* on her twentieth birthday. Anna wrote the message, "For Sue dear–with heaps of love and best of wishes for a very happy birthday–from Anna." Inside the front cover she drew a profile of Sue with four men looking at her in adoration from the facing page. All four were looking up at her, probably symbolic of Sue's spell over her male suitors.

Sue's picture was featured on the society page of the *San Francisco Call* on September 30, 1906, just after she had met R.H. at Santa Cruz:

> Miss Sue Nicol, whose photograph is shown today, has the distinction of being exceedingly popular in a social way in two of the leading cities of the State, her home being in Stockton where she is a decided favorite, but she has visited here so much that she is almost as well known as though she were a San Francisco girl. Miss Nicol, who is a vivacious, attractive girl with vivid brunette coloring has, with her mother, spent the summer at Belvedere, but returned recently to her home in Stockton.[5]

Her popularity was an easy introduction to the society circle of San Francisco. She did not need the introduction of her father's, uncle's and aunt's names or the money of her family. Her personality served Sue well as it would continue to do so throughout her life.

Frank felt strongly about his family obligations. After many visits to his mother's bedside, Margaret died from pneumonia in Columbia in late November of 1892.[6] She and her husband had celebrated their fiftieth anniversary four months earlier. She was buried at the family plot alongside her three children and her brother-in-law, Colin, who had died from a stray bullet. Alice still lived at home and cared for her father. George was nearby in Sonora and Frank was a frequent visitor to the area. Their father continued to work on his farm and in his orchard until his death in June of 1900[7] at the age of seventy-five.

The day after services were held for James, daughter Alice passed away from heart failure at the family home. She was only fifty-one and had dedicated her life to caring for her parents. The family that had traveled twice to Columbia now numbered only three. Susan Nicol Johnson still resided in Columbia, George was in Sonora and Frank in Stockton. The parents, a brother and four of their children were buried in the cemetery behind the Columbia schoolhouse.

Frank frequently visited the area where he had been raised. Often he brought his eldest son, Edwin, and they fished the Stanislaus River and ventured on several photography expeditions to Yosemite. George would join them when he could and they would camp and fish along the river. On one expedition, Frank followed the Stanislaus further upstream than he had on previous excursions. He had visited the giant redwoods in eastern Calaveras County but never had he ventured any further. He fell in love with the high country along the river and vowed to return.

Frank shared his interest in the eastern Calaveras County area with several friends in Stockton. It was not long until the owners of a select 160 acres, east of the giant redwoods on the Stanislaus River, were located. The Board brothers of the Linden Meat Market in Linden were owners of the property. They no longer used the property for running their cattle but an older brother retained a third interest in the land. All three needed to agree to sell the land.

Several trips were made to the property by following the road east from Stockton to Angels Camp in Calaveras County and on to the Big Trees Hotel. The county had figured prominently in the literature of Mark Twain in his *The Celebrated Jumping Frog of Calaveras County*, a story set in Angels Camp. Mark Twain had lived for five months in a cabin near the border of Calaveras County during the winter of 1864-1865, while he wrote his famous story. The county was also the site of the Calaveras Grove of Big Trees, the first sequoias discovered in 1854. There Frank and his party would spend the night at the hotel in the redwood grove. The following morning, they would travel to Dorrington and follow the cattle trail to the river. The Board brothers offered the use of their homesteaders' cabin so Frank, Dr. Wallace and their guests could spend the night at the little, two-story shake cabin.

Finally in October of 1902, the Board brothers sold their 160 acres to Frank Nicol and Dr. Wallace of Stockton for $2,000. This was the beginning of the camping expeditions to the Stanislaus River at Board's Crossing, a location that was to become increasingly important both socially and financially to the future generations of Nicol descendants.

Sue continued to reside with her parents in Stockton while she often traveled to nearby cities to attend social functions. Edwin graduated from Stockton High School in 1902 and enrolled in college. Lawrence followed suit and both of the boys were busy making plans for their business futures. Helen, the youngest, was still attending school in Stockton.

Their father, Frank, began to have increasing bouts of illness that the family doctor was unable to diagnose. A few days of bed rest with a prescribed diet and he seemed to improve. Frank felt his energy subsiding and began to have grave concerns for his family, his business and his children's future. When the young Smith approached Frank and asked for Sue's hand in marriage, Frank consented. He liked the young lawyer, his ambitions and his foresight in investments and finance. As a father giving away his eldest daughter, he felt R.H. and Sue were a fine match with a bright future.

Following the engagement luncheon at the Fairmont in San Francisco, Aunt Ruth traveled to Stockton to help plan the wedding with Sue, her mother and grandmother. R.H. felt increasingly left out on his frequent visits to the Nicol residence. When his future father-in-law was feeling well, they would travel to the Calaveras County property, now known as Board's Crossing and spend their time exchanging stories of legal escapades and fishing.

The spring passed quickly and Wednesday, June 24, arrived. Many of the wedding guests from out of town had arrived in Stockton the previous evening. Preparations began early on Wednesday morning for the evening wedding. The wedding party arrived at St. John's Episcopal Church for the nine o'clock evening ceremony with seven ushers and groomsmen, seven bridesmaids and a matron of honor. George Cameron stood as best man and Miss Anna Peters as maid of honor with Aunt Ruth as the matron of honor. More than six hundred guests filled the church to overflowing.

R.H. presented Sue with a diamond crescent to wear on her wedding day. Her imported gown was made entirely of princess and point lace with a court train of several yards in length. The most striking costume was that worn by the matron of honor, Mrs. Washington Dodge. It was from the design of a magnificent gown made entirely of opal beads worn by Calvé, the French soprano opera star, during her latest visit to San Francisco.

On Saturday, the *Stockton Daily Evening Record* reported:

> The most brilliant wedding of the season in this city was that of Miss Susan Alice Nicol, daughter of Mr. and Mrs. F.D. Nicol of this city, and Robert Hays Smith of San Francisco.[8]

The Sunday *San Francisco Chronicle* had the following to say about the wedding:

> With three large weddings and an important engagement to its credit this week, society temporarily lost its jaded mien, and a perceptible ripple of excitement had pervaded the dead calm of the summer dullness. The whole world loves a lover–it is equally true that all society loves a wedding–on Wednesday evening, Miss Sue Nicol and Robert Hayes [sic] Smith plighted their troth at St. John's Episcopal Church at Stockton.[9]

The society page article continued, saying the wedding was a "notable gathering of San Francisco society folk."[10] Following the ceremony, a dinner for 150 was served at the Nicol residence.

The yard was enclosed with canvas and decorated with shasta daisies and green tulle. The bride's cake yielded gifts to the attendants of a gold heart, a gold coin and a gold ring. Each of the groomsmen received a handsome stickpin from R.H. and Sue gave each of her attendants pins with circles of sapphires and pearls.

At midnight, Sue changed into her traveling suit and hat and the two whirled away from the crowd in R.H.'s new automobile. They spent the night in the small town of Byron. The following day they continued to the southern part of the state, vacationing for the most part, but R.H. made several excursions to check on business investments for himself and his clients. When they returned to San Francisco their residence at the Fairmont was ready.

Quick preparations were made for the rest of their honeymoon in last-minute consultations with the Dodges. All four were planning to meet in New York and then continue together to England. This was to be the first trip abroad for R.H. and Sue. They would see Ireland and England and then would travel through Europe. The Dodges would depart for home in late summer, but the Smiths had decided to continue their trip. Before meeting the Dodges in New York, R.H. wanted to introduce Sue to his family in Pennsylvania. They had not made the trip to California for his wedding. It is possible he had not invited either his parents or his brothers and sister. Financially it may have been difficult for his family to make the trip. Whatever the reason, the newlyweds planned to take the time to spend a day while enroute to New York.

～

The summer abroad passed quickly and the couple returned to San Francisco in late September. On their return R.H. became engrossed in his business affairs and Sue in the social whirlwind that encompassed most of her life. The Dodges had returned previously so that Washington could attend to political business. In 1896, Dodge had been elected to the San Francisco Board of Supervisors and served in that capacity for two years until he accepted the Democratic nomination for City and County

Assessor. His political interests had first been recognized by his previous father-in-law, Dr. Lampson.

Dr. Dodge was a good-looking man with deep-set eyes, dark hair and a neatly trimmed beard. He dressed impeccably. He had been born in Jamestown in 1859, the eldest of Eliza and Mark Tyler Dodge's two children. His early education was in the local public schools. He graduated from San Francisco Boys' High School and went on to obtain his medical degree from the University of California. After an early career of teaching in public schools, he returned to San Francisco to practice medicine.

In 1891, he married the eldest daughter of Dr. R.M. Lampson, one of the pioneer physicians of California. Dr. Lampson had been politically active and finally served as a state senator. His daughter, Mrs. Alice Lampson Shepherd, brought one daughter to her marriage with Dr. Washington Dodge. Dr. Dodge built a large and lucrative medical practice. His politics were best known as progressive. The election in which he captured the Board of Supervisors seat also elected James Duval Phelan as Mayor of San Francisco.

As supervisor, he was an ardent supporter of Mayor Phelan and his progressive politics. Reform was on the minds of several San Francisco politicians and Dr. Dodge concurred. He was a member of the minority that supported Mayor Phelan's efforts to control quasi-public corporations and reduce their excessive charges for services to the people. Dr. Dodge tried to have the Board of Supervisors, acting as a board of equalization, raise the valuation of the property of the quasi-public corporations, especially that of the street railways. Failing in this, he accepted the nomination on the Democratic ticket for City and County Assessor, pledging to the course he had recommended as a supervisor.

In the fall election of 1898, Dr. Dodge was elected Assessor by a handsome majority of eight thousand votes.[11] His promises to the public were so promptly fulfilled and his services in his office were so satisfactory to the taxpayers that he was returned to office and re-elected by an overwhelming majority. His plurality was over seventeen thousand,[12] the largest ever received by any candidate for public office in San Francisco at that time.

His following campaign became known as his memorable "blackboard" campaign.[13] He would use a blackboard to demonstrate the inequalities in taxation and what he had done to rectify the matter. Simply put, Dr. Dodge had increased the assessments of the quasi-public corporations, including the street railways, the gas, electric, water and telephone companies by over eighteen million dollars, while other moneyed interests and "newly" discovered personal property swelled the assessment roll by more than fifty million dollars. He then reduced the assessed valuation of old improvements, chiefly homes, by more than five million dollars, providing relief to over ten thousand taxpayers. These were the lowest rates in years to a majority of personal property owners. Revised assessments earned San Francisco the reputation of one of the most fairly taxed cities in the United States.

Dr. Dodge continued to run for assessor and won each election with overwhelming majorities. His political career looked bright. His personal life, however, had some difficulties. He and his wife had one child, Henry Washington. In 1901, Alice left Dr. Dodge and the following year he was granted a divorce by decree of desertion. He was awarded the custody of their eleven-year-old son.

In 1906, he married Ruth, a French lady, who had lived in England. The following year they had a son, Washington, Jr. It was Aunt Ruth that Sue had spent so much time with before her marriage. Every excursion to San Francisco found the two women shopping and socializing. Ruth was only eleven years older than Sue and the two had much in common. Their friendship grew. Ruth was the matron of honor at Sue's wedding.

The Dodge family suffered greatly after their rescue on April 14, 1912, from the maiden voyage of the Titanic. They had been abroad and were returning from Liverpool, England to New York City when the British luxury liner struck an iceberg. Of the 2,200 people aboard, more than 1,500 lost their lives. Among the survivors were Dr. Dodge, his wife, Ruth, and their young son, Washington.

The weight of social opinion settled heavily on Dr. Dodge. Accused of pre-empting space from women and children, he quickly came to his own defense. After numerous newspaper interviews in New York and in San Francisco, he prepared to speak about his experience. He delivered a speech entitled "The Loss of the Titanic" before the Commonwealth Club in San Francisco the following month. The club had been founded in 1903 to investigate and discuss problems affecting the welfare of the Commonwealth, the State of California, and to aid in their solutions. Membership in the club was open to persons interested in the issues of the day. It frequently held lectures open to the public. Dr. Dodge may have been a member of the club. It is also probable that his speech was requested as he was a public official of that city. The Commonwealth Club was interested in clearing Dr. Dodge's reputation.

Defending his rescue, Dr. Dodge stated that many women elected to stand by their husbands while lifeboats were being lowered without being filled to capacity. After the rescue by the Carpathia, his skills as a doctor were needed to aid many victims who had been subject to exposure. Dr. Dodge's political career culminated when he resigned his position as San Francisco Assessor in July following the Titanic ordeal. This was six weeks after his speech. The *San Francisco Call* printed a flowery editorial on Dr. Dodge's service to the city:

> When an able and faithful public servant—a man, fair, firm and of scrupulous integrity—retires from office, the community does indeed suffer loss. San Francisco owes much to Dr. Washington Dodge. It is not only the capable and honest administration of the assessor's duties that counts—it is the admirable example set during fourteen years of service.[14]

Pursuing a career as a banker, he again gained prominence until his suicide on June 21, 1919. He lingered for a week in St. Francis Hospital before he died. At the time of his death Dr. Dodge was personally being sued by two former associates from Anglo California Trust Company for misrepresenting the value of stock of the Poulson Wireless Company. The suit was for $57,615 in damages. During the last seven years of his life after the Titanic disaster, Dr. Dodge had received frequent negative coverage in the press for his investments, a car accident in which he hit a former fellow assessor and the mysterious appearance of his bathrobe on a San Francisco beach.

The tarnishing of his reputation, beginning with the question of his rescue from the Titanic, was considered the reason for his suicide. Ruth, his wife, found him in the garage shot through the head with a revolver.

BOOK THREE:

FRANCIS NICOL SMITH

When I arrived at Belmont Boarding
School the boys would say, "We've
heard of goldsmiths and silversmiths,
but never a nicolsmith."

> *Nicol Smith*
> *Quote from an interview*
> Times-Herald Tribune, *1947*

5

THE FAIRMONT BABY

San Francisco did not fully recover from the ravages of the earthquake and fire of 1906 for several years. Reconstruction was proceeding, but private residential housing was still scarce. The Fairmont Hotel was one of the first hotels to reopen after the earthquake and many society families of San Francisco took up residence there. The earthquake had not cracked any of the structure of the building. It had ten floors and was designed for six hundred guests. Each room had a private bath. The going rate was $2.50 per day. This is the way the hotel advertised its amenities:

> The Fairmont offers a wide range of dining accommodations....
> One may dine in full or in street dress—may have service in
> any style or in any manner.... Luncheons and dinners, private
> receptions and social gatherings may be held in many parts of
> the Hotel, and will have the most flawless of service and ap-
> pointments. The Hotel is operated on a distinctly unique plan
> in that it specializes in its departments to meet special tastes
> and requirements....[1]

The Fairmont Hotel had opened its doors one year after the earthquake on the anniversary of the city's disaster. The opening was a grand event with 935 places laid for dinner and hundreds more hoping to get seated but could not be accommodated.[2] Among the guests was R.H., now an advisor to and member of the staff of the Governor of California, James N. Gillett.[3] The young man listened attentively to the speeches. His interest was deeply sparked by the discussion of the Isthmian Canal and the proposed harbor improvements. He could envision the business opportunities the completion of these projects would offer for San Francisco.

The year before their wedding, both R.H. and Sue attended many events at the Fairmont Hotel. R.H. was with the governor when the Atlantic Fleet was welcomed to California waters. He helped host the banquet at the hotel to honor the Secretary of the Navy, Victor Howard Metcalf. Six hundred guests were invited. During the spring of their engagement, R.H. took Sue with him on several goodwill excursions aboard the Navy ships. Following each visit to a ship, Sue faithfully recorded in her diary-like book, *Chap Record*, the names of the young men who impressed her. Among the several ships she visited were the Tennessee and the Kansas. After each, the welcoming committee would invite the officers to a banquet in their honor at the grand hotel.

On April 2, 1908, R.H. held a luncheon for Sue. He invited his friends and business associates for her to meet. Among those most noted by Sue in her diary was young George Cameron, the close friend and business partner of R.H.'s who later became the publisher of the *San Francisco Chronicle*. Sue wrote about George, "never enough are the good things I had heard of him.... Fascinating man."[4]

The luncheon was probably an announcement of their engagement since the wedding date was the following June. It is not known if R.H. simply wanted to introduce Sue to his friends or if they used this occasion to make their engagement public. The *San Francisco Call* had carefully followed Sue's social life about town during the preceding years but neglected to mention this important event. But Sue carefully wrote about each man she met. Her engagement to R.H. did not tame her wandering eye.

⌖

The residence of the newlywed Smiths was logically chosen at the Fairmont Hotel. During the first four decades of its existence, it was primarily a residential hotel. Many of San Francisco's wealthiest families were still without homes after the fire and the hotel was among the earliest to open. The Fairmont provided everything from teas, card games, musical concerts to grand banquets.

Both R.H. and Sue Smith had a passion for San Francisco and wanted to live nowhere else. R.H. spent every moment in the great city when he wasn't attending his business in the oil fields of Coalinga and the Kettleman Hills, while Sue hoped to reside in San Francisco. She had spent many summers there with her Aunt Ruth and Uncle Washington Dodge. For Sue the center of society was in the hotel and for R.H. his business entertaining took on a grand style at their residence.

Sue and her Aunt Ruth continued to be close, although Sue began to develop her own San Francisco social circle. Living at the Fairmont, she began to entertain in her apartment and in the restaurants on the main floor, no longer needing the home of her aunt. Sue's acquaintances included the other residents, the scions of San Francisco society. Her friends were the Tobins, the de Youngs, the Floods and many other prominent California families.

Sue quickly found herself caught up in events at the hotel. R.H. was often out of town to attend to his various business concerns. Sue was an inveterate card player and enjoyed the games at the opulent residence. She began giving private card parties in their suite with her closest friends. As Sue was a lively and sparkling young lady her parties became quite popular. She was a delightful entertainer and her guests enjoyed her vivacious personality even more than the card games.

As Sue's first pregnancy progressed she became confined to her room. One particular bridge luncheon was unexpectedly interrupted. Suddenly Sue laid her cards on the table and asked her guests to please leave because the game was over. It was time for her first baby to arrive. The ladies went home, the doctor and a nurse were quickly summoned and then her Aunt Ruth and R.H. were called to her side. Later that day, January 10, 1910, Sue gave birth to their first and only child, a boy, Francis Nicol Smith.

~

Francis Nicol Smith came into the world known as the "Fairmont baby." The hotel chef baked a cake and the maitre d'hotel presented the baby with a silver cup. He was the first baby to be born in the hotel. Immediately a nanny was hired, Henrietta Lincoln Washington Alfred, who resided with the Smith's. She wore striped shirtwaists and lace bonnets and was an immense Negro lady, weighing nearly 250 pounds. She and the baby, Nicol, became fast friends. Nicol wrote many years later:

> She had the same fat face I had as a child and we became fast friends long before I realized what friendship meant. I was never to become integrated. I was born integrated. As a baby my dearest friend was black....[5]

Henrietta Lincoln Washington Alfred became known as "mammy" to baby Nicol. She wheeled Nicol in his baby buggy around Nob Hill, the ostentatious San Francisco neighborhood of the wealthy. He was dressed in a rather moth eaten, ermine coat and cap which some distant relative had sent as a gift. It was said that the gift originated from the country of "Bolivia," but that was understandable. When mammy didn't know where something came from, she would automatically place its source in Bolivia.

Frequently passersby stopped to peek into the perambulator and commented on the darling baby. Mammy contended that often they would ask, "What great merchant prince or captain of industry's son is this that rides about in ermine?"

"Laws a massy," she would boast, "It ain't nothing at all to what he's got for Sunday and holiday use."

"What does he wear then?" she would be questioned.

"Chinchilly and sables," she replied and then winked happily at the baby as they rolled on. Mammy always swore that baby Nicol would then wink back.

Life at the Fairmont was delightful for Nicol. Mammy gave him constant care and companionship. The hotel had a completely equipped school and outside play area, plus activities, including dance lessons, for the children of the hotel. Nicol began to cement lifelong friendships with the other youngsters residing in the hotel. During this period, R.H.'s business ventures continued to flourish, as did Sue's social activities. They traveled abroad with extended trips to the European continent in 1910, 1912 and 1914. Each trip required traveling to New York to depart by ship for Europe after a visit with R.H.'s relatives in Pennsylvania.

On the 1912 and the 1914 excursions Nicol was taken as far as Oakville, Pennsylvania to stay with his Aunt Myrtle, R.H.'s older sister. In 1912, R.H. and Sue originally planned to travel with her Aunt Ruth and Uncle Washington and their son Washington Jr., known as "Bobo." Business matters delayed the trip for the Smiths and they rescheduled it for later that year. This was a fortuitous change because the Dodge's return trip was aboard the ill-fated maiden voyage of the Titanic.

Nicol's earliest memories of his relatives in Pennsylvania were from his stay at Aunt Myrtle's when he was four and a half. He and his cousin, Elizabeth Smith, spent hours playing together. They were nearly the same age. One afternoon Nicol was missing. Elizabeth was not particularly concerned but followed Aunt Myrtle as she frantically looked for Nicol. After a complete search of the house, they headed to the barnyard. There Nicol was found in the pasture with the bull. As Nicol edged toward the bull he called "Here nice bully, nice bully bully." Aunt Myrtle was afraid to climb the fence to rescue him or raise her voice for fear the bull would charge the small boy. Finally she got Nicol's attention and coaxed him toward her where she quickly pulled him to safety under the fence. He was sternly admonished since he had been told to stay away from the bull. Little Nicol looked into Aunt Myrtle's eyes and replied, "But he is such a nice bully." This began Nicol's ventures in life with unlikely pets.

The next occurrence of the visit made an even stronger impression on Nicol. One summer afternoon he and cousin Elizabeth were playing on the floor when they ended up in a tussle. Before Aunt Myrtle could separate the children, Elizabeth accidentally kicked Nicol in the abdomen. The children continued to play but Nicol complained the next day of a pain in his stomach. The pain refused to go away and Nicol became quite ill. Finally a doctor was summoned. When he arrived at the house, he found Nicol had appendicitis and needed to be operated on promptly.

The rest of the visit, until his parents returned, was spent quietly recovering. The day R.H. and Sue were expected, everyone was up early and went to meet the train as it entered the station. As soon as his mother and father stepped off the train, Nicol started yelling as he ran to greet them, "I broke Aunt Myrtle's

Beethoven. I broke Aunt Myrtle's Beethoven," over and over again. Poor Nicol had accidentally broken Aunt Myrtle's favorite piece, a bust of Beethoven. But Myrtle had told Nicol he need not confess the accident to his parents because she was afraid he would be severely scolded. The weight of his folly was too much for the honest child. His confession preceded a greeting from his parents.

The Fairmont Hotel residence soon seemed small for the entertaining Sue loved. In 1915, R.H. began to search for a new home for the family and soon leased a suitable house. The move to the three-story brick home at 2324 Pacific Avenue introduced a new personality into Nicol's life. Mammy retired to take care of her ailing mother and Miss Linette Whitman was hired as Nicol's governess. Mademoiselle, as she was called by all the members of the household, was to have a singular influence on Nicol's life. She was a tall, thin French woman, with her hair pulled into a bun at the nape of her neck and she had a stern demeanor. In photographs she always appeared with Nicol by her side, ramrod straight, firmly gripping the adventuresome youngster's hand as if to prevent a child's curious meandering. She taught Nicol to speak French as a youngster, which was invaluable to him later during his years of travel and his service with the Office of Strategic Services (OSS, predecessor to the CIA) in World War II.

The governess impressed other lifelong lessons upon Nicol. Toys, she explained, were soon broken, out of style, or taken by older children. In her estimate, toys added up to a frivolous expenditure. It was on his sixth birthday that Nicol received his first lesson on the value of money. He was invited to a ranch for his birthday. The ranch owner was Etta Sayre, a close friend of his mother's, who lived on her family's prosperous dairy ranches in Madera in the San Joaquin Valley of central California. Sue, Nicol and Mademoiselle made the trip south to the ranch.

Before the excursion, Mademoiselle had given Nicol a long, black cotton stocking. She had coached him in his reply to the inevitable question, "What do you want for your birthday?" Nicol would sweetly respond with, "A silver dollar please, for my black stocking. I am saving for a rainy day." Her expectation was that most people would be so surprised at a six-year-old saving for a rainy day that they would give two or three dollars instead of a lone silver coin.

From an early age, Nicol was willing to take a chance. It was a rainy, stormy day when they arrived at Aunt Etta's ranch that January. She was not a relative but his mother insisted on Nicol calling all her close women friends "aunt." He was always happy to oblige. Nicol was also warned to be on his best behavior because there was a very famous lady staying in the house. The Australian soprano opera singer, Nellie Melba, was visiting at Aunt Etta's. Nicol asked his mother if he should call her Aunt Nellie and his mother replied with an adamant "No."

After their arrival, Nicol was asked his age, to which he replied that he was six. When the women inquired what type of toy would he like, he replied seriously that it was not necessary to buy him a toy. The answer seemed to please his mother until Nicol continued, "I would prefer a silver dollar if you don't mind. I am saving for a rainy day." Nicol extracted the carefully folded, black cotton stocking from the pocket of his jacket. There was a sudden silence in the room. Nicol could hear the grandfather clock ticking in the hallway.

Dame Nellie Melba was the first to break the silence. "A most admirable virtue. There is nothing like thrift, and most unusual at such an early age." She opened her reticule and reached down into its cavernous folds for a coin purse. She counted out six silver dollars, one for each year and dropped them into the outstretched top of the black stocking.

Aunt Etta left the room and returned with six additional silver dollars. They were added to the collection in the stocking. The age of toys was over and saving for a rainy day had started. Nicol and Mademoiselle were both pleased.

Mother had not been impressed and said so to Mademoiselle on the return trip to San Francisco. But Mademoiselle held her ground and replied that this was how she trained the young people. She had done it with others. She had slightly intimidated Sue from the beginning, so no more was said.

Nicol continued collecting coins in his stocking. He was elated at his early success with saving. Unfortunately no one else had been invited to his birthday on the ranch in Madera so he waited until his return home to continue the rainy-day savings. On occasion he could advance his forthcoming birthday a bit and fill the stocking with more coins. Finally the silver dollars had to be redeemed for larger coins as the stocking became too heavy. Four years passed when Sue called Nicol into her room one morning. He knew she had been out late to a poker party. From her expression, Nicol could guess she had lost. He was right.

His mother asked how much he had saved in his black stocking. Nicol replied $872. He had counted the hoard so often he always knew to the penny how much was there. His mother said, "Nicol your rainy day has arrived. I lost $850 last night in a poker game." Nicol retrieved the stocking and she counted out $850, leaving the balance of $22 in the stocking.

Sue promised to pay Nicol back but she never did until she passed away. When she died, she left a list of all her borrowings. All the sums were correctly totaled. It was thirty-nine years later that Nicol had his rainy-day sum returned.

↵

The years on Pacific Avenue were comfortable. Mademoiselle tutored Nicol in French and geography in addition to the education he received at the Pacific School. A chauffeur drove Nicol the few blocks to school and returned to pick him up at the end of each day in R.H.'s Jordan touring automobile. Nicol was a good student and particularly enjoyed his classmates. The French lessons continued until he could speak English and French equally well. He and Mademoiselle frequently conversed in French.

Dancing lessons were added to his schedule. He learned to dance with childhood playmates, who remained his lifelong friends—Patricia Tobin, Peter McBean, Frank West, John Drum and many others. Nicol's first friends were the offspring of the great families of California. The Tobins were descendants of a prominent California family and the founder of San Francisco's largest savings bank, Hibernia Savings and Loan Society. Peter McBean's father, Atholl, was connected with R.H. at Associated Oil Company and was on the board of directors of Crocker First National Bank and Pacific Telephone & Telegraph Company, to name only a few of his business responsibilities. John Drum's father was also a lawyer and a banker. Frank West was the son of a distinguished lawyer. The list of noted names continued, among them families such as Bancroft, Flood and Fleishhacker.

Nicol's first informal introduction to society and its gala gatherings occurred in an unusual manner. Sue was great friends with Elsa Maxwell, the well-known hostess, songwriter, author and entertainer. Elsa had spent her childhood and teens in San Francisco. On her thirteenth birthday she borrowed, without permission, the motor launch of a neighbor to take several children on a cruise around San Francisco Harbor. This was her first experience as a hostess.

It was a later party, to which she was not invited, that inspired her career as an international hostess. The rejection caused Elsa to decide that she would give great parties to which everyone would want to come. After returning from abroad on a tour with a Shakespearean repertory company and a circuit as a piano accompanist in South Africa and the first sales of her musical compositions, Elsa began to give parties. She had an unconventional style of entertaining and believed that dinner and cocktail parties were dull. She began to include games and claimed to invent the scavenger hunt.

Elsa borrowed other people's homes for her entertaining. The Smith home became host to one of Elsa's parties shortly after her return to the United States. Nicol had been strictly instructed to remain upstairs and not disturb the important guests. But curiosity overwhelmed the boy. Quietly stepping outside his upstairs door into the hallway, Elsa was sweeping past in a gown with a long train. She was about to make her grand entrance down the staircase to the drawing room. Nicol accidentally stepped on the train and tumbled down the stairs wrapped up in the lovely dress. Sue was horrified. Elsa was amused. She invited Nicol to her party. The evening was spent avoiding the wrathful eyes of his mother and tagging along with Elsa. The party cemented their friendship.

R.H. was prospering in his business ventures. Sue was involved in the whirlwind of society. The exposition in San Francisco brought new excitement to Nicol's life. Recovery from the earthquake and fire was complete by 1915. San Francisco celebrated both its recovery and the completion of the Panama Canal with a world's fair, the Panama-Pacific International

Exposition. The fair was also meant to assert the importance of California and the American West. It opened on February 20 and closed on December 4. Nineteen million people visited the exposition on the extensive fill built along the city's bay front. It created a magnificent fairgrounds. Unlike previous fairs, its buildings were designed as permanent structures for civic and cultural use. Among the buildings, the Palace of Fine Arts still stands.

The exposition became the final showcase of the American Renaissance.[6] It opened with an optimistic view of the future, of peace, prosperity and progress. A new era had dawned in the great city of San Francisco, but World War I had begun in Europe. A new era had indeed dawned.

Nicol enjoyed the exposition and wanted to visit as often as possible. He and Mademoiselle made almost daily excursions to the many displays. Although he was only five years old, the pavilions of far away places intrigued the child. His first exposure to the secrets of the world lay at his door that year in San Francisco. The close of the exhibition brought more excitement to the Smith home on Pacific Avenue. R.H., in his unfulfilled desire to see China, repeatedly visited the China Pavilion. When the fair closed in December, he purchased the entire China exhibit. Their three-story home was filled with the tapestries, vases and urns that had been on display. R.H. was finally able to satisfy his insatiable curiosity about China.

6

EDUCATION: CALIFORNIA TO CONNECTICUT TO CALIFORNIA

Nicol never forgot the day he left for boarding school. He was only nine at the time and had never been away from home except to stay with relatives or to go on a short excursion with Mademoiselle, whom he had grown to know probably better than he knew his parents. The school that had been chosen for him was Belmont, which was a boarding school of approximately fifty students, located in the hills behind the town of Belmont south of San Francisco on the peninsula. The campus was beautiful with spacious grounds and excellent quarters for the students. Each boy had a large room to himself with a washstand. At the end of the hall there were showers, an amenity Nicol never chose to use more than once a week.

While Nicol attended Belmont Boarding School he began referring to his parents, his pets and the hired help as "the family." As an only child with his parents frequently monopolized by their business or social engagements, Nicol made close friends among the help employed at the Smith home. The child endeared himself to the servants, his governess and tutor with his thoughtful disposition and the winsome stories he spun about his daily escapades. Nicol was an adorable, cherubic and mature child. He tried to please everyone. During the years he spent at the boarding school his parents purchased a home in Burlingame. The family moved from San Francisco to the mansion, The Crossroads, in the quiet residential town nestled in the hills on the San Francisco Peninsula. R.H. retained the lease on the Pacific Avenue house but he and Sue wanted a larger home in the fashionable residential community south of San Francisco. Many great estates had been established in the elegant suburb by the progeny of the creators of California and important American business people. The child heiress of Woolworth stores, Barbara Hutton spent her formative years in Burlingame and became a good friend of Nicol's. They spent hours together learning to ride horseback.

Within a week Nicol decided that a boy from Central America would be his best friend. He was not wrong and soon developed a friendship with Rudolph Rosales. The boy was from Tegucigalpa, Honduras, and his father was a general in a military faction. Rudolph spent many holiday breaks with Nicol in San Francisco and later at the family's new residence, The Crossroads in Burlingame, California. The two boys became inseparable.

Rudolph Rosales had brought a wonderful alligator skin to school from his home and displayed it in his room. Nicol admired the tanned skin which still had all its teeth. His fascination with the hide continued. After months of listening to Nicol's incessant questions about alligators, Rudolph finally gave him the hide. Nicol moved it to his room and draped it over his bookshelf where all his friends could marvel at the preserved alligator.

No young boys ever had a better time than the nine-year-old class of 1919 at Belmont. Nicol remembered nothing of what he studied but his recollections of the hours of play are vivid with details.

The unbroken country behind the school was vast to the boy. Nicol walked as far as he desired and never came upon a fence. There were unexplored canyons. On investigation they yielded tumble-down shacks that he considered the haunts of daring bandits and robbers of another day. Often prying into the shacks, he found that earlier students were responsible for the make-shift buildings. But Nicol spun stories about robbers and bandits anyway to the delight of his classmates.

Clubs were organized with secret initiation practices for membership. Every boy wanted to join and hoped a club would ask for his membership. No club was particularly pursuing Nicol. One boy, Tubby Bengizer, frequently showed displeasure with Nicol during the first few months at school. Tubby, upon knocking Nicol down, would straddle him and rub his scalp with his fist as rapidly as possible. Nicol howled his protests but it was no use. Tubby had discovered early in life that a show of force was impressive and his size made his power displays easy. When Nicol was asked to join the club Tubby was a member of, he did so immediately. It was a most satisfactory arrangement because Tubby never bothered Nicol again. They became good friends.

The most sought-after student was Nicol's neighbor, Michael Cudahy from Chicago. Most of the boys received a weekly allowance from home of fifty cents, but Michael received five dollars. All winter was spent determining how to win over the skeptic Michael. It was a particularly damp winter and the clubhouse roof developed several leaks. Nicol was considered the most persuasive of the group. He was nominated to entice his neighbor to visit the clubhouse. Nicol succeeded in arranging the visit, but traveled along the wrong secret path, leading his blindfolded guest through a poison oak patch. A few days later, Michael broke out with poison oak and never joined the club.

Each year the students performed a pageant for parents and family on the front lawn facing the Senior House. The year Nicol participated he was chosen for the part of an ambassador for the pageant, "King Arthur and the Knights of the Round Table." Nicol asked his instructor to tell him where the ambassador was from? When he did not get an answer, he proceeded to check out his costume. It resembled a burlap bag. Nicol was chagrined. No one ever determined where the ambassador was from, but Nicol was listed on the program and that pleased the family. Sue told Nicol that ambassadors were always important people. They ranked at social events above almost everybody except a king, and he was too young to be a king.

Unknown to Sue, Nicol decided to brighten up his costume when he spent a weekend at The Crossroads. A fellow student told Nicol he looked like a "bag." Infuriated, Nicol decided a "bag" had never been in the family.

> Father's family have been here for so long I bet that they were in at the beginning with the Indians and mother's is lost in the clouds of antiquity. Why we have been here for generations, right here in America, and we have never had a bag in the family yet![1]

Nicol borrowed his mother's long chain of matched crystals. After all, he knew his mother would be pleased. The crystals were wonderful. The big lights in front would play upon them like diamonds. Nicol felt more brilliant than a king. The night of the pageant arrived and soon every seat was taken. The clash of the cymbals announced the beginning of the spectacle. Nicol's part was near the middle. He thought the minutes would never pass and then as his turn approached, the moments passed too quickly. He was anxious for everyone to see him as the "ambassador." At last, his cue came and in swept Nicol, crystals and all:

> How those beads did flash. I knew I looked swell and it sure was fine. Once before the king's throne I turned, and facing the audience, spoke my lines. I did them just swell, strong and powerful like. My voice squeaked once in the middle, but I coughed to hide it and then the big flourish at the finish. I had been practicing that flourish for weeks. It was something between a grand opera singer's toss of the head and a railroad terminal's sign dropping. It was tremendous but it was my undoing. The toss was too much for the crystals. The string broke and they rolled in all directions. I heard a scream from the audience. I had been found out.[2]

Nicol quickly exited from the stage and disappeared into the trees. At final count, there were seventeen crystals missing.

The years at Belmont passed quickly. There were boys from as far away as Russia to Latin America. One of Nicol's favorite upper classmates was Peter Donlan. He spent time with the younger boys helping them with their swimming and diving. Peter went on to become an Olympic class swimmer. At age thirteen, Nicol's Belmont days came to an end. Sue planned to send Nicol east to a preparatory school, but first he would spend a year at home with a private tutor.

~∽

The scholar, Mr. John Moran, spent the next twelve months with Nicol, including a summer excursion to Tahoe, followed by a trip to Western Canada and Alaska. To Nicol he seemed to be an ancient gentlemen, but Moran maintained a distinct feeling of youth. He had been a tutor for Senator Phelan when the U.S.

Senator was a boy.[3] Though certainly an octogenarian, his mind was as lucid as that of a man tens of years his junior.

He was a perfect Latin and Greek scholar and had endless knowledge of the classics. Nicol felt the man read a miraculous number of books and retained everything from his readings. Nicol avoided mathematics as much as possible. He concentrated on the languages and history, though he did not have much success except in French.

Meanwhile, Sue and R.H. were planning the rest of Nicol's education. On a trip east, R.H. wrote from the home of a friend, Frank Hitchcock, former Postmaster General, that he was visiting preparatory schools, including St. Paul's in New Hampshire:

> The years have flown swiftly by and now I am planning the college career of my son, Nicol. His mother, who has a big say in the planning, wants him to prepare at St. Paul's, and I suppose that will be our decision. Before returning to California, I expect to go up to New Hampshire to see about his entrance there.
>
> It is a great thing to have a boy going to college. His doings will bring back more vividly to me the things we used to do at Carlisle....[4]

Nicol's cousin from San Francisco graduated from preparatory school that June. Washington Dodge finished his last year at Choate School in Wallingford, Connecticut. Aunt Ruth was widowed by the time she decided to send her stepson to Choate. It removed Wash, as he was called, from the stigma his father's suicide cast upon the Dodge family in San Francisco. Wash flourished at Choate. Aunt Ruth strongly influenced Sue's decision to send Nicol to Choate. On July 2nd, 1925, the application for Francis Nicol Smith to attend the renowned preparatory school was completed and mailed.

The application included all of Nicol's academic achievements. It stated that he was to be prepared to enter Harvard. The personal recommendation listed his cousin, H. Washington Dodge, and for financial references Sue wrote "Any San Francisco Bank."[5] Nicol's acceptance at Choate was received by telephone later the same month. Preparations began for his departure in August.

↙

Judge William G. Choate founded the school for boys in 1896. Twelve years later Dr. George C. St. John was appointed headmaster and was in that role when Nicol entered Choate. During St. John's time, the college grew and gained its reputation as a leading college preparatory school. When Nicol arrived at Choate, there were 361 boys in attendance, from the ages of fifteen to nineteen. When the cook handed the acceptance telephone call to Sue, she was informed that Nicol was accepted into the third former. She had requested the fourth former on the application which would have resulted in Nicol's spending only three years at the institution. His academic achievements did not merit the advancement and he entered the third former. At age fifteen he was slightly older than many of his classmates and would be nineteen when he graduated. The next four years of his education were spent at Choate.

Assigned to a cottage with several other boys, Nicol quickly made friends. Among them was Armar Archbold who Nicol sat next to at dinner. Armar was older and in the fourth former that year, although he was new at Choate also. After the evening meal, he introduced Nicol to his younger brother, John. The two fifteen-year-old boys met that sultry, August day and settled down to their studies and activities at Choate. John and Nicol were in the same former and became inseparable friends. After the four years at Choate, their friendship spanned their lifetimes. It was a friendship that lasted through marriages, a war and around the globe.

Armar and John Archbold transferred to Choate from their previous schools, Alden and St. George's, respectively. John had been unhappy at his former school and convinced his mother, Anne Archbold, that Choate was an excellent school. Anne researched the school and decided to send both of her sons to the same institution. Her decision, as so many of her future decisions would, influenced the remainder of Nicol's life.

Nicol enjoyed the years at Choate. He made friends easily and developed many relationships that lasted a lifetime. The school scheduled speakers from different countries and walks of life. Lectures were presented by the explorer Lowell Thomas on his trips around the world and to Afghanistan. An Arctic explorer, Vilhjalmur Stefansson, described his northern explorations.

During these years, Lindbergh made his initial flight from St. Louis to New York.

Exploration and travel began to interest Nicol, along with a few academic subjects. His studies started poorly the first year, but Nicol continued to improve as each year progressed. He excelled in history and French, while geometry and chemistry were dropped. Algebra and Latin were required, but Nicol struggled with these subjects. He joined the French Club, the Kodak Club and participated on the boxing squad the first two years. But competitive sports required physical discipline which disagreed with Nicol. Instead he became the assistant manager of the baseball team and joined the literary magazine staff, the dramatic club and the oratorical contests, all of which allowed him to excel in areas in which he was talented.

His earliest efforts at writing were made during 1928 to 1929. His first publication was in *The Choate Literary Magazine* in May of 1928 and was titled "The Calcutta Sweepstakes."[6] The short story was about an English gal, Mona, who spent a pound note to gamble on a horse race to win her fortune. After almost winning, her chosen horse stumbled and fell. Mona had dreamed of riches, but the story ended with a dose of Nicol's viewpoint of reality, one that was well-established during his upbringing in a wealthy and prominent society family. Concern for money matters were trifling annoyances:

> Pound notes were looked at once or twice, sometimes three times, but never more. There was a chance that one would win, if one was lucky. What did a pound note matter, anyway?[7]

Nicol's story stimulated an interest in writing and brought him praise from his classmates and instructors. The following school year Nicol wrote several more articles for the magazine. A story titled "The Black Baron"[8] was his longest and most notable fiction. It was a story about a curse upon a noble family of England who had dislodged an old woman, previously a family nurse. The curse, carried out over many years, culminated in the twelfth baron who was born black to the otherwise white family in 1956. The baron, Lenoir, was secluded from public view but was well educated at home. Finally, Lenoir escaped and married a white woman and became the leader of the United Black Races of the World. The story culminates in the future year of 1992 when Lenoir led a terrible battle:

> In '92, as you remember, there came the terrible battle. In which the outcome of the great struggle was assured the complete victory of the white races and the subjugation of all the colored.[9]

Nicol wrote himself into the story as a detective from Scotland Yard. He was called upon to investigate the curse and determine the cause of the racial battle. He concludes with his observation to his Scotland Yard cohort that the curse was strange and turned the world upside down. "I have run up against many queer cases, but for just damned queer ones, without any sense at all, that of Lenoir takes the prize."[10]

Why Nicol chose 1992 as the year for the battle of the white and colored races is unknown. When he was recently questioned about the date, Nicol remarked it seemed like a good number and was so far in the future that surely the racial problems he could recall during his youth would be resolved. He had limited exposure to racial issues at the time he wrote the story. His closest friend at his previous school had been from Central America. Nicol witnessed the humiliation and degradation of his friend Rudolph Rosales from other students. Unfortunately my reading of Nicol's story coincided with the Los Angeles riots of 1992. Nicol's teenage hope for ending racial strife seemed idealistic. The stories printed at Choate are the only fictional work Nicol did during his lifetime. He was developing his taste for the unusual and the element of intrigue.

Nicol did not apply to Harvard at the end of his last year but instead looked back to California and Stanford University. Ear problems had persisted during his entire time on the East Coast and he felt the drier climate of the west was more agreeable. Unfortunately his ear problems had landed him in the school infirmary one holiday, instead of on the yachting trip he was scheduled to take with his classmate, Larry Mellon and his extended family that included Andrew Mellon, U.S. Secretary of the Treasury. Nicol never forgot his bitter disappointment about the missed excursion aboard the Mellon yacht, the sleek double-hulled, teak-planked, 224-feet long, Vagabondia.

Nicol's parents visited on occasion. His father appeared enroute to a business deal. His mother arrived in New York at her apartment in the swanky Ritz Carlton, she would ask Nicol to bring his friends and she would entertain them there in grand style. His friend's found Sue delightful. She was charming and witty and entertained the young men with her stories. But Rudolph Spreckels became Nicol's most frequent visitor. Since childhood he had been Uncle Ruddy to Nicol. Although they were not relatives, Uncle Ruddy was dearer to Nicol than any of his related uncles. Rudolph Spreckels first became associated with R.H. after the San Francisco earthquake and they remained business partners until the onset of the Great Depression. Rudolph respected the business acumen of his partner and admired his savvy wife, Sue. Nicol, always an adult-like child, won the heart of the sugar king and they became closer than Nicol was to his own parents. Even after animosity developed between R.H. and Rudolph in the thirties, Nicol and Uncle Ruddy continued their relationship, as did Rudolph's and Sue's.

Uncle Ruddy listened to the exploits of the boy as if he had nothing else to do with his time. He visited Nicol at each of his schools, wrote letters, sent telegrams and brought gifts. Often his correspondence provided more information about events at The Crossroads than Nicol's parents provided. Nicol's favorite gift from Uncle Ruddy was given to him in New York where he spent the Christmas holidays during his last year at Choate. The paper was shredded as Nicol removed the wrappings to find a beaver fur coat. Fashioned in the latest trench coat style, the luxurious fur coat remained in Nicol's possession for forty years. The coat was not worn after the first few winters, but the memories it recalled of his dear uncle kept Nicol from parting with the gift.

Among his friends, Charles Nichols, John Archbold and many others, Nicol became known as "Uncle Nicol." He developed his own story-telling technique, much like his mother's ability. Nicol could tell a story to his peers like only an elder uncle could. Thus evolved the new title, and it was one of respect among his classmates.

In June of 1929 Nicol graduated from Choate. Next to his picture in the yearbook a quote that described him to classmates said: "Greatest wits have a touch of extravagance." His stories, like his mother's, were often exaggerated tales of everyday occurrences. Nicol could find a delightful tale in the simplest, daily task. His friends often wondered if he experienced the same mundane daily routines as they did, for no one among them could see the event as an amusing story. Nicol had a gift and he entertained friends for hours with his stories.

R.H. and Sue came from California for graduation, Anne Archbold came from Washington, D.C., and the parents of many other classmates arrived at Choate. After the ceremonies, R.H. asked Nicol to introduce him to his instructors. Nicol willingly obliged since his instructors found him to be an enjoyable pupil. On his application to Stanford one instructor had written:

> We are going to miss Nicol's cheerfulness and friendliness a lot next year. Nicol has made a large place for himself in our hearts, and our affectionate interest will follow him always.[11]

The introductions turned out to be insightful for Nicol's future. One instructor in particular mentioned to R.H. and Nicol that perhaps he might want to consider a career of travel abroad, followed by lecture circuits in the United States. R.H. did not comment, but Nicol never forgot that idea, that was planted like a seed in his youthful mind.

With graduation over and an application submitted to Stanford, summer preparations began. That spring, one of the housemasters had planned and organized a summer trip. The six-week excursion included travel through Europe and Asia Minor. Nicol was excited as he packed for his first trip abroad.

7

THE ODYSSEY

N icol packed and re-packed his luggage during the end of the school year in anticipation of the Odyssey Tour. His parents were easily persuaded to allow him to go after they received the official information with a note from the organizing house master and his French teacher, Mr. Newell. Some of the other young men who wanted to go were not so fortunate. They would not be going abroad until family members accompanied them.

Traveling with some of his best friends from Choate seemed ideal to Nicol. Sue and R.H. had made several trips to Ireland, England and Europe but Nicol had never gone with them. He was sure he wanted to venture to more unusual places than his parents visited. His best friend and Choate schoolmate, John Archbold, and good friend, Frank West, from Stockton, California were in the Odyssey group.

After graduation, Nicol packed the remaining personal items in his room and shipped them home to California. Saying goodbye to his friends, instructors and specifically the headmaster, Mr. St. John, and his wife, Nicol left Choate with a lump in his throat. This had been the most difficult farewell of his life. Many of the people seemed closer than his own family. With his luggage stashed in the Stetson's car, he was off to spend a few days with classmate Bill Stetson and his family before the trip.

The days crept by. The watch his father gave him at graduation seemed barely to move its hands. Finally the morning of June 27 arrived, the day prior to the Odyssey Tour departure.

Nicol headed to New York. After picking up his passport and tickets, he stopped at his mother's suite in her favorite hotel, the Ritz, where he cleaned up to spend an evening on the town with another classmate, Charles Nichols. Charles had planned a grand evening with dinner on the roof of the Astor, followed by a musical review of "Keep it Clean."[1]

John and Frank met Nicol after the review and they boarded the ship to settle in their cabins. Nicol shared an outside cabin which he liked immensely with three other Odyssey Tour members. His roommates were Rob Riddle from Louisville, Kentucky, Bob Waggemen from Washington and a delightful fellow who Nicol found very amusing named Mills from Middlesex, New Jersey.

The next morning Nicol awoke at sea. The ship had gotten underway during the night. Breakfast did not appeal to him, but he played some deck games and began reading a mystery novel written and sent to him by his friend Kathleen Norris, the popular California novelist. After lunch, he was invited to the first-class deck to play poker. That evening he danced with several young ladies who were also on their first trip. Nicol was impressed to find that the passengers were a first class list and not a "tourist thud."[2] His society upbringing was apparent from this remark recorded in his diary.

The following morning he awoke quite seasick from the rough seas during the night, but he quickly gained his sea legs. Feeling better by evening, he even enjoyed the challenge of dancing on the swaying floor.

At noon on July 4, after only six days at sea, the ship arrived at Cherbourg, France, the seaport town on the English Channel. The transfer from the boat to the train distressed Nicol. The porters were stubborn and refused to carry his bags the full distance without a larger tip. It seemed that everyone wanted a tip or demanded a larger tip. The fence along the train tracks was lined with women in pitiful clothes, holding their babies. Most of them were begging. Observing the masses, Nicol wondered if this display of humanity was unusual. He was relieved when the train got underway. His sheltered life of boarding and preparatory schools had not prepared him for his first exposure to poverty.

After he settled into the hotel in Paris, Nicol and his friends hired a cab for a moonlight drive about the city. They stopped at a small pub to have a beer. Nicol was persuaded to order a beer and he took one sip. He didn't care for it and he also did not want to break his promise to his father.

At age fifteen, Nicol and his father had made a pact before he left for Choate. Nicol's father had told him that at school he would meet young men with different values. New opportunities, freedom and pressure from peers could lead a young man astray, but he hoped Nicol would uphold his morals and especially stay away from smoking and drinking until the age of twenty-one. Only an occasional glass of wine with a meal was permitted. As an incentive, his father then informed him that $125,000 had been placed in a bank note for Nicol to receive when he came of age, if he upheld his part of the deal. Nicol planned to receive the money at the predetermined date. From his observance, drinking on the part of his friends only made them silly and ill. He had no desire to participate. His parents had smoked as long as he could remember and it did not interest him either. His friends tried smoking and coughed and choked on their first cigarettes while claiming it was enjoyable.

The following day the Odyssey Tour began at the Eiffel Tower. Nicol found it disappointing. It appeared to be a "victim of advertising, its subject being at present the new Citrogen Six, 'a car that any family can afford,' too bad."[3] But the view from the top was magnificent. Nicol wrote, "All of Paris laid at our feet."[4] After quickly having his caricature done by the artist at the top of the tower, Nicol and his friends went straight to the National City Bank. There they met John Utter, who for many years had been the tutor for the Archbold children.

> He took us to a place for lunch, where never in my life have I tasted such good food.... The lunch was great. We had some wine that was excellent, and for dessert, little pancakes cooled in Fine Champagne, a morsel which is surely meant for the gods, for it is too good for mortals.[5]

The afternoon included a visit to his mother's friend, Madame Verdier, who owned the City of Paris dry goods store in San

Francisco. She spent a part of each year in Paris. Madame Verdier enjoyed Nicol's companions, John and Frank. She kindly provided the use of either of her cars to the young men. Off they went in her Chrysler.

Among Nicol's earliest purchases in Paris was the book that became the diary of the Odyssey Tour. The tan leather cover was trimmed with a gold design and the pages had gilded edges. Each glossy page was of the best quality paper Nicol could find. He carefully numbered the 280 pages and copied the daily entries already made on sheets of paper into the book. The diary remains intact with Nicol's keen observations, stories of adventure and records of the many fabulous meals he enjoyed. Included is a list of all his purchases on the final pages.

He seemed to be a mature, young man of nineteen. He sometimes found the exploits of his companions to be ridiculous. On occasion his friends would drink too much and end an enjoyable evening in a drunken stupor. One fellow landed face down on the dance floor, lost the gallon of beer he had consumed and had to be carried to bed. This escapade ended Nicol's intriguing conversation with the possible president-elect of Austria midstream. Nicol hoped the man hadn't noticed.

Pursuit of women of favors was of little interest to Nicol. He did accompany his companions to a show followed by a tour of the house by the madam:

> We went to [a] house on a street not far away. The Madame met us at the door, and told us that for fifty francs we could have half of everything she had to show, and for the other fifty the other half. The first show on the list was the thirty girls probley [sic] seen in houses of this type in every big city in the world. This was followed by an act put on by a hermaphrodite and an assistant....[6]

This was followed by act two:

> A dance by a young lady of the desert, from the Sahara. She, however, had her costume in the wrong place concerning only certain outward, or rather, I might say, upward extremities. Such contortions of the abdomen, as well as other parts, would do credit to a cobra, and it is a wonder to me....[7]

Nicol recorded the entire visit, observing the madam and her girls, the different rooms with mirrors in "all the nooks and crannies." Nothing tempted him, although he left poorer but wiser. The madam flattered Nicol by telling him she had taken a personal liking to him. Nicol wrote:

> An honor indeed, to spend the rest of one's days as a procurer's husband. My French is indeed meager, but in the best that I could command I told Madame that I considered her charming, but that life is much more interesting, when the gal lies always in front, and the fruit has not yet been tasted.[8]

This was the only visit Nicol recorded of personally visiting such a house, although he noted in his diary of the other young men occasionally exiting for an evening adventure of ill-repute.

In Vienna, Nicol and his friends visited the avenue famous for its streetwalkers. He observed that some were well-dressed as if they were ladies of great wealth, but others looked terribly poor, which was evident by the quality of their costumes and the lines in their faces. Nicol had watched the women walk by for ten minutes, when one of the desperate cases accosted him. John Archbold and Nicol quickly departed for an amusement park and left their two companions behind who later managed to collect two women of the better class.

He met young women throughout the Odyssey Tour. Always respectful, he enjoyed dancing and pleasant conversation above everything else. At times he appeared too mature for his age, always sure to turn in at a reasonable hour in light of the activities planned for the following day:

> Went for another walk before diner [sic], and after diner [sic] played some more roulette, was again lucky, had a wonderful waltz with a beautiful Austrian divorcee, a Mrs. Seels, to the tune of the Blue Danube, and then to bed early, as the trip down the Danube in canoes was to start early the next morning.[9]

Nicol met people of all ages. He talked to everyone and, in turn, he seemed to be liked by all. He acquired a way with cards, inherited quite naturally from his mother who was a confirmed player, and he was invited to numerous games. Each day he recorded the games he played and he seldom lost. Time after time he "was very lucky, and won the small ship's pool which was a most pleasant surprise."[10] On the train from France to Switzerland "a little roulette was played, quite profitably."[11]

History had been a favorite subject in school. While traveling through Europe, he was intrigued with the history surrounding him. In his diary he wrote what he had seen each day, including long paragraphs capturing the past of every place he visited. He knew of the monarchies, the family connections to other countries and the architecture. It seemed to flow from his fingertips onto the pages of the diary. He also shared his love of history with his traveling companions. The other young men did not have the same interest, and therefore, spent little time listening to Nicol's historical dialogues. Instead they preferred his tales of adventure.

Spelling and punctuation did not seem to concern Nicol, except in the cases of proper names of people and places. Throughout the diary, title is "tital," dinner is "diner." Penmanship also received little attention. The diary would have been difficult for anyone else to read, but since Nicol did not intend for anyone to read his diary, he probably did not bother to write carefully. Later in life, Nicol began to print. His handwriting never did improve. Being a remarkable letter writer throughout his life, he occasionally heard complaints about the difficulty in reading them. Friends were relieved to receive his correspondence either typed or printed in blocked-capital letters.

Adventure is a theme in his diary. Nicol took part in every possible new experience, especially those offering a thrill. The earliest adventures that he recorded of the Odyssey Tour occurred in Switzerland. A boat trip across Lake Zurich was followed by a train ride into the mountains. The last lap to the overnight lodging was an aerial railway that took them to a small hotel in the mountains:

> The arial [sic] railway was a wonderful experience, hanging or rather passing over hanging gorges hundreds of feet in the air and knowing that only one little cable lies between you and death is enough, I should think, to thrill anybody.[12]

The hotel, nestled at the foot of the snow-covered mountains, was at the six-thousand-foot elevation. After dinner, he went to bed early because the climbing group would be rising at two in the morning. The next day was to be spent climbing the mountain, Glärnisch, in the Glarus Alps of east-central Switzerland.

Rising time came too early and Nicol really didn't want to get up. It was very cold. He dressed as warmly as possible in all the sweaters and coats he could lay his hands on. At 2:30 A.M. everyone lined up outside shivering. Nicol found himself next to a woman, an English author, who proved to be interesting company. Within an hour, the group crossed the snow line and continued upward. The climb got harder and harder as the incline became steeper. The English woman and several others turned back.

At the halfway point groups of five were tied together with ropes. They moved onto a glacier and the distance to the top looked about twenty feet to Nicol. But it was many times that number and took nearly two hours before the summit was reached:

> At last we arrived at the top, and what a sight. The sun rising over the tops of some of the grandest mountains in the world, all the famed mountains of Switzerland.[13]

The cold was intense and chilled Nicol thoroughly. Food and hot drink were necessary before descending the mountain, but first a location must be found where everyone could rest. One of the guides spotted a big rock:

> We reached it by way of a narrow ledge some two feet wide, flanked by two tremendous cliffs. So to this rock we made our way inch by inch, and when we finally arrived at the rock, I was so ill I didn't want either the bread or the hot drink.[14]

Finally everyone managed to eat and the descent began. The group arrived at the hotel before noon. Nicol determined he didn't care if he ever saw a mountain again.

↝

The following morning they departed for Innsbruck. Nicol enjoyed the breathtaking scenery from the train window. On arrival, he and his friends immediately went for a swim at the hotel. Nicol felt quite uncomfortable in the pool because his conservative American bathing suit seemed quite conspicuous. Although the costumes of the bathers left nothing to the imagination, he vowed to purchase local attire to wear for his next plunge.

The long-awaited canoe trip down the Danube River was to begin the following morning, so it was early to bed once again for Nicol. They started downstream about 8:00 A.M. near Linz, the large river port on the Danube. It was not long before Nicol began to feel warm from the intense summer sun. After about an hour of paddling, the canoes were tied together to form a train, which could be led and kept in motion by only a couple of the boys. The remaining boys swam or rested. Nicol elected to rest. The country was beautiful. They floated past splendid castles, abbeys and ruins. They reached Melk, Austria, early in the evening and Nicol headed straight for bed. He had a terrible sunburn and a painful headache.

He was ready to go the next morning. Because of his bad sunburn, he was lucky to be seated in the guide's canoe and was able to enjoy the trip even more from that vantage point. They discussed history, the peasants and country people on the tiny beaches they floated past. They marveled at the scenery. Vienna was the final destination, but Nicol was sad to see the canoe trip down the Danube come to an end.

From Vienna, the Odyssey group traveled to Budapest, Hungary, and on to Yugoslavia and the coastline of the Adriatic. They followed the shoreline to reach their destination of Ragusa. The shopping and marketplaces intrigued Nicol in every city. A scrupulous shopper, he selected his purchases on the basis of their potential return value at home, except items he planned to keep for himself. The buzzing marketplaces provided colorful costumes and unusual goods. John and Nicol both bought local clothing for a complete costume to wear at home.

The second part of the Odyssey Tour was a cruise that began in the Adriatic Sea. Not all of the original Odyssey group continued with the yachting expedition. Good-byes were said and the forty or so who had signed up for the cruise boarded the boat and lifted anchor. Nicol anticipated this part of the tour more than the previous one. He was interested in the ancient history of the regions through which he was traveling. He had not met many travelers from these areas. He had often heard about Europe from family and friends who had traveled to many parts of the continent, but he wanted to go somewhere a little unusual. Recovered from the rigors of his first climbing expedition, he now climbed another mountain:

> We were on our way. It was a drive of some hour and ten minutes duration, and at the end of that time, we were to start on our donkey climb. I happened to be the first off, and called my donkey, Antonius. He was the most sensible I think I have ever met, and riding him was more comfortable than a drawing room in a Pullman Palace Car Special. Up and up we went until we were at about 6,000 feet.... Here we left the donkeys, and started the last part of the 8,000 foot climb on foot. It consisted mostly of going straight up a great mound of shale and loose rock. An hour and a half saw us at the divide on the top, where all but eight decided that they had climbed enough. We decided, however, that as we had come as far as we had, we might as well go on further and get to the top most peak in the surrounding country.[15]

When they reached the top, Nicol enjoyed the view while some of his companions began throwing rocks into the valley below. After a few minutes, several yells from below were followed by a pistol shot. The fellow who started the rock throwing claimed the bullet had whistled by and they all left in a hurry. The descent took about a fifth of the time the ascent had taken. Back on the donkeys, the climbers were able to enjoy themselves again.

The ride was uneventful but still interesting. The local women sat on their cabin porches spinning yarn as American women had done in the past. Shepherds herding their flocks passed on the trail.

Athens was the next stop. Nicol went ashore in a lifeboat. John had acquaintances in the city who were friends of his mother, Anne Archbold. One was kind enough to lend them a car for their use and off they went to find another family friend who was in charge of an irrigation project in Macedonia. Nicol enjoyed meeting Mr. Monks, a noted engineer, and found him an interesting man. Nicol questioned him in great detail about the project, even taking notes which he later copied into his diary. He was already developing a technique that he used for many years when preparing lecture material about his travels.

Shopping was next on their agenda. They drove to the place where Anne Archbold had purchased many furnishings for the mansion she had just completed in Washington, D.C. There they were introduced to the young princess who was in charge. She was an English girl who had married a Prince of Georgia. She had a brother living in Santa Cruz. The world seemed small to Nicol as he purchased a wall hanging and some embroidered cloth.

Ever since Nicol had seen a play in New York where a man was lowered over a cliff in a fish net, he had wanted to try the same. One afternoon in the Pindus Mountains of Greece, he came across two fishermen who were lowering their nets down a cliff. Nicol got an idea:

Finally the monks were persuaded to lower me. I was taken out onto a tiny platform overhanging the rocks far, far below. I was placed in the net, the rungs were put inside the hook, the platform was kicked back, and there I stood, or rather sat, suspended in the air.

The doctor who was there from the yacht took a snapshot, and immediately upon its completion, I was lowered, very slowly, and yet with each foot down, it seemed like the last. Once there was a terrible squeak, and I thought the tiny cable had broken. It however was strong enough, and finally terra firma was reached with one young Californian more dead than alive.

A little boy who was there for the purpose to let me out of my prison, and for at least five minutes I just sat too weak to move far. I suppose that it was safe, and yet it was a very terrifying experience.[16]

Only one other traveler tried the fishnet ride as Nicol did, and later, they agreed it was an experience enjoyed more on reflection than in reality.

The cruise continued through the Greek Islands to the Hellespont, the ancient name for the Dardanelles, a strait thirty-seven miles long and up to four miles wide that separates the Gallipoli Peninsula from Asia Minor and links the Sea of Marmara to the Aegean Sea. An entire day was spent cruising between the continents of Europe and Asia. Constantinople, a place he longed to visit, became a reality for Nicol at last. It was no longer a dream. He arrived at the city. The passports were cleared while the young men remained on board. First on the agenda for Nicol was what he called "the dream of all travelers, the famous Mosque of St. Sophia." He toured the city from dawn to dusk each day seeing all the sights he could take in and buying items of value he hoped would turn a profit when he reached home. Among the most interesting sights he enjoyed was the jewel collection of the former rulers of Turkey. It contained the largest emerald in the world. Lingering over the fabulous jewels, Nicol almost missed lunch. Hurriedly, he returned to eat a quick bite before the next outing.

Following lunch the group traveled to the Black Sea and stopped at a yacht club to prepare for the swim across the Bosporus, the narrow strait between European and Asian Turkey, linking the Black Sea with the Sea of Marmara. The distance was slightly less than a mile but the swim was against a strong current:

> This we swam, I believe about thirty did it and it was a very easy swim. Taking only twenty-two minutes and thirty-one seconds for yours truly, and the others doing it more or less in the same time.[17]

Nicol's first landing in Asia was reached by swimming across the Bosporus from the European continent. The return trip was in a small boat to the club where they dressed and returned to their yacht.

After dinner, Nicol left to tour Constantinople by twilight. He enjoyed the ruins of the walls that used to protect the great city. The next day there was time for shopping before anchor was lifted for the return to the Hellespont. Here the real test was to come.

The morning activity was to swim the Hellespont. Shortly after sunup, the swim began. The swim seemed like it would last forever. The ships passing through the channel were terrifying. The boys could not tell if a ship would pass before or behind them as they swam:

> The ships always seemed, however, to decide at the last minute to go the right way, and it was always behind. Toward the middle, Bill McCarter, one of the directors who was in the little row boat that came along with us, saw a dolphin and for a moment was quite worried that it might be a shark. A shark, however, it was not, poor English but great good fortune for me.[18]

With the tide in their favor, the last half of the swim seemed to go more quickly than the first half. The distance was about four miles and they all successfully finished the adventure.

The trip back to Europe from Asia in the little rowboats was more difficult. Rowing against the current, the sailors could barely handle the wind and the waves. The boat Nicol was in leaked so badly that it might have been easier to swim. Finally, washing ashore on the European side, they walked a mile in their bare feet to reach their point of departure.

Nicol returned to Asia that same afternoon in a Ford truck, rather than by swimming. The trip to Troy was hot and grew even warmer as they traveled inland. Nicol enjoyed seeing the camels that were used for transportation and labor. At Troy Nicol was disappointed:

> It looked more like the deserted basement of a large house after an earthquake than anything I could think of. It is very tiny and is set up on a hill with very broad plains below it. Behind are a lot of vineyards, and in the distance is the sea. It is not a beautiful spot....[19]

Once back aboard the ship, the travelers left the Hellespont behind and the swimmers celebrated with champagne. Nicol indulged in just a few sips and turned in early. At five-thirty the next morning he was awakened by a wave washing over the top deck. The weather worsened and by ten-thirty Nicol was miserable. A little later, he felt he had lost all the food he had eaten in the last month. The first attempts to dock on the Greek Islands were not successful because of the gusting winds. First, the island of Tenos was approached. Finally the ship was able to dock at Syros, the commercial center of the Cyclades Islands.

The boys made straight for land. Once the telegraph office was found, Nicol sent a cable to his parents and another to Uncle Ruddy telling them about his successful swim across the Hellespont. Feeling better, the young men found a candy store and were finally able to eat.

The trip continued on to the volcanic island of Thera and south to Crete. Two days were spent on Crete and then they went back to Athens to see the Acropolis by moonlight. The boat departed next for Naples and crossed the Mediterranean under heavy seas:

> The water became terribly rough, and once we were in the Mediterranean, we knew it. The waves had become as big as mountains or so at least it seemed, and it was not long until I was feeling pretty miserable. There was a stiff wind blowing, and little waves were beginning to break over the bow of the yacht. I began to feel worse and worse in my deck chair, and, in fact, felt like I soon would have no feeling at all.... A tremendous sea running with the wind lashing the foam over the bow, and into your face, and with streaks of lightening and claps of thunder overhead, and about you.... In a storm never to be forgotten. The streaks of lightening come nearer and the thunder got louder. The storm minute by minute became worse.[20]

Nicol could not bear the thought of going below to sleep that night. Being violently ill, he went to bed without any dinner on a deck cot in the shelter of an overhang. Others joined him, but one by one they were driven below by the rain. Having cover from the rain, Nicol stayed on deck all night. And a wild night it was, with cots and chairs flying by in the wind and rain blowing under the shelter with such force that he had to hold a camp cot over his body for protection. Sleep was impossible:

The sun looked very ugly, and what made it even more fantastic.... a red glow could be noticed coming from the volcano,
and this gave the black waters a very uncanny appearance.

The old devil of Stromboli[21] had been awakened by the
storm. Rain, wind and waves, intermittent thunder and lightening, and so on into the morning.

Staid [sic] in bed, or rather on the cot on deck all morning. The night before had been such a terrific strain for me, at
least as far as my stomach was concerned, and I would be
willing to bet a very large sum or for that matter any sum at all
that there were others who were in exactly the same condition. In fact, John was worse off than I was.[22]

The last leg of the yachting trip was made to Naples and a
train bound for Rome was boarded. They spent a few days there,
then went on to Florence and Venice.

Italy fascinated Nicol—the history, the art and the shopping.
He had enjoyed many shops and markets throughout the trip,
but now as it neared its end, he would not have to pack his purchases so often. Mr. Newell was helpful to the young shoppers
intent upon making purchases of value. Often following his
advice, Nicol bought jewels, art and icons with the intention of
reaping benefits upon his return to California.

The last pages of the diary carefully detail the forty-five items
Nicol purchased throughout the trip. On these pages each item
is numbered and carefully described with the place of purchase,
followed by the price paid and then the valued price. Nicol spent
approximately $675 on the items he bought and with the help of
Mr. Newell and the other chaperone, Mr. Lorando, he valued
them at $2,887.

Shortly after returning home, the icon purchased in
Constantinople for eight dollars was priced by an American col-
lector at two thousand dollars. The three brocades were valued at
seven hundred dollars. At home the family appropriated many
of the purchases for The Crossroads. Already Nicol had developed a discerning eye for art and jewels which stayed with him
throughout his travels.

Before departing for Switzerland from Venice, it was necessary to pack and ship many of his purchases to California. Nicol

hoped they would not take too long to reach home as it was only a short time until he too sailed.

A letter arrived from his father and another from his mother with a note from Uncle Ruddy. He enjoyed his mail from the family. He saved the few letters and telegrams he received on the trip, often rereading them at mail stops when he did not receive additional letters. His mother and father both wrote interesting letters, but cables better suited his mother because her social engagements left her little time for writing. His father was extremely busy with the Carson Case and his other business ventures, so his letters were short, although they arrived more frequently than his mother's. Uncle Ruddy, although equally involved in the Carson Case, had written as regularly as his parents and usually provided all the news about life at The Crossroads.

With his packing complete, Nicol made one last visit in Venice. A short trip with a guide to St. Mark's Square was in order to satisfy his curiosity. It looked just as it had when his mother and father were photographed there in 1908 on their honeymoon.

The train trip to Switzerland with Frank West was uneventful and Nicol looked forward to seeing John again. Once the cruise was over, John had departed for Lausanne, Switzerland, on Lake Geneva to meet his mother, Anne, and younger sister, Moira. John would be spending the next year at the University of Geneva.

Nicol and Frank spent the night in the resort town of Montreux, Switzerland. They received a call from John the next morning and plans were made to meet for lunch. They eagerly dressed and took the train to Lausanne to the small station where John would meet them. From the station, John drove them to the chateau where they were staying. After lunch, the travelers shared their adventures and Anne displayed her purchases for Nicol. Frank, John, Anne and their hosts decided to take a ride in an outboard on the lake. Moira and Nicol declined.

This was the first time Nicol had met John's younger sister, Moira. He found her quiet and shy. He hoped to become ac-quainted with Moira because he enjoyed the Archbold family. After the others left, he proposed a canoe ride. Moira seemed to brighten at the prospect and did not seem the least bit shy with only Nicol as company. The two paddled away from the dock:

Moira and I went for a canoe ride. I told Moira that I believed in the continental idea, at least as evidenced in the Near East, namely that the woman do the work, and therefore, she did the paddling. We had quite a talk, and went in for a dip.[23]

Their first visit together was a pleasant one. Nicol found Moira sweet and attentive. Listening to Nicol's stories she appeared to enjoy his conversation and his company. Questioning Moira, Nicol heard about her trip and her plans for the year in Switzerland. She was apprehensive about living at the school she would be attending away from John. Her life had been spent in the company of John or her governess, Eva. Nicol realized her life had been more sheltered than his since he was always alone, except when he had a nanny or governess. Moira had never been alone. In addition to a governess, she had two older brothers and a sister, all very close in age.

The afternoon ended too quickly and Nicol had to return to his hotel with Frank. He wished Moira good luck for the coming year and promised to write to her as soon as he reached home. Accompanying the boys to the train station, she again looked like a shy and helpless younger sister. She stood next to John as they waved good-bye.

~

The trip home through Paris to Cherbourg was uneventful. After crossing the Atlantic, Nicol boarded a train in New York and headed west. Even after shipping many of the purchases home, Nicol had seven suitcases at every train station. At the Oakland depot, Nicol disembarked for the last time, wrestling with the pile of luggage. He was eager to see a familiar face. He waited for almost an hour and still no one had appeared to welcome him home. He looked for the nearest telephone but kept an eye on his luggage. He rang the house in Burlingame and the cook answered that the chauffeur was at the picture show and no one was available to meet him. The family thought Nicol was arriving the following day.

Nicol managed to board a ferry to cross the bay and to hire a cab for the drive from San Francisco to Burlingame. Much to the surprise of the family Nicol was home. To their greater surprise, there was a large sum to be paid to the cab driver.

~

8

THE NUDIST COLONY

While Nicol traveled abroad with the Odyssey Tour, Stanford University reviewed his application for admission. He had completed it in February but admission could not be granted until all of his grades for the school year were recorded. To his relief, by the time that he returned home his grades had arrived by mail. He had received the "A" in history that he had hoped for and his professor had written a note to his parents saying:

> I do hope Nicol's heroic efforts in History were rewarded by success on the College Board examination. I see no reason why Nicol should not be considered prepared for Stanford, or for that matter, for any other college. We have worked our hardest to secure his acceptance for the fall quarter and shall continue to do so at any opportunity that may present itself. If this proves to be impossible, we shall be mighty glad to give Nicol any testimonials we can to procure him admission elsewhere, or at Stanford later.[1]

Nicol ranked seventy-first in his Choate graduating class of ninety-three students. His academic success had been hindered by persistent ear problems each winter. In spite of this he had persevered and completed all the courses successfully. The headmaster, George St. John, said about Nicol:

> Nicol has so much in him that we have great confidence in his development. In many ways he is a very rare person and is

with older people, at least, a genius for friendship. We have every reason to believe that Nicol will be entirely successful in his college work. He is one of the most interesting boys in his class.[2]

Even with these glowing references, Nicol was denied entrance to Stanford. His father was distressed and contacted the registrar's office at Stanford every few days. His application had been mistakenly processed for advanced standing. R.H. telephoned Choate and requested assistance. A few weeks later, an instructor sent another letter to Stanford explaining Nicol's application and that he was not asking for advanced placement. This last letter corrected the problem and he was given a tentative admittance. He was advised to spend the next year at Menlo College and then transfer to Stanford at the end of the academic year. His father was satisfied.

Nicol's father, recently a new member of the board of Jordan Machines in Cleveland, Ohio, surprised him with a new, special order, Jordan Playboy Roadster with a two-tone brown paint job and red wire wheels. According to the shop that sold it to Nicol and his father, it was the only one like it in California and would reach nearly 100 miles per hour. The Playboy, first produced in 1919, had quickly become the most popular model of Jordan automobiles. The Jordan was not manufactured but assembled with parts with the look of a custom car. It was built with a Continental engine, Bosch ignition, Stromberg carburetion, Fedders radiator, Bkjur fuel feed and a Sparton electric horn. Together they made a nice package. The racy wire wheels, standard equipment for the car, caught Nicol's eye. Relishing his new freedom, he vowed never to drive under sixty if possible.

Rules were set at home, however. The family required him to spend weeknights at home, but Friday and Saturday he could do anything he wanted. And he certainly did. In mid October, Nicol wrote to John Archbold, "I haven't had a dead moment yet." He had been to a poker and bridge party and the weekend had netted him $100 which seemed like old times on the yacht.

The fall of 1929 continued to be good times for the Smiths. The conclusion of the Carson Case provided R.H. with funds just in time to finish purchasing Capitola-by-the-Sea, a California coastal town between Santa Cruz and Monterey. It had been on

THE NUDIST COLONY

the auctioneer's block that August. The quiet seaside village, situated on the Soquel River, had long been considered an ideal place for a resort town with campsites, beach frontage and a nearby golf course. R.H. wished to develop it into a working man's seaside resort. He purchased it from intermediaries for an undisclosed price.

Nicol's investments were beginning to suffer the woes of the stock market. He wrote John in Switzerland "the stock market is going from funk to worse." One of the stocks he had bought while at Choate no longer appeared on the quotation list. But R.H. was wealthy. Sue's social engagements encompassed all her waking moments. Nothing was spared at The Crossroads. The twenties had been a prosperous decade for the Smiths. The move to Burlingame, the elegant suburban residential community south of San Francisco, located the Smiths among their wealthiest friends. Joining the Burlingame Country Club, the first such club to be established in California, they entertained lavishly. At one well-remembered party they employed Beniamino Gigli, the Italian tenor, at five hundred dollars per song for entertainment.

Nicol enjoyed his roadster and his independence, especially when his parents were absent from The Crossroads. His father was frequently in Capitola-by-the-Sea, overlooking his investment, or off to Wyoming to search for oil, while his mother often traveled to and from New York. Sue and R.H. discussed the possibility of purchasing a coach car so their train travel would be more comfortable, but instead they continued to use the Crocker's private coach for trips to the East Coast.

Menlo School and College had previously been a school for boys until the junior college was founded in 1927. Located in Atherton, the college was growing rapidly when Nicol began attending. Clubs were being formed and Nicol soon joined the Junior College Social Committee and became the secretary for the English Club. However, the year at Menlo was difficult. Nicol enrolled in a heavy class load and worked diligently to maintain good grades. His ear problems had disappeared and his hard work paid off. The next spring brought confirmed admittance to Stanford.

Nicol found himself alone at Menlo. Most of the young men lived on campus and were involved in college life. The student union was popular and he made a few friends there. At home, he spent his time studying or visiting with the cook and the chauffeur.

Each day he checked the mail for letters from his Choate friends. Relishing each sentence, he quickly would write back with his latest events and plans. John seemed so far away in Geneva, but Nicol hoped they could travel together the following summer. He hoped to persuade Frank West to go along also. A house master at Menlo was organizing a two and a half month trip to the interior of China, Korea and Japan. Nicol had asked his father's permission in October. He could go if his school work was satisfactory. When Nicol submitted his application, R.H. paid the initial installment for the China trip. Nicol wrote his concerns about his grades to John, "so you never can tell," and worried his work might impede his desire to travel. Nicol closed with, "Give my love to Moira."[3] The words love and Moira were carefully underlined. This was the first indication of his feelings for John's younger sister.

After Christmas, Nicol approached the family about moving from The Crossroads to the Stanford campus. He had made several friends who attended school at Menlo and lived at Stanford anticipating the next year on the latter campus. In early February, he rented an apartment with two other students, David Morris and David Huntington. With hard work he had received an average grade of between eighty-five and ninety percent on the midterms in the six courses he was carrying. He was at the top of his class and with continued effort, he would enter Stanford at the sophomore level the next fall. Writing about his studies he said, "Oh John, what a long, long cry from the days at Choate." The letter continued with:

> We have a wonderful apartment. It consists of a dining room, a living room, a sleeping room enclosed like a porch, a bath room, [sic] a kitchenette, and what is even more important, the last mentioned room has ice which is made by some snappy process while you wait. Then there are two garages for the cars and to cap it all, we have our valet.... We entertain at poker parties, have a great big Victor radio so are planning dances there being plenty of room. What a life and I never take a drink because I am still hoping to collect the hundred and

twenty-five next year. I have been terribly cold in poker believe it or not. All the old luck has vanished. The car runs beautifully and so far have escaped a ticket, even though I have never been known to go under sixty.[4]

With his studies, social life, golf and boxing, Nicol was busy. He began to write a book about his previous summer's trip. R.H. hired a secretary to help him with the typing. With all of his educational and social commitments and the planning of the China trip, Nicol still longed for the times past. He wrote to John:

It seems a thousand years ago that I was at Choate and yet it always will remain to me among the happiest days that I have ever had, notwithstanding the infirmary and all the ear trouble.[5]

Spring break found Nicol on his first short trip to Mexico. When he returned to school, he found the China trip had been canceled. The problems in China with Japanese aggression did not make it a favorable place to travel. Nicol began to look for an alternative. Settling on the South Pacific, Nicol began to put his plans in place. He invited John once again, "Write soon and tell me you are willing for a jaunt out to some strange corner of the old world."[6] But John was unable to persuade his mother, Anne, to allow him to accompany Nicol. John had gained admittance to Princeton for the fall and summer plans were already arranged by Anne.

Nicol's spring grade report was the best he had ever received. R.H. agreed to pay for a trip to the South Seas. Nicol would be gone for six weeks, three weeks in the islands and ten days each way on board the ship from San Francisco. Nicol enjoyed the South Seas, visiting the Pacific island groups of Marquesas, Tuamotu, Society and Cook. He experienced every adventure available. From Tahiti he wrote about the coral reefs, fishing, meeting the natives and even sleeping in the bed of a princess who was gone for the weekend.

Unexpectedly, a storm blew in while Nicol traveled to Tahiti. The ship sank and the passengers were rescued by another craft carrying a load of French convicts bound for the penal colony at New Caledonia. News of the sinking reached the states and the story about a young society man on the ship made the front page of a San Francisco paper. His mother and father were frantic. They sent cables throughout the South Sea Islands to ask if anyone had seen their son. Finally contact was made with Nicol in the Fiji Islands and his parents informed him that future travels would need to be to more civilized parts of the world.

Initially Nicol agreed with his parents, but his gravest concern was not the sinking of the ship but an incident which occurred on the island of Moorea the day before he departed for Tahiti and the trip back to San Francisco. A maiden Polynesian, Tiari or "Little Plum Blossom," invited Nicol to a native celebration on his final evening. Nicol had frequently seen the three-hundred-pound woman spying on him at the plantation where he resided while on Moorea. He accompanied her to the celebration and was enticed to take part in dancing that resembled the Hawaiian hula. As the music grew faster and faster, Nicol wiggled faster, thanking his stars that none of his American friends were there to see his uncoordinated, frenzied attempt at a native dance.

Suddenly Little Plum Blossom deftly tripped Nicol and wrapped her arms around his mid-section. She dragged him into the jungle as if he was a bale of hay. Nicol protested to no avail and was convinced that he was being kidnapped. None of the other celebrators paid any attention to his cry for help.

After some distance, Little Plum Blossom stubbed her toe and fell, sprawling on top of her kidnapped date. Nicol kicked, squirmed and bit in an entirely ungentlemanly fashion. As soon as he got to his feet, he sprinted for the plantation where he stayed for the remainder of his visit. He piled his luggage against the bamboo door hoping to prevent another kidnapping attempt. The next morning he hired three natives to guard him on the short walk to the dock. Little Plum Blossom never reappeared.

As he left the South Seas, he and his traveling companion, Eddy Christianson discussed the possibility of a return trip. Nicol found the climate pleasant. He would like to rent a house next time and enjoy an extended stay. But his next trip was already in the planning stages. He was searching for travel companions and he would need to appease his parent's wishes for a safer trip. Perhaps he should return to Europe. Possibly he could arrange a short stint in Russia without upsetting them.

Nicol spent the winter persuading his father to send him on a trip the following summer. He wanted to see the northern countries of Europe and spend a week or two in Russia. R.H. was reluctant but finally relented. Nicol's studies at Stanford were progressing well even with the heavy load he carried.

He headed to Pasadena, California, as soon as school was out for the summer and met his two traveling companions, his fraternity brothers, David Huntington and John Myers. The latter had a new Chrysler Imperial Roadster called Bessie. With no rumble seat and fourteen suitcases lashed on the back, the young men drove across the states to New York.

They made numerous stops crossing the country, including one at Aunt Myrtle's house in Pennsylvania. Nicol never missed the opportunity to visit his father's older sister. She made Nicol his favorite meal of fried chicken. The next morning they left for Washington, D.C., to visit John Archbold. A few poker games later and John owed Nicol $259. Promising to pay in full upon Nicol's return, John asked for an introductory letter to Nicol's dear friend, Barbara Cates from Burlingame who now lived in New York. John hoped to meet her over the summer when he traveled north. Nicol and Barbara, or Bobbie as she was known to friends, had been quite fond of each other several years previously.

Upon arriving in New York the young men drove Bessie aboard the Olympic, and they sailed for Europe. After landing in early July, they made Paris their first stop, followed by London, Belgium, Holland and Berlin. From Berlin, Nicol would travel alone to Moscow for two weeks, then back to Berlin and on to southern France and Spain, finally back to Paris, then by ship to New York and another drive across the United States.

Prior to their departure from New York, Nicol had purchased a book to read while crossing the Atlantic. According to Nicol, it was the first of its type to be published by a reputable house, Knopf & Company. The book was about nudists and nudist colonies and was a great success among the Olympic passengers. He lent it to anyone who asked and found it intrigued many of the passengers.

Nicol wanted to visit a nudist colony while traveling in Europe, but David was skeptical and doubted one even existed. If it did, they would never be allowed in. He also voiced concern that it would not be good for their minds. He was so sure they would be denied entrance that he bet Nicol ten dollars they couldn't get in.

On their way from Lübeck, Germany, to Copenhagen, Nicol remembered the book had mentioned a nudist colony in the vicinity. Following the directions given in the book, they reached the gates of the Frielisch Park Klingberg. Upon ringing the doorbell, they were greeted by a young lady wearing nothing but glasses. Nicol was so surprised that all he managed to blurt out was "pardon me." She was the first nude he had ever met in the open doorway of a house and he was startled. David and John couldn't say a thing and just stared. Finally Nicol was able to stutter they would like to see the head of the colony. A moment later, a nude man appeared and Nicol explained he had read about the colony in a book. The man's eyes lit up because the book had glorified his place and he asked Nicol for his letter of introduction. Quickly Nicol responded:

> Listen, we are seniors at an American university. The youth of America are fed up with cocktails and gangsters. We'll give them nudism instead. We'll spread it from coast to coast. Another three years and everyone in the United States will be naked day and night.[7]

Nicol apparently put so much fervor into his brief speech that the man decided they could stay for three days providing they behaved. They were led to his office and were provided with a list of rules to review. The price of the nudist colony was about two dollars and fifty cents a day for room and board. This included daily exercise routines and horseback riding which Nicol decided he probably did not want to do in the nude.

Since it was nearly bedtime, the three young men were taken to a little cottage where they unpacked and proceeded to remove their clothing and climb into bed. Promptly at 7:00 A.M., Nicol awakened by a young woman tapping him on the shoulder. She informed him it was time for the morning exercises. Nicol asked her to awaken the other two. She obliged by tapping David on the shoulder. David opened his eyes and with a surprised shriek he jumped out of bed. Then jumped right back in, pulling the bedclothes over his head. Nicol knew David startled easily and chuckled at what he suspected was one of the most amazing experiences of David's life.

Now John was awake and Nicol motioned to him to engage the girl in conversation while he jumped out of bed and slipped into his robe. The other two managed their robes while Nicol spoke with the girl and then they all followed her up a hill to the location where the nudists were exercising. The exercises were more exertion than Nicol was used to so early in the morning and he attempted the regimen only halfheartedly. Everyone was friendly and helpful and soon the group walked down the hill to breakfast.

Following the simple meal, Nicol decided to sunbathe. Retrieving a blanket from the car, he headed to the shore of the lake. Carefully spreading his blanket, he lay down in the middle so the prickly ground cover would not poke at his bare flesh. Suddenly a toe nudged him. He looked up to see a beautiful young German girl who claimed to have forgotten her blanket. In a beseeching voice she vowed there was room for both on the blanket as she plopped down beside him. Nicol did not move an inch all morning. The sun became hotter. At the left edge of the blanket were the prickly bushes and to the right the beautiful nude fraulein. Hours later and thoroughly sunburned, Nicol finally escaped for a swim in the lake.

The afternoon was spent taking moving pictures and photographs of everyone. No one minded at all if they could also photograph Nicol and his friends in return. The young men wondered if they would appear in the family albums of the nudists. Knowing that none of their friends ever went to northern Germany gave them a sense of security. Many photos were taken of John and Nicol among the groups of Germans.

After seven days at the colony, they stayed some additional days since Bessie was undergoing repairs. It was raining when they left, so they donned their clothing and continued the trip. The young men were unaware that a photo of David and John with two German girls had been misplaced at the nudist photography department. Several months later, one of the girls found the photo and sent it with a letter to John in Los Angeles. John had made a favorable impression on her. Unfortunately, John was not home at the time and his mother opened the letter from far away Germany to see if there was any news of special importance that should be forwarded to her son or if it could wait for his return. The woman was astonished at the photo that fell from the letter. Nicol felt John's mother was always a little cool towards him after this exposure.

When asked later why he hadn't moved into the shade, Nicol replied he just didn't. There was something about a first day in a nudist colony that kept one from wandering around. He just stayed put. David spent seven hours in the lake the first day and immediately went back to the cottage after his extended swim. Nicol found David just wasn't made for nudism and never got into the spirit of the colony. But pay up on the bet David did. Nicol demanded payment in full in Deutsch marks.

On his return to Berlin, Nicol visited the Intourist office to find that he had been granted permission to enter Soviet Russia. He paid a sum that was the equivalent of twenty-eight dollars a day which included transportation, hotels, meals and the services of a girl guide employed by the Intourist Bureau. The following evening, he left his two friends in Berlin and boarded the Paris-to-Warsaw Express. He was embarking on a journey he had anticipated for many months, a journey which was to be astonishing to him and that launched his career.

Arriving in Warsaw, Poland, the next morning, Nicol had only a few hours to tour the city before boarding the next train for Russia. At the border another train change was required. After exchanging money at the train station, Nicol boarded the Russian train, deposited his luggage in his berth and proceeded to the dining car. Finding that a sandwich and tea cost two dollars and seventy-five cents in American money, he returned to his compartment without dinner.

As he entered the compartment he found two young women, one of whom was half undressed. Confused, he begged her pardon and withdrew into the hall. He checked his tickets and verified that he was in the correct compartment, so he opened the door and thrust his ticket towards the partially clothed woman, demanding to see hers. They were for the same room. Nicol was aghast. The turmoil had brought the passengers of the neighboring compartment into the hall. The two women in his compartment nonchalantly reported to the gathering in the hall that the embarrassed young American was sharing their room. Nicol had reached the Soviet Union. Here members of both sexes traveled in the same compartment on a train. It was considered acceptable. Nicol didn't sleep a wink.

Disembarking in Moscow, he was greeted by a lady in her late twenties who was assigned to him as his Intourist guide. Nicol's bags were carried to a beautiful new Studebaker waiting beside the curb. Commenting on the car, Nicol assumed he would walk or ride on streetcars in Russia. His guide scornfully interrupted, informing him that only lies were spread about her wonderful country. She told Nicol he would see for himself how wonderful her country was.

The hotel room seemed comfortable enough and after the experience on the train he was relieved to find he did not have to share it. A washbasin was the bathroom portion of the room while the rest, including the shower, were down the hall. Each time he used the bathroom it cost two rubles. Each American dollar had been exchanged for one Russian ruble. A trip to the bathroom down the hall cost two dollars.

He attempted his first bath in the washbasin in his room:

> The washbasin must have been a Peter the Great relic. I turned on the faucet and six and one half drops wended their way out. When the half drop backed up in, I tried a second time. The six and a half drops appeared again, but the mass formation only peaked [sic] at me, and then withdrew, leaving the half drop like a melted pearl in my hand. As a result, my tooth brush suffered, and the bird bath I gave myself would hardly have ruffled a sparrow's tail.[8]

He went down to the dining room, ravenously hungry because of the skipped dinner the night before. It was a huge room filled with tables, magnificent palms and dirty linen. Four others were expecting breakfast and each was handed a huge menu. Seven waiters stood to one side of the room talking and apparently avoiding the customers. Finally one broke away from the rest to wait on the patrons. Nicol pointed to several items, since the menu was all in Russian and hoped for the best. Everyone received identical meals regardless of what had been ordered.

> In the due course of time, I received what everybody else was given, a small piece of ham, a biscuit, and a cup of coffee. The ham was almost like rubber, it was so pliant, I automatically rolled it into a ball and bounced it onto the table. The biscuit was harder than the ones my mother baked on the semi-annual occasion when she enters the kitchen. And at that time, I didn't drink coffee. Being ravenously hungry, I attempted the biscuit, and lost a comfortable filling in an already crumbling molar, which my good friend, Dr. Sharp, the dentist in San Francisco, had done his best to save. The consummation of my breakfast did not take long. I was in an ugly frame of mind when I approached Miss Lithuania in the lobby.[9]

Miss Lithuania, Nicol's nickname for his guide since she had been born in the province of Lithuania, interrupted Nicol to tell him he was just a bourgeois American and was too fat anyway. She turned and marched out of the hotel. Nicol trailed behind as she haughtily asked him if he was ready for his first tour. Nicol was ready, but the Studebaker was not in sight. Inquiring about the automobile's whereabouts, Miss Lithuania laughed and informed him it was off to pick up the next tourist. They would be walking and she expected he would thin down a little during his visit. Nicol protested. He did not want to thin down but rather liked himself as he was.

Walking past the Kremlin, where Stalin was living, and through Red Square, they approached the palace of the Romonoffs. To Nicol the palace appeared to be in a state of disrepair and he observed only meager furnishings of mediocre craftsmanship. He asked his guide where the displays were. "Sold for the public good," she replied noncommittally. Walking through the palace, Nicol was repeatedly disappointed. His guide could show him where Catherine the Great had once slept, except the room was empty. Again his guide replied to his inquiry to where her bed was, "Sold for the public good."

The return trip was made by streetcar, which was completely empty when they boarded to Nicol's surprise. Remarking to Miss Lithuania that he had believed all streetcars were crowded, she retorted, "Lies, more lies about our wonderful country." Miss Lithuania was beginning to sound like a gramophone record, playing the same old tune. Several blocks went by before the streetcar reached its next stop. Hordes of people boarded. The same occurred at each subsequent stop, until the streetcar was bulging and Nicol was sweating. He gratefully disembarked at the hotel.

Lunch was still being served when they entered the hotel. The service was better than breakfast, but the food was scarcely more appetizing. Nicol received an unrecognizable soup, eight slices of cucumber, a small piece of meat and ice, not ice cream, for dessert. It was necessary for him to order an extra bottle of water to drink, which cost an additional one dollar and twenty-five cents.

A moving picture was the next item on the tour agenda. Nicol hoped to see a Russian version of an action-packed adventure but instead it was a dull and poorly made documentary.

> We went to the moving picture and saw a film dealing with one of the great problems the Soviet Government has had to contend with, namely, the caring for the homeless children, the so called wolf children, or Bezz Brizoni. In 1923 and 1924 there were reputedly a half a million or so children between the ages of six and sixteen, who, as a result of famine, pestilence, and the break up in the family home, and the absence of relatives, were waifs, sleeping on street corners and in cellars, robbing and stealing. The Russian Government, realizing that something should be done, built homes for them where they might learn an honest trade, and as a result, more than ninety percent of these children have been made into honest citizens. This moving picture, The Path to Life, dealt with this problem.[10]

The next two weeks provided many new experiences for Nicol. The marriage and divorce bureau intrigued him. A bribe of half a cake of Ivory soap persuaded Miss Lithuania to marry him. It was easily done and took not more than ten minutes and two dollars and seventy cents to complete the permission forms and the ceremony. The divorce bureau was in another part of the same building. It was necessary for both parties to appear for a marriage but only one need appear for a divorce. Married for eleven minutes, Nicol and Miss Lithuania signed the papers for a divorce and were told they were both liable for half the support of any children. When only one party appeared for a divorce, the other was informed by mail.

During the week in Moscow, Nicol met a Russian girl at a museum who spoke six languages and she invited him to her mother's apartment for dinner. She worked as a secretary for an American engineer and her mother was connected to the aristocracy both in Russia and in England. The appointed evening arrived and he was called for by the other guest, an American newspaperman. He stopped the car in front of an attractive three-story building of gray stone.

Climbing the stairs to the third floor, he followed the other guest to the last door in the hallway. Nicol assumed the entire building was their home and was astonished to find their residence was not much larger than a good-sized pantry in an American home. The room contained no closet space, two chairs, a single bed and four nails in the wall for hanging items. Nicol commented that their quarters seemed crowded. The girl's mother replied that they were lucky. Even though they shared the same bathroom and kitchen with twelve other families, they had not been ordered to provide their floor space as a sleeping area for a stranger as had happened to people they knew.

In the privacy of their room, Nicol questioned them on what they thought of the Soviet government. Neither of the Russians answered. They knew people who had been arrested when they spoke too freely about their government. The dinner was enjoyable, although the mother had spent seven hours in lines to get the groceries.

At a work farm near Moscow, Nicol was allowed to talk with the men. He found the conditions deplorable and the men were unwilling to answer his questions about Russia, although they were all well informed on subjects concerning unemployment in America or on any other negative aspect of capitalism. Later when questioning an American who was living in Russia on why anyone would want to remain, Nicol was told, "In America you have only your own future and the future of your children. In

Russia we have the future of our countrymen and my countrymen's children as well."

With Miss Lithuania, he went everywhere, to factories, palaces, hospitals, museums and bathing beaches. The second week was spent in Leningrad touring palaces, museums and meeting interesting people. At the close of the second week, Nicol traveled by plane from Leningrad to Berlin. He anticipated his first flight with excitement and he wrote to his friend John, "I will travel by plane from Leningrad to Berlin."[11] To his amazement, he flew over eight countries on his first flight. He flew from Russia over Estonia, Latvia, Lithuania, East Prussia, Danzig, Poland and landed in Germany. That evening he ordered the largest steak on the menu in a Berlin restaurant.

↵

9

CAPITOLA

Nicol arrived at The Crossroads after his extended trip to Europe and Russia to find the press interested in his travels. The local newspaper requested an interview of his impressions of Russia. His travels to Russia occurred during the time when it was an outcast among nations. It was not until 1933 that the United States officially recognized the Soviet Union. People were curious about the country. American attitudes toward Russia had in fact been changing during the preceding decade.

The newspaper article attracted widespread attention and culminated in launching Nicol in his lifelong career. The Foreign Relations Committee of the Women's Club of Coalinga, California, invited him to speak at their next meeting, offering him a seventy dollar honorarium.

R.H. offered to match the fee Nicol received from the speaking engagement and for his future lectures. He did not believe Nicol would be interested in a speaking career for any length of time. He envisioned Nicol as a businessman or a lawyer like himself, or grandfather Frank Nicol or the judge, Uncle George Nicol. R.H. was skeptical about forthcoming engagements for a lecture circuit based on travel experiences. Nicol later recalled that his father's friends would tell R.H., "Nicol won't continue to lecture for long." Everyone believed he would tire of the profession after a couple of years and return home to settle into business with R.H.

Nicol's success in Coalinga was overwhelming. His speech, consisting of sensational stories, attracted a full house at the women's club. Nicol was a sensation. It was forty-four years later that he retired from the travel-adventure-lecture circuit. Needless to say, R.H. did not continue his fee-matching agreement indefinitely.

Nicol began to make adventure his business. Blessed with the ability to tell fascinating stories, a talent he no doubt inherited from his mother, he began to plan trips to distant places. He wanted to take one trip each year to an unusual place, followed by a lecture circuit in the United States and possibly Canada. Nicol liked people and naturally tended to focus on the people of faraway places. Adventure was inherent in the places he chose to travel.

Nicol planned continually. With every new travel idea he would write to his old Choate buddy, John, and invite him along. The Odyssey Tour was their only joint excursion during their lifelong friendship. But due to their closeness, they always considered each other as the first choice for a traveling companion.

John was busy with his schooling at Princeton University and his mother, Anne, planned the summers for her children, frequently sending the boys to camp in New Hampshire. Each summer also included a family camping trip with the children, their closest friends, and their governess or a counselor from camp. The summer after the Odyssey, Anne brought her children to California for a camping trip to Yosemite. There she and her children enjoyed the scenic grandeur of the seven-mile glacial valley surrounded by the sheer granite walls of Half Dome and El Capitan and the thunderous waterfalls of Bridalveil Falls. Nicol was invited and he enjoyed the trip with the Archbold family immensely. Excursions were planned for each day.

Nicol became quite popular with the Archbold family during the trip. Each day he participated in the same itinerary as everyone else, hiking and exploring the wonders of Yosemite. At the end of each day Nicol entertained everyone with his amusing stories. John shared Nicol's nickname with his family. He had acquired from his Choate peers the name of "Uncle Nicol." It suited the young man since only an uncle could tell stories and yarns with Nicol's innate ability.

Moira and Nicol vividly remembered their prior meeting at Lake Geneva in Switzerland. During the Yosemite trip they hiked and explored together, ending their day talking around the camp-fire in the evenings. Moira found Nicol's travels exciting and loved listening to the gregarious young man. Nicol found Moira's adoration to his liking and went out of his way to be kind to Moira. Moira, the quiet one of her family, felt comfortable talking with Nicol and he made her feel her conversations were equally interesting.

The Yosemite trip culminated at The Crossroads with the Archbold family meeting R.H. and Sue. Sue entertained them in grand style with a welcoming party of Burlingame society, while R.H. took Armar and John to the hills southeast of the San Francisco Bay near Patterson. There he gave them a tour of his latest investment in mining. The Archbold's departed. Moira and Nicol promised to write.

~

Nicol returned to Stanford for his junior year. The family remained at The Crossroads with a new addition to the household. Just as Sue loved to play cards and gamble, so did Nicol. Throughout boarding school and the years at Stanford he spent much of his free time playing poker or backgammon—always for money. Nicol claimed he earned his own spending allowance from his winnings. His correspondence with John Archbold during those years attested to the truth of this statement. Nearly every letter thanks the payee, or asks when he can expect payment. John frequently owed gambling debts the sums of $100 to $250 in the early 1930s, a substantial sum for a young man in college.

After returning from Russia, Nicol was playing backgammon one evening with Herbert Fleishhacker Jr., the son of the well-known benefactor of the Fleishhacker Zoo in San Francisco. Frequent gambling partners, Herbie suggested that the stakes were dull. He proposed a change. If he lost, Nicol would receive a baby Nubian lion from the Zoo. If Nicol lost, then Herbie wanted a rare type of snake. The game proceeded and Nicol won. Not giving the debt any credence, Nicol forgot about the wager. A few days later, R.H. was tending his rose garden when a truck pulled up from the Fleishhacker Zoo. R.H. summoned Nicol when the driver insisted on leaving a lioness cub on the lawn.

Amused Nicol led the cub into the house, and they soon became warm friends.

He named her Chaquita and she slept on the foot of his bed until she became too big. Then she slept on the floor. Chaquita adopted Sue's Great Dane, Nuts, as her mother.

As the months passed, Chaquita accompanied Nicol everywhere. She always rode in the front seat of his convertible Jordan Playboy with her paws on the door and her ears straight back in the breeze. Whenever Nicol commanded, she would roar at passersby, which frightened more than a few motorists. R.H. had never been fond of animals, and Chaquita positively disliked him. By the time she was one year old, she was the size of a large Airedale dog, but she never hurt Nicol or attempted to bite him.

One night, R.H. awoke and decided to go to the pantry to fix himself a sandwich. As he went by Nicol's door, which was ajar, Chaquita saw her chance and began to stalk him. With his back turned in the pantry while he made a sandwich, his nightshirt fell open and Chaquita quickly nipped R.H. from behind. The next morning R.H. was upset and the maid gave notice claiming that when she had been employed the question of working in a house with a lion had never arisen. R.H. could not sit down for several days and he said either Chaquita had to go or he would.

Nicol hated to see Chaquita leave and insisted if his father had been wearing pants instead of a nightshirt the problem would never have occurred. As usual, the decision was up to Sue, since she made all the important decisions. Sue decided in R.H.'s favor and Chaquita was given to an artist in Saratoga, a small community in the Santa Cruz Mountains. Occasionally Nicol stopped to see Chaquita and to attempt to collect on the debt the artist owed. He promised Nicol one of his paintings when he received Chaquita. Nicol would visit Chaquita, who had grown to the size of a circus lion, whenever he stopped. Nicol had a passion for animals and the lioness was the first of the unusual pets he adopted during his lifetime. Nuts, their Great Dane, often took the place of Chaquita, and rode in the front seat of the automobile.

Nicol convinced R.H. to pay for his trip to the South Seas when the Menlo College China expedition was canceled. The following year, it took him months to convince R.H. to foot the bill for the European trip.[1] Nicol's father asked to see his planned itinerary and wanted to know who would be traveling with him. Once R.H. felt assured that Nicol's plans were arranged, he agreed to pay the expenses.

But each year it was becoming more difficult to cover the expenses of the household, plus Nicol's education and travels. Although 1929 had been unfavorable to many investors and businessmen and R.H. lost large sums of stock in companies he had invested in heavily, he managed to get payment from the Carson Case during the economic downturn. When he received his portion from the Carson Investment Company from the settlement of the case, which totaled seven million dollars for him alone, he invested in real estate. Already involved in extensive oil speculation in Wyoming, he had connections along the California coastline.

It had been several years since he had met Henry Rispin in San Francisco. Rispin had made his money in oil in the Colorado area and had purchased Camp Capitola,[2] a scenic section of coastline south of Santa Cruz along the Monterey Bay, established in 1879. Rispin had grandiose dreams for the area and purchased the whole town, including the beach front, the Hotel Capitola with 160 rooms, the wharf, bathhouses, a number of lots and the campground, in addition to the eight-acre parcel he already owned west of Soquel Creek. He made his investment in 1919 by buying out the heir of the town's originator, Frederick Hihn.[3]

Rispin attempted to carry out his dream for the small town by improving the streets, building a new bathhouse and a movie theater. He moved buildings to new locations where he felt they were better suited. In 1923 his twenty-two room mansion was complete on the acreage west of Soquel Creek. With the advent of the automobile, Capitola-by-the-Sea would become a vacation haven for well-to-do San Franciscans. He even went so far as to offer the mansion to Calvin Coolidge as a summer retreat.

R.H. traveled to Capitola-by-the-Sea to have a look at Rispin's dream. Impressed by the location and the Rispin Mansion, he decided to invest. On July 27, 1929, it was announced that all of Rispin's holdings were to be auctioned off on a summer evening in August.[4] With his available capital already committed to oil investments, R.H. convinced an intermediary to purchase the entire property. The auction took place in a large, striped, circus tent erected on the beach for the occasion. For an undisclosed price, the land was purchased by R.H.'s designated bidder. A few months later, with his financial situation more liquid, R.H. became the owner of Capitola-by-the-Sea. The land, the beaches and beach front, the automobile campground, the wharf, the streets—even the sewers belonged to R.H.

He purchased the Rispin Mansion separately for a sum of $19,800. To oversee the development of this investment into a burgeoning seaside resort, he hired bankrupt Henry Rispin. With the land purchases, R.H. reactivated Rispin's corporation, the Capitola Company, which had been formed in 1919. In addition, the Pacific Coast Jockey Club and the Ocean Shore Railway Company resumed business. Additionally he formed two new companies: the Freehold Land Company and "Nicol and Smith." Each of the corporations was designated to manage certain aspects of the Santa Cruz County investments.[5]

All recreational land, including the country club and golf course, was held by the Pacific Coast Jockey Club, and the Ocean Shore Railway Company was designated for railroad and streetcar holdings. R.H. continued to carefully organize each investment, not only for his purposes but also in an attempt to control Rispin's expenditures.

A groundskeeper was hired for the former Rispin Mansion, now called the Capitola Place by the Smiths. Sue liked the mansion and planned to have a hand in the refurbishing and decorating. But R.H. attended the Flood's estate sale and filled the Capitola Place with the furnishings he bought at the sale. Sue was appalled. She felt less pretentious furniture should be bought. After all, it was a beach house for entertaining their friends. Despite her objections, everything was hauled to the mansion. Sue never again visited the Capitola Place while it remained in her family's possession.

The investment in Capitola was proving costly and Rispin's demands to R.H. for funds were frequent. Sue was unhappy about the partnership with Rispin. She had distrusted him from the beginning. Sue was sharp when it came to people and the first day Rispin entered The Crossroads, she disliked him. She told R.H. it was going to be a poor "investment" but her husband did not listen to her ill-boding.

The dichotomy was that R.H. liked his new partner and entrusted large sums of money to him. On one occasion, Rispin requested eleven thousand dollars from R.H. during a brief stop at The Crossroads. R.H. wrote him a check for the amount and ignored Sue's dire warnings. Unfortunately, Sue was correct and Rispin spent the entire amount on himself rather than the bills he promised to pay that had been incurred by the Capitola Company.

Whether it was Rispin and Capitola or dry speculation in the oil drilling taking place in Wyoming that caused R.H.'s financial downturn and ultimately his loss of everything except The Crossroads is not known. These congruent situations with his major investments surely determined his financial future.

In 1919, R.H. had written in a letter that he was worth in excess of three million dollars by conservative estimates.[6] In Nicol's letters to John from 1929 to 1931, Nicol mentions his father's good luck in oil speculation and drilling. Obviously, R.H.'s hard work and speculation had brought him wealth.

Following Nicol's twenty-first birthday, his father offered him the $125,000 that had been put aside for this occasion. Nicol kept his promise and never smoked nor drank, except with dinner. Using his better judgment, Nicol asked his father to reinvest the money at R.H.'s choosing until he graduated from Stanford. Nicol planned to use the funds to begin his career. Little did he know that R.H. would no longer have the funds when he graduated in December of 1933. The Depression was taking its toll on the Smith family and on R.H.'s business partners. It was to have an impact on Nicol's plans for his future.

↜

Nicol began to plan a trip to China, hoping to go during the summer of 1932. He wrote to John, asking him to be his traveling companion. Nicol's interest in China seemed to reappear annually. Whether R.H.'s early fascination had any bearing on Nicol's travel plans is unknown. Writing to John, he had two comments about money, one in conjunction with his travel plans, the other concerning the Depression-era stock market:

> If you feel too poor—take your time over the backgammon of last June but if you don't I would appreciate the results of our friendly fight.
> I hope to go to China in June, and am planning a wonderful trip which if the market does not get worse it may materialize.[7]

The trip did not materialize, so Nicol decided to attend summer session at Stanford. Feeling the full effects of the Depression, he did not reach mainland China for another seven years.

He enrolled in seventeen units for the summer session and studied diligently. The heavy load meant he would be able to complete his course work during fall quarter. Prior to leaving Choate he had taken the Scholastic Aptitude Test and ranked in the forty-second percentile, considered a C average at that time.[8] His parents, particularly his father, had been disappointed. R.H. hoped his son would follow his example as valedictorian of his graduating class.

Nicol applied himself during the year at Menlo College and maintained a B+ average for both semesters, completing eighteen units and twenty-two units during the fall and spring semesters, respectively. When Stanford admissions received the records from Menlo, they wrote asking for clarification. Apparently the discrepancy between the grades on his previous application when he left Choate and the more recent application from Menlo College was observed by the admissions committee. In a letter to Dean Vandervort at Menlo Junior College, the committee stated the application was being deferred until further explanation was received.[9]

Within three days Dean Vandervort replied, stating that Nicol's grades were correct. He had maintained a B+ average and shown his true abilities as a student. Since he had completed his course work successfully, he hoped the committee would immediately clear up the matter for Mr. Smith.[10] With summer quarter over, Nicol enrolled in thirteen units for that fall. On January 6, 1933, Stanford University conferred the Bachelor of Arts in History degree to Francis Nicol Smith.

↩

BOOK FOUR:

THE ADVENTURER

Tomorrow begins for me the greatest
adventure of my life....

> *Nicol Smith*
> *Letter to John D. Archbold*
> *Written from*
> *Nickerie, Dutch Guiana, 1935*

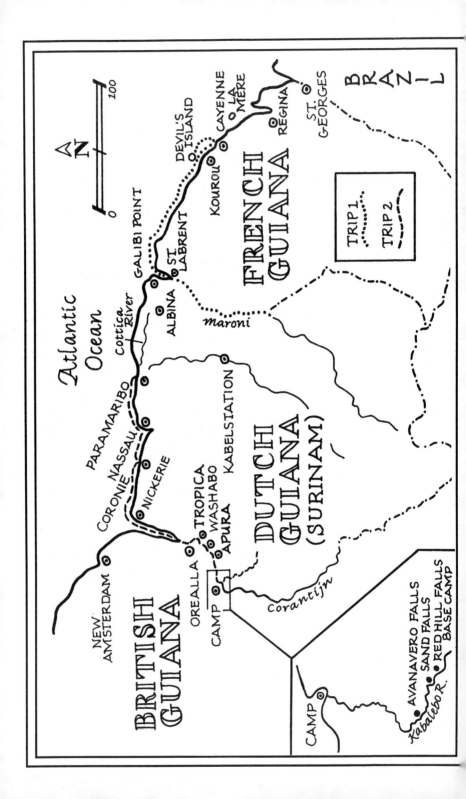

10

LETTER FROM NICKERIE

N icol's educational goals were completed with his
graduation from Stanford University. He thought his history degree would be appropriate background for a travel and
lecture career and he was poised to launch his next adventure.
Sue and R.H. were supportive of Nicol's desires but neither were
enthusiastic. R.H. felt more education was in order, at least some
practical business experience. Since Nicol's $125,000 was cur-
rently invested by R.H. and not readily available, travel plans were
put on hold. Nicol began to plan an expedition for later that
year. Meanwhile, he agreed to R.H.'s wishes and went to work
for him.

Working for his father did not bother Nicol. R.H. probably
hoped to introduce his son to the business world and turn him
toward business and finance and away from adventure and travel
that Nicol craved. Nicol never considered employment with his
father as anything more than temporary. It was a way to pass the
time and pacify his parents until he was able to finance his next
expedition. After all, he had made money at his first lecture and
he had paid to attend lectures by noted explorers.

Nicol's responsibilities were mundane and generally involved
trips to oversee investments. Frequently he handled the bank
transactions, including deposits for the payrolls, followed by delivering the payroll to the business location. His favorite delivery
was to a magnesite mine near Patterson, a quiet farming community in central California only several hours away. The delivery took Nicol an entire day by the time he left home, picked up

the payroll at the local Patterson bank and delivered it to the mine.

One afternoon he had a prolonged wait at the Patterson bank while the payroll was prepared. With nothing to do, he sat down on the bench inside the door. Striking up a conversation with the young man next to him, he found they knew some of the same people. Nicol had several classmates at Stanford who attended Santa Monica High School where this fellow had graduated in 1927. Asking what his business was, he learned the fellow needed a loan to harvest his crop of peaches.

When the payroll was ready, Nicol stood and reached out to shake the man's hand. He introduced himself and the man did likewise. Art Hall was his name. He gave Nicol instructions on how to reach his ranch and maybe they could look at pictures of their mutual acquaintances in his old yearbook. Nicol accepted the invitation and promised to stop by on his next trip. For many months, Nicol stopped at Art's ranch each week after making the payroll delivery to the mine west of town. That fateful introduction at the bank was to shape both their lives in the years to come.

❧

Nicol found his work dull. There was no adventure to feed his spirit. Occasionally he met interesting people, but that wasn't enough. While waiting for his coffers to become well lined, he began to turn his past adventures into stories. Each evening at his desk he diligently tried to put the excitement he had felt on paper. The following morning, he asked R.H.'s secretary to type the stories and make any necessary corrections. Page after page accumulated. He wrote about the nudist colony, his trip to Russia, escapades in Paris and exploits in the South Seas.

Sue and R.H. occasionally glanced at his work and asked what he planned to do with it. Nicol said he planned to publish his adventures in short stories and hoped a magazine would be interested. Busy with their own affairs, his parents did not give it much thought. Nicol continued, undaunted by their lack of interest.

One day, while watching a Hollywood-style, adventure movie at the local theater, he yearned to resume the travel exploits of his college days. An adventure was what he needed to bring spark back into his life. But where would he go? He knew Europe fairly well. He had explored the South Seas. What next? He found South America beckoning him. Not the South America of conducted cruises, with their hasty glimpses of civilized cities, but of countries more mysterious, more remote.

As he boarded the train for New York in May of 1933, Nicol tentatively planned a trip to Venezuela. In New York he visited his old friend John Archbold and they discussed his idea. Talking over his plans, John agreed South America sounded intriguing. John had a connection and thought he could get Nicol an introduction that might help him plan his trip. Consequently, the next day Nicol booked passage on a boat bound for Venezuela in two weeks. He still felt uncertain. Then two days later, he received an invitation from a Dr. Rice to come to his home to discuss his plans.

Dr. Hamilton Rice, an internationally known explorer and authority on tropical diseases, was noted for mapping unexplored country in South America. When Nicol arrived at his home, he met Dr. and Mrs. Rice and two other colorful characters, Sacha Siemel and General Rafael de Nogales.

Gathered in the front room of Rice's lavish Fifth Avenue home were three men and a woman who knew the jungles of the South American continent as few others did. Sacha Siemel was known through Julian Duguid's book *Tiger Man*,[1] in which Siemel was the main character. He had spent fourteen years in Matto Grosso,[2] one of the wildest regions in Brazil and had hunted jaguars. General de Nogales was known for his escapades in Central America, as well as his maneuvers as a Turkish General in World War I.

It was astounding to Nicol that these people had gathered to help him plan his trip. For two hours he listened, fascinated, as each described a region of the Americas. Secretly he had always wanted to visit the Orinoco River of Venezuela and the countries directly south of it, particularly the colony of French Guiana and its district of Cayenne and Devil's Island.

Wondering if they had been to these countries north of Brazil, he asked what they might know about them. Siemel replied he had been to both French and Dutch Guiana but had only touched on them in the course of an expedition up the Maroni

River, which was the boundary between French and Dutch Guiana. The previous year he had journeyed there and he could provide Nicol with many letters of introduction.

> Siemel had with him among the photographs that he was showing to the doctor several taken on the Maroni River. The waterfalls and the country were so beautiful and the story of escaping convicts encountered so fantastically interesting that I left the house with my mind made up that this was the section of South America that I intended to visit.[3]

Nicol invited the group to have lunch with him two days later at the River Club. Only Siemel and de Nogales were able to meet him for the luncheon. Young, exuberant Nicol, accompanied by de Nogales in his uniform and Siemel in expedition dress, caused a stir at the exclusive club. Upon their arrival, the doorman disapprovingly stared at the three gentlemen. The luncheon progressed smoothly, even though Nicol felt his group was the center of attention. The waiters hovered near their table trying to catch every word of the adventures they discussed. By the time the luncheon was over, Nicol's trip was definitively outlined. He parted from his new acquaintances with letters of introduction safely stowed in his jacket pocket. He promised to contact his new friends on his return.

Excitement gripped Nicol. The delays and working for his father were over. With his adventure planned, he changed his reservation and began to pack. Before his departure, he wired John and thanked him for the lucrative meeting with Dr. Rice. Next, he wired the family in California to inform them of his decision. He planned to travel for several months. He would notify them when he returned to the states.

Armed with advice from the seasoned explorers, his first stop was Haiti. This country of towering mountains and sheltered valleys offered the young traveler a valuable transition period before venturing on to the jungles and swamps of French Guiana.

Nicol had a letter of introduction to President Borno. Presenting it on his arrival, he was invited to a dinner party at their villa near Port au Prince. Nicol found the family gracious and President Borno, actually ex-president by this time, charming and astute. During the remainder of his stay in Haiti, Nicol dined with the former Haitian minister to the United States, a famous author and Stenio Vincent, the then head of the government.

While visiting Haiti, Nicol wrote in his diary:

> The whole feeling of color seemed so unimportant here. This is a beautiful island, with a perfect sky and the blue Caribbean with the giant mountains reflected in its waters. But the color question was important here, terribly important. The majority of the people who were three-fourths white would have given anything to have been four-fifths and the one-half, three-fourths. The peasants in Haiti are as contented as any of the black peoples of the world, if not more so, but the upper classes are not. On the surface there is brilliance and etiquette and polish. All this is true, but underneath it, there is sadness at the thought of having to remain on the island. The majority of the upper classes are trying to become white and yet the son of one of its most prominent members is just as desirous of appearing black.... Now that his education is completed and he has returned to his island home, his extensive land holdings necessitate a great deal of personnel supervision, thus the need to be black.

After meeting with Henri Borno, the ex-president's son, Nicol wrote in his diary:

> Henri Borno, the son of the ex-president said to me after I had been in their country for only a month or two, "Nicol you act as if you have always lived on our island with us." I remember saying, "Henri I feel that way, but I perpetually feel that way wherever I go."[4]

Nicol found the question of color to be disturbing. A believer in the equality of all peoples, the American whites in Haiti had drawn a strict color line. But the French whites did not seem to have the same divisions based on race. From an early age, Nicol's dearest friends were of other colors. He always welcomed his friends, regardless of race, and his warmth was reciprocated.

Nicol arrived in French Guiana several weeks later. After a stay in St. Laurent, a port city on the Maroni River, he traveled to the capital city of Cayenne, the center of the French penal settlements. He took passage on a boat that was transporting three escaped convicts who had been caught in Columbia. Viewed from a distance, Nicol found the penal islands to be as beautiful as any of the South Sea Islands he had visited.

Devil's Island, with its two companions, Royale and St. Joseph, were within a stone's throw of each other. The three were known as Les Iles de Salut or Isles of Salvation. During the trip he learned from a ship hand only three hundred of the five thousand prisoners in the colony resided on the three islands. Devil's Island was only for the political prisoners from France. At the time, seven prisoners lived on the island. Inquiring about writers who had previously visited the islands, Nicol was informed that was a thing of the past. France did not like the publicity from such visitors, which was often exaggerated. Nicol knew of *Au Bagne* published in 1923[5] and he had just read *Cayenne* by Alexis Danan.[6] Both books dealt with political prisoners in the French colony. Nicol wondered what the reaction would be if they knew of his intent to write about the infamous islands and their inhabitants.

As always, the people interested Nicol more than the islands themselves. He found it hard to believe that three islands with palm trees, set in an azure ocean, were dens of punishment rather than a high-priced tourist resort. He began to ask questions. Meeting convicts in Cayenne proved easy. Nicol inquired at his hotel and the next day he was escorted to the penitentiary, where the men were willing to tell their stories to Nicol. At times they seemed to want to frighten the naive American with their tales of heinous crimes. Upon returning to the hotel room after each session, Nicol sat down at his portable typewriter and turned the stories into a manuscript. He was gathering these stories to add to those he had already written at home.

An interesting opportunity came about when Nicol inquired about a white-haired woman whom he saw repeatedly at the Hotel Des Palmistes where he was staying in Cayenne. Another hotel guest mentioned that the lady had once owned and lived on the island of La Mère with twenty-four convicts, her husband being one of them. Nicol was determined to meet her.

As the days progressed he spoke to her as they passed in the hallway or the dining room. Finally he sat down with her at an

evening meal and introduced himself. Nicol invited the elderly
woman to join him in his sitting room one afternoon. They
began to visit on a regular basis when he was not away exploring
some unknown region of the tropical countryside. Slowly, speaking in French, she began to tell him of her past life. It had been
a tragic one culminating in the death of her French husband,
Edmund Duez.

≈

Madame Duez had been the wife of a Parisian lawyer, Edmund
Duez. In 1906 the great division in the affairs of the church and
state took place in France. At the time, Edmund Duez was assigned as the administrator for the diversion of church funds to
the government. A few years later, however, a large sum appeared to be missing. Duez was accused of stealing forty million
dollars of the Church's money. He protested, knowing he had
requested approval from government officials for all of his
department's expenditures and wages. The department for the
diversion of the church's money had not been funded by the
government. It was necessary to use the collected funds to finance the government-approved operation. Needless to say, he
was found guilty of a political crime the government had sanc-
tioned. Sentenced to twelve years, he was destined to be sent to
the penal colony. Any judgment exceeding five years automatically brought exile. All sentences required an additional term of
equal length as a libéré, or freed prisoner, who must then earn
his living in French Guiana without leaving the country. Sentences exceeding seven years were automatically commuted to
life as a freed prisoner after the first portion was served on Devil's
Island. Essentially Duez was sentenced to life. Twelve years on
Devil's Island followed by a life sentence as a libéré. His life in
France was finished.

As the case unfolded in France, Duez vehemently refused to
implicate any of the French officials who granted permission for
this unusual method of funding his department. Duez never
believed he would be found guilty, let alone be sentenced. As
events progressed, several of his faithful friends promised to appeal his case as soon as possible. The trial dragged on for eight
months. Finally he found himself thrust into the hold of a prisoners' ship. His wife remained in France. She divorced him to

protect her remaining dowry which otherwise would have reverted to the state to help reimburse the lost funds. She disappeared from her previous social life and saved every penny so that she could join her husband twelve years later in French Guiana.

Each year Edmund wrote an appeal for release to the French government, but to no avail. At Devil's Island, Edmund, a model convict, had been entrusted with the prison correspondence and had free reign on the island. After ten years, he was transferred to the mainland penitentiary at Cayenne. At the same time, one of his so-called friends, Millerand, become Prime Minister of France. Again, he won the respect of the prison officials for his honesty. Duez hoped for release with the help of the new Prime Minister, but his appeals went unheeded, although he was led to believe his sentence as a libéré would be commuted and he would be allowed to return to France.

Madame Duez joined her husband when he completed serving his prison term and began his libéré sentence. With only her dowry to live on, they could not afford to stay in Cayenne, an expensive city by French Guiana standards. For a pittance she purchased the uninhabited island of La Mère, meaning "The Mother," three miles off the coast of French Guiana and twenty-two miles from the capital, Cayenne. She hired twenty-four convicts, including her husband as the butler, to build a home and help with the chores. There the couple lived year after year while each appeal was denied.

In 1929, Duez was offered 750,000 francs by a French syndicate to write his memoirs. They wanted him to name the political personages who had been involved with him during the notorious scandal. He refused, saying that freedom meant more to him than the money. He knew if the true names were divulged, he would never be granted a pardon. He claimed he had learned from reliable sources his pardon would be granted in 1932. That year arrived and again his appeal was denied. He was informed he would never be pardoned. He must remain in the country of French Guiana until his death. Later that year he died. For twenty-two years he had not lived as a free man while his friends in France were elected to esteemed offices. On his deathbed he told his wife to avenge him and to divulge to the world the list of his cohorts. He had recorded everything in his black notebook.

Before Nicol's departure from Cayenne, Madame Duez entrusted him with the notebook filled with her husband's handwriting. Duez's story, carefully penned in French, was told in intricate detail in the black notebook. Giving it to Nicol, she hoped the story was of value to him since justice for her husband had never been realized.[7]

Nicol was excited when she finished the story. Writing as she spoke, he had tried to capture her emotions during each session. Now, with the original notebook, a chronicle of the actual events, and pictures from her life, Nicol believed he had found a story better than those written by earlier authors and more wrenching than the Captain Dreyfus story, the political célèbre who had returned to France. He hid the black book[8] among the clothing in his trunk. He intended to keep it safe.

Writing to John Archbold that evening, he began to repeat the story. After some thought, he decided to wait. He hoped to publish the Duez story when he returned home. By telling it too soon he might lose his opportunity.

After six months of travel, Nicol, in November of 1933, revisited Haiti on his way home. His excitement about the Duez story precipitated a quick return to the states. Nicol edited and retyped his notes on the Duez story. Finally, more than two years after listening to Madame Duez relay her tragedy, he succeeded in finding a publisher for the story. The story was printed in *The Saturday Home Magazine* of the *New York Evening Journal.* The article was headlined on the front cover as "Revelations of the 'Widow of Devil's Isle.'" This original one-thousand-word, feature article filled two pages and was titled, "Strange Love Tragedy of the Rich Widow of Devil's Isle."[9]

Perhaps Nicol sought more publicity or this first publication drew notoriety, but three months later in the Sunday edition of the *San Francisco Examiner* a similar story was printed entitled "Poignant Love Tragedy of the Rich Widow of France's Devil's Island."

Eighteen months after this second publication, Nicol sent a copy of his original story, accompanied by a letter, to David Lewis at Warner Brothers Studios:

Pursuant to our conversation on Saturday morning, I am enclosing the story of Madame Duez as you suggested. This story, as included in these pages, is authentic in every detail, and in all my expeditions to remote corners of the world I have never found a love story or human interest story that I felt was comparable to this one.

Hoping that you will find this material of interest....[10]

Nicol had previously held a telephone conversation that acknowledged Warner's interest to turn his story into a motion picture. It is probable he used his personal connection with Jack Warner, who had established a studio in Hollywood, to promote his story. Nicol did not include the sensationalized version of the story that had been featured in the two newspapers, instead he sent his original manuscript. A problem arose with the copyright ownership. Finally, a full three years after the first story was printed, Nicol received the reassignment of copyright from King Features Syndicated, the publisher of *The Saturday Home Magazine*. After much confusion, Nicol could now resell the story and copyright, as he soon did.

In January of 1941, Nicol signed his second copyright agreement on the Duez story giving all motion picture, radio and television rights to Warner Brothers Pictures, Inc.[11] Nicol received an initial $2,500 for their purchase of his story and was to collaborate on the screen play. More money would follow. Meanwhile Nicol, traveling the country on a lecture tour, was informed he must secure a letter of approval from Madame Duez for the proposed picture.

It was not until seven years after his first visit to French Guiana that Nicol returned and inquired about Madame Duez. But she had left Guiana and returned to France. When the governor attempted to contact her, her whereabouts were not discovered. She was presumed dead. It was on this later trip that Nicol decided to visit the island where she, her husband, and the convicts had lived. Nicol and his photographer, Loren Tutell, ventured to the island and were greeted by one of the three remaining convicts still living on La Mère. Loren even photographed Nicol sitting on the veranda of Madame Duez' house.

Nicol never received the letter of permission to produce a motion picture from Madame Duez as desired by Warner. In

April, a Warner's employee submitted an outline of a screenplay. An interoffice communication stated, "This is the story outline. I don't think very much of it so I am returning it to you for your files."[12] This ended the potential movie that Nicol had hoped for.

Presumably Nicol never saw the screen play version nor the accompanying memo. Warner Brothers informed him a movie could not be produced. Supposedly, negative sentiments had been expressed by French politicians concerning the coverage the Duez story received in the American press. A movie would exacerbate ill feelings between France and the United States. Nicol was intensely disappointed. The reason seemed plausible to Nicol and he never questioned the source of this information. Years later he still believed Warner Brothers abandoned the Duez movie due to French intervention. When he was presented with the memo concerning the attempted screen play, Nicol was dubious about the timing. He felt the memo was written after the movie idea had already been scrapped.

Meanwhile, Nicol had returned from his second expedition to French Guiana and made plans to write a book about his experiences. The Madame Duez story would be the final section of his book. Again the problem of copyright ownership surfaced. Nicol hoped to write a bestseller travel book and wanted to include the Duez story as a major attraction.

After three months of lengthy correspondence between his publisher Bobbs-Merrill Company, and Warner Brothers, another copyright agreement was signed. Nicol held the copyright on his book, *Black Martinique, Red Guiana,* which included a twenty-thousand-word version of the Madame Duez story, the longest version to be written. Warner Brothers maintained all cinema or radio rights and also the rights to an abbreviated fictionalized version. The expanded story in the book would have the copyright notice printed on the back of the page directly preceding the story. Bobbs-Merrill agreed and Nicol's book was finally published in 1942.

This ended the Madame Duez story. The exact reason why a movie was never made is not clear. The only factual evidence to date is in the internal memo that accompanied the outline. Nicol was never paid an additional sum nor was he consulted for a screen play. Why Warner Brothers retained rights to the story remains unclear.

The "black book" also became a mystery. Nicol kept it in the safe at The Crossroads for many years. But in 1991, when a thorough search was made for the "black book" and for the pictures provided by Madame Duez, only one picture was found. The only remaining pages of the "black book" are those that were photographed to be included in Nicol's book, *Black Martinique, Red Guiana*.

↩

The financial situation at The Crossroads continued to worsen during Nicol's absence. R.H.'s oil speculation had not been fruitful and Capitola and Mr. Rispin had taken their toll on his remaining finances, but R.H. continued to feel infallible. He promised the family that riches were on the horizon. Meanwhile, Sue's automobile had been repossessed and she was taking a taxicab to her social engagements. Nicol's twenty-first birthday trust fund was gone. It had been used to prevent the loss of the Capitola property after Rispin drained R.H.'s financial resources. To replace the lost money, R.H. signed the deed to the Capitola Place mansion over to Nicol.

Before his departure, Nicol had inquired about renting a cottage at the Burlingame Country Club. One became available during his absence and Nicol anticipated living in a place he could call his own, but his move to the cottage was delayed when he caught a severe cold. After recuperating and completing the move to the snug bungalow, he made a trip to Patterson to look up his friend, Art Hall. Finding Art in great form, they enjoyed sharing their stories. Nicol was full of his adventures and Art could match his tales, word for word, with his local experiences. Before the evening was over, Art let Nicol in on a secret. Sworn to secrecy, Nicol was elated to hear that Art and the young Mattos girl planned to marry. The Mattos family leased the Hall ranch, while Art worked for them in return. Virginia Mattos would be graduating from high school in June and they planned to elope. Nicol promised to meet them when the date was set.

The trip to French Guiana had been his first experience taking moving pictures. After recovering from his illness, the footage was developed. Nicol was pleased to see the results were outstanding and began editing the film into a presentable moving picture. Writing to John Archbold, Nicol recaptured the adventure of his travels:

It was the greatest experience and adventure that I have ever had and the moving pictures turned out really quite satisfactory. I am sorry that you were not able to be with me as I think you would have enjoyed it. I found Devil's Island and the Convicts of Cayenne something unbelievable....[13]

Now to set his career in motion.

Making the proper contacts was not difficult for Nicol. With a repertoire of adventure stories and moving pictures of remote lands and people, he now needed to capitalize on the potential financial aspects. With numerous social connections and many lifelong friends, he searched for an opportunity.

During the next year and between trips, Nicol spoke at seventeen clubs and schools in California. He then contracted to do twenty-six fifteen-minute radio shows after his return from his next trip to Dutch Guiana. Nicol's childhood governess, Miss Whitman, introduced him to her close friend, Miss MacAleer. She owned and operated a secretarial school for young women in San Francisco. In the fall, he began teaching French at Miss MacAleer's Private Secretarial School.

Making an income was critical. Nicol had planned to use his birthday trust fund to finance his next travels. With it gone, he needed to raise money to travel. Camera equipment was expensive. The cost of developing moving pictures and traveling to speaking engagements amounted to no small sum. He planned to capitalize on his adventures in every possible way.

Before Nicol's departure for Dutch Guiana, Art Hall and Virginia Mattos eloped to Santa Cruz. Nicol met the clandestine couple and gave Virginia away. After the short ceremony, Nicol handed them the key to the Capitola Place and told them they were welcome to use the mansion for their honeymoon. Wishing them well, he returned to his bungalow.

His plans were in place to return to Dutch Guiana and make a river trip into the jungle. He had already scheduled lectures on his return with a sponsor, Alice Seckels-Elsie Cross. His first presentation was at the Fairmont Hotel Ballroom, a location he fondly remembered from his childhood. The radio show was ready to start in October and the class at Miss MacAleer's the month before. Nicol departed and hoped to return with more tales of adventure.

Nicol left the steamer at Paramaribo, the capital of Dutch Guiana, with no real plan. As he states in his book, *Bush Master*, "If adventure promised itself, I could stay on. If Dutch Guiana had anything to show me, let her trot it out."[14] Seeking a new adventure, Nicol planned to stay only if an opportunity presented itself.

Nicol had several letters of introduction and planned to present himself to the individuals. Checking into the Palace, the only hotel in the city, he proceeded to unpack and cabled home to tell of his safe arrival.

He never waited long for an exciting venture to search him out. Within days, he had met an Austrian doctor, known as Herr Doktor E.V. Heidenstamm, who introduced himself as the Bush Master to Nicol, hence the title *Bush Master* for his next book. The mysterious man invited Nicol to travel with him into regions previously untouched by an American. In his book, *Bush Master*, Nicol appeared to eagerly accept the opportunity even after numerous warnings from the Bush Master's acquaintances. His letter to John Archbold portrayed his true feelings:

Dear John:

Here I am at the tiny town of Nickerie the last outpost of civilization before I enter the jungle. I have been to Cayenne, Devil's Island and many more extraordinary places where I had the most amazing adventures.

Tomorrow begins for me the greatest adventure of my life. I am going up the Corentijn River to its source and then down tributaries, never yet visited by a white man, to Brazil and possibly to the Amazon. I am going with a brilliant Austrian scientist who has made already two trips in this direction, spending over a year and a half in the interior and now his plans are complete for this the greatest adventure of all. He has discovered a tribe of Indians who live high up in trees. We will visit them this trip and than [sic] continue into country that even the Indians are afraid to go as they claim that there are headhunters. So I don't know if you will ever see your little backgammon partner again. We are going to hunt for another specimen of the deadly Labaria, the most poisonous member of the Bushmaster family, and hope to bring back several alive. The doctor has already brought one back, the first to be captured alive on this continent. You die in three minutes from its sting and of the same symptoms as with Infantile Paralysis. He hopes to make an anti-venom.

I don't know when I will reach civilization again but will communicate with you immediately when I do. I wrote Moira but never heard from her so suppose she has forgotten me.

I only wish you could be with me as I know you would enjoy it.

As ever
Your old friend,

PS. Please telephone Charles Nichols and tell him that I wanted to say good-by and to his family also, and his charming wife.

Nicol[15]

The concerns he voiced in the letter were quite valid. The man known as Bush Master proved to be unreliable, although the upriver excursion was truly an adventure. Nicol had been forewarned in Paramaribo before his departure with this man. Even though he had a good idea of the risks he was taking, the reality of the situation seemed to be clear by the time he wrote the letter to John.

Nickerie was a small town that lay at the mouth of the Corantijn River[16] where it flowed into the Atlantic Ocean. The upriver expedition would follow the river until the tributary, the Kabalebo River, was reached. Then they would proceed as far upstream as possible. The headwaters would bring Nicol nearly to the border of Dutch Guiana and Brazil. The river flowed for 450 miles from Brazil through dense tropical forests. Only canoes could reach the upper portions.

The doctor planned to capture snakes for museums and zoos in America and Europe. He was specifically looking for the Gada-Ouri, a snake from which the doctor hoped to extract the venom to use as a cure for infantile paralysis. Since the venom of this particular snake caused symptoms similar to the dreaded childhood disease, polio, the doctor hoped to find a cure in the snake venom.

Perhaps unwisely Nicol paid the Bush Master as soon as he could wire for the money. He did not want to risk losing this opportunity. He had been promised adventure.

The upstream trip progressed smoothly and was full of sights, interesting villages and people. But each day the Bush Master became more sullen and uncooperative. Finally, at the commencement of the adventuresome portion of the trip and at the height of his cantankerousness, he left the expedition at the distant village of Washabo, supposedly returning for additional supplies, while Nicol proceeded upstream with the aid of the guides. Setting up a base camp at Red Hill Falls, Nicol and the guide waited for the return of the Bush Master. None of the guides had previously been this far upstream.

By the time they reached the falls, located deep into unexplored country, Nicol experienced several unsettling situations during their day excursions. Meeting a jaguar face-to-face as he prepared for bed unnerved him, as did some threatening natives and escaped convicts from French Guiana who appeared near his encampment. A deserted hut with a rare butterfly collection and no inhabitant baffled the group. And the Bush Master failed to return.

The daily explorations provided plenty of adventure stories for Nicol's repertoire. The group finally gave up waiting for the Bush Master and returned to Washabo downstream from the confluence of the Corantijn and Kabalebo rivers met. When Nicol arrived, he found others were also waiting for the Bush Master. The Bush Master had not paid any of the suppliers or guides who had taken their party upstream. Nicol found the people of Washabo were owed many guilders by the Bush Master. When Nicol explained that he had prepaid for the expedition, it was concluded the Bush Master had left the country with their money.

The people of the jungle village belonged to the Arawak tribe. Grateful to Nicol for his honesty in exposing the Bush Master who had repeatedly absconded with money and supplies, they inducted him into their tribe with a celebration.

Returning to Nickerie and then Paramaribo, Nicol again wired for money. He had given the last of his funds to the river guides. At the town's only bank, he politely told the banker of his travels up the Corantijn River. The banker replied that just days earlier, another man had also mentioned that he had been on the same river. Nicol surmised that the Bush Master had cashed in Nicol's money and left the country.

Despite the Bush Master's thievery and disappearance, Nicol was pleased with his latest thrilling adventure. Upon his safe return to the states, he was greeted with an invitation for yet another expedition.

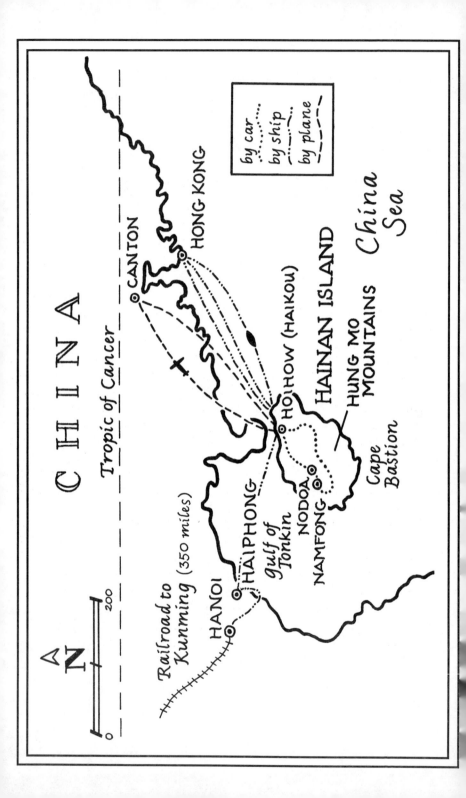

11

EXPEDITION TO HAINAN

The bungalow at the country club was just as Nicol had left it. He quickly deposited all his bags and headed to The Crossroads. When Nicol called from John Archbold's to announce his return to the states and arrange for the chauffeur to meet him at the train station, the cook told him there was no longer a chauffeur employed. His parents were not in and they had not returned his call from John's on the East Coast before he left for the trip to California.

Arriving at The Crossroads, the grounds appeared unkempt, except for R.H.'s rose garden. It was perfect, just as he had always kept it. R.H. took great pride in his hobbies and his roses were always admired. Seeking the cook, Nicol learned that Sue was upstairs preparing for a job interview and R.H. was at the garage where his automobile was being repaired.

A job interview! Nicol took the stairs two at a time. He had never considered the possibility of his mother working. What would she do? Not that she was not talented, but in a day-to-day job? Nicol immediately assumed the financial situation at The Crossroads must be dire. Hearing Nicol, Sue rushed from her sitting room to greet her son. Assuring him that everything was fine, she said she was just looking into a small job, possibly writing an occasional column for the newspaper. In fact, she was having lunch with William Hearst and one of his editors to discuss the opportunity.

Nicol was relieved. Maybe things weren't too bad after all. This sounded like a social engagement rather than a business luncheon. Nicol recalled meeting William Hearst when the family had spent a weekend at his home in San Simeon. Otherwise, he knew only his sons from their childhood parties at Phoebe Hearst's home, the Hacienda, in Pleasanton, California. Reassured, Nicol learned the chauffeur was no longer needed with only one automobile. Sue would take a taxicab or a friend would call for her and they would go to an engagement together.

Nicol waited for R.H. to return. He arrived shortly. R.H. planned to have a business discussion with Nicol. He needed help. Finances were tight and he needed more for his oil speculation in Wyoming. The magnesite mine in Patterson was closed and his new golf course was not attracting many people during the Depression. He had let Mr. Rispin go since the plans for Capitola had not progressed and money continued to disappear. Sue had been adamant, so R.H. hadn't any options. He was afraid foreclosure proceedings might start on some of the Capitola real estate. He had kept the payments current on the mansion, but only one caretaker was still employed there.

Answering Nicol's questions about his Uncle Ruddy, R.H. said their business connections were no longer welcome. Rudolph Spreckels had his own financial problems and the two had separated their respective business concerns. Although their business partnerships ended amicably, R.H. was resentful. Nicol's Uncle Ruddy still regularly visited The Crossroads, usually to see Sue. Nicol should ask his mother about Uncle Ruddy as they visited often.

During their conversation, the doorbell rang. The cook had handed Nicol his messages and mail and had left for the day. Nicol answered the door to find the milkman from Borden's Dairy standing on the stoop. The man explained to Nicol the delivery bill had not been paid for many months and he wondered if he could collect. Nicol offered to pay and to his astonishment the bill totaled seventy-four dollars! Surely there was some mistake. He rushed into R.H.'s study to inquire. R.H. resignedly answered that the sum was probably correct. Opening his safe, he sadly handed Nicol a leather pouch.

Instructing his son to pay with the gold dust in the pouch, R.H. turned away, his shoulders slumped. Quietly he told Nicol that the pouch and the gold it contained had been mined by his ancestors when they arrived in Columbia, California, during the gold rush. When he and Sue married, his father-in-law, Frank Nicol, had given it to him as a wedding gift. R.H. planned to give it to Nicol when he married. Now there was nothing else left.

Nicol poured the contents of the bag into the cupped hands of the astonished delivery man. The man was still standing on the stoop when Nicol closed the door and returned to R.H.'s study. He asked his father how much gold was in the bag. R.H. replied he wasn't sure, but he knew it was more than enough to pay the bill. Borden's continued to deliver milk and never again came to the door requesting payment.

Nicol left feeling melancholy. Surely his parents' economic situation would soon improve. He knew times were hard and had seen what several of his friends had experienced. Uncle Ruddy had a particularly hard time, but he never lost his spirit. He knew his father was a speculator and often his business associates got the best of him. But what would happen now?

Returning to his bungalow, he wrote a cable to John announcing his safe arrival in California. He sat down at his typewriter and wrote a long letter to Moira. There was not a letter from her among the mail the cook had handed him and he had not heard from her for some time. Nicol looked through the rest of his mail. Finding a letter from Leonard Clark, a noted adventurer and San Francisco author, his curiosity was piqued. They had met only briefly at a travel club and he wondered what precipitated his writing?

↩

The engagements Nicol had arranged before his last trip were successful. His lectures, radio shows and teaching added up to savings for his next venture.

His first speaking engagement was announced by a full-paged flyer headlined with his photo and name, "NICOL SMITH in a Travel Talk 'AN ADVENTURE IN DUTCH GUIANA' (Illustrated)," followed by two photos taken on the river trip. The following description was provided about his topic:

Nicol Smith is a young Californian whose adventures in far away places have brought him into the limelight. His lecture will deal with his most recent expedition into the primitive jungle of the Kabalebo country of Dutch Guiana.

This dense jungle has been visited only once before, by the famous Dutch explorer, Dr. Stahel, in 1925. Nicol Smith's expedition went even further into the interior. Dr. Stahel did not make moving pictures of this country and congratulated Mr. Smith upon his success in having this photographic record of this unexplored Kabalebo country, including its magnificent waterfalls of unbelievable beauty.[1]

The flyer continued with a list of the specific topics the explorer would cover while showing his films. Nicol's moving pictures were a sensation. He was becoming an accomplished photographer. With each expedition he captured scenes never before viewed by the American public.

With a projectionist assisting him, the picture was shown while Nicol stood on stage and narrated. His ability to tell an enthralling story, while the moving picture film reeled out a travel experience of its own to his audiences. Afterwards at the reception, Nicol would meet the audience. His ability to remember names and faces was phenomenal. Standing in a reception line he was briefly introduced to several hundred people. When an individual left the reception, Nicol frequently said good-bye to each one by name.

This ability endeared Nicol to many people. Not only did he remember them, but he could recall a detail they had repeated to him and rattled off their address without any effort. His storytelling also was truly a talent. Few lecturers, regardless of their hair-raising adventures, could tell a story that enraptured the audience as Nicol could. The combination of his storytelling talent and his amazing memory, destined Nicol to a lucrative lecturing career.

That fall, Nicol began to teach French at Miss MacAleer's Private Secretarial School. Miss MacAleer was a tall, imposing woman with white hair and an ample but attractive figure. She had a dramatic air about her. After an introduction by his childhood governess, the two had become friends. Nicol agreed to teach a French course at her school. They also discussed the possibility of an economic geography course, but Miss Mac, as Nicol called her, didn't feel it fit the curriculum. The French class seemed appropriate since it offered a touch of culture to the course of study.

Miss MacAleer had opened the school in San Francisco for the sole purpose of providing young women with secretarial skills and proper etiquette for future employment. During the Depression, the tuition to attend was twenty dollars a month, often a substantial sum for a family to send their daughter to school.

Nicol was the only male teacher at the school and he probably made an impression on many of the young women. Whether he made much money teaching French is unlikely, but he was given unlimited secretarial services. Nicol needed a typist to assist him with the stories he was turning into manuscripts. Even if he was not paid, the services and the experience were valuable to Nicol at the time.

Nicol also provided a colorful flourish to the young women's education. He escorted each class, along with several other teachers in attendance, to the Capitola Place for a picnic on the beach. He brought several of his friends to the school and introduced them to his class. Among the most noted were his childhood friend, the Woolworth store heiress, Barbara Hutton, and the renowned California author, Kathleen Norris.

He approached his classroom in the most professional manner and he expected respect from his students. One young student spent hours typing for Nicol in Miss MacAleer's office. There Nicol would sit with his papers spread about him while he dictated to Miss Lois Ferguson. The adventures were foreign to her. She had been fortunate in attending the school through the good will of her aunt who lived in San Francisco. Raised in Klamath Falls, Oregon, typing for Nicol seemed worlds away from her upbringing. Diligently the two worked together throughout the year, turning the Guianas into a presentable manuscript.[2]

Nicol and Miss MacAleer remained friends for the duration of her life. Nicol only taught for one year before his profession took him to another corner of the world. He stayed in contact with Miss Mac. Nicol frequently sent her flowers from wherever he was when she moved to a rest home after her retirement. Having difficulty with her investments, she turned them over to Nicol to manage for the remainder of her days. When she visited him at his lodge on the Stanislaus River, she was elderly and so feeble that the chauffeur, Bill Greene, carried her into the lodge. Their friendship was characteristic of the loyalty and gratitude Nicol felt for his close colleagues. He never forgot those who were dear to him.

His first radio show began that same fall. Once a week Nicol broadcast for fifteen minutes and told a tale of intrigue to the listeners of the San Francisco area. He carefully outlined twenty-six shows, each with a different story. On his first airing he told of the penal islands of French Guiana. As the weeks passed each of the trips unfolded on the air. Madame Duez, the nudist colony, Russia and the South Seas became adventures he shared with hundreds of listeners. Nicol liked the radio show, but preferred the audience of an auditorium. His stories flowed when the spectators responded. He found it more difficult to tell the stories over the silent airwaves.

As the year came to a close, Nicol decided he could plan his next trip with a little more savings. He wrote to Leonard Clark, accepting his offer of a proposed trip to China. Specifically they would be the only white men to visit the interior of Hainan Island. *National Geographic* desired a story of this little-known area. Perhaps the island had potential for an American military base.

 ⌒

The island of Hainan had belonged to China for approximately two thousand years, yet the Chinese occupied little more than its shores. The hinterland was a vast, unknown region, never before explored by an American. Crossing the China Sea from Hong Kong, Nicol and Leonard Clark stepped ashore on June 26, 1937. The city of Hoihow was at the northern tip of the 150-mile-long island. A drive of sixty miles brought them to the city of Nodoa where the expedition would leave as soon as coolies and servants were hired.

It was more than three sweltering weeks later before the expedition finally departed for the interior. Numerous difficulties arose. Nicol finally returned to Canton on mainland China to obtain a special permit that allowed him to take photographs and moving pictures. Once the permit was issued, the return flight encountered a typhoon which meant back tracking to Canton. When the storm ended several days later, he came down with the flu and spent two days recovering at his friend's, George Flynn. Finally, he managed to return to Hainan by airplane.

Nicol's diary described the island as egg-shaped, 150 miles long by 115 miles wide, lying fifteen miles south of mainland China. The south and central portions were mountainous with peaks reaching seven thousand feet.

The tribespeople of Hainan were known as the Lois. They were the original inhabitants of the island. Repeated invasions by the Chinese had driven them into the mountains. The Lois were made up of many tribes whose dialects were Malayan in origin. Although there were differences among them, their customs and dress were similar.[3]

The tribespeople cultivated rice fields and gardens on the steep mountainsides and hunted and fished for their livelihoods. There was little money exchanged since cattle were the currency of the interior. Nicol found the Lois to be uniquely different from the people of mainland China. A characteristic he found particularly unusual was their disinterest in bargaining. Used to bargaining for native wares in his travels, Nicol could not budge the Lois even a few cents. All they wanted were silver coins or tobacco for their goods. Nicol bought beautifully embroidered jackets, bone hairpins and jade, always paying the demanded price.

Departing from civilization, Leonard and Nicol were warned of the hazards of the jungles. In Hoihow, the port city of the island, and Nodoa, twenty miles inland from Hoihow, they lodged at a Presbyterian mission. Hoihow was a town of several thousand inhabitants, where they hired their porters and purchased more than a ton of supplies. While obtaining the supplies, they were notified by the government that their travels would be delayed due to an imposed martial law. A cholera epidemic was spreading and martial law kept the people from fleeing en masse into the surrounding countryside and spreading the epidemic.

In Nodoa, Reverend Melrose again warned them about the malaria outbreak. Since the bubonic plague was rampant in Nodoa and they feared that governmental problems on the mainland might cause their long-awaited passports to be revoked at any moment, the two men felt they couldn't delay until the height of the malarial season passed.

Early on the morning of July 20, their boxes and bags were loaded into a Ford, which Nicol was told had once belonged to the actor, Wallace Berry. They drove down the narrow military road to Nam Fong, the Chinese-Loi market town a few miles away. From there they progressed on foot.

The expedition included of a cook, a guide, several interpreters and twelve Chinese porters. All in all, there were as many as five interpreters working with one another since different tribes were encountered along the trip. The weather was hot and muggy. The first day on foot they covered sixteen miles. Often Leonard, Nicol and the guide would travel ahead, while the porters with loads averaging sixty pounds apiece brought up the rear.

On the second day, a terrible rainstorm overtook Leonard, Nicol and the guide. Taking shelter in a Lois hut, they decided to turn back to meet the porters who had fallen a few hours behind.

The downpour ended shortly and they quickly reached the banks of the last stream they had crossed. In one hour it had gone from a narrow stream that had risen to their knees when they forded, to a rapidly swirling rush of water more than ten feet wide. Nicol decided to cross the stream by wading as he had done earlier. Before he knew what happened he was knocked down by the current and dragged toward the center of the stream. He had on his heavy rubber boots which quickly filled with water. Swept downstream, he spotted two rocks. He feared that his time had come. Miraculously, he passed safely between the rocks. Still there was nothing he could do to break out of the current. Spotting a big bamboo overhanging the stream, he knew it was his only chance. If the bunch of bamboo held, he was safe. Wildly grabbing the clump, it gave, but was just enough to drag him toward the edge to shallower water. He dragged himself up the bank, still clutching the mass of bamboo.

Returning to the Lois hut, the guide offered to backtrack to the porters by an alternate route. After a few hours, he returned with their mosquito nets, dry clothes and canteens. Never had such meager supplies looked so good to Nicol.

The next night found them camped on a jungle ridge, surrounded by a mahogany and rosewood forest, about twenty miles due west of Hung Mo, the "Mountains of the Red Mist." Nicol and Leonard discussed the fascinating name, speculating on its origin. Studying the map they found a peak that was unnamed. While they relaxed under their tarpaulin, Nicol named it after Moira. The afternoon rainstorm brought flashes of lightening that burst around the mountains. By sunset the storm had subsided to a drizzle. Nicol cried out to Leonard to view the horizon. The entire sky over the mountains had turned an intense red. The red mist was uncanny and lasted about twenty minutes until the sun had set.

The porters appeared afraid. The interpreter informed Nicol they felt it was a warning. The red mist was an omen from the Loi devils, warning them of trouble to come. Unbelieving, he and Leonard slept peacefully through the night.

The next morning, two of the porters were sick with malaria. Their loads were distributed among the other men so they could travel on until help was available. Later that day, two Lois were hired to replace the Chinese coolies. That evening each man was given ten grains of quinine in hope of preventing a further outbreak of malaria.

Nicol nearly met misfortune again the following day when he barely missed stepping on a bamboo snake, which was feared by Hainans as much as the deadly king cobra. That evening six more men were down with malaria. Now with only five coolies remaining, they began to realize why Hainan had not been thoroughly explored.

The following morning, six days into the expedition, Nicol could not rise from his cot. Though he drank only boiled water and ate only from the canned supplies, he began to vomit. His nausea continued all day. That night a runner returned to the village where the Ford had been left. The next morning he arrived leading a pony and Nicol was lifted into the saddle. Nicol and the sick coolies backtracked while Leonard continued into central Hainan.

Leonard selected only the essential items: food, forty pounds of medicine, camera and films and trading articles. Suffering from an aching back, which was a symptom of malignant malaria,[4] he took twenty grains of quinine that afternoon. Early the next morning he departed. Nicol planned to return to the mission to recover his health. By the time he reached the mission two days later, he had lost eighteen pounds.

It was a week before Nicol was feeling fit. He considered rejoining Leonard in the interior jungles, but was unsure if his guide would be able to locate the other party. Jean Clark, Leonard's wife, had arrived at the mission the day before and discouraged Nicol from making the trip. He was thin and could not risk another bout of illness. Seeing the sense of Jean's statement, Nicol passed the remaining weeks with tribes of Lois, spending nights in each village, completing his pictures and writing in his diary.

After recovering at the Presbyterian mission, Nicol ventured to the hinterland to photograph the tribes he had met with Leonard. It proved to be very difficult. The Lois believed they would die if anything happened to their photographed likeness. Nicol decided it was unwise to show them any finished photographs. After much haggling and finally paying various tribesmen, he succeeded in shooting only one hundred feet of film the first day. Knowing he needed much more in order to have a feature movie, he proceeded to work with a head tribesman until all the village clamored to be in his moving picture. The people were shy and very superstitious, both of which continued to cause him difficulty with his photography.

The following day he shot seven hundred feet in all by bribing a village with several red scarves. Often the older people would stay and pose while the younger ones quickly scattered. Nicol tried to tell them he had traveled far for these pictures, but his hand signals and words made little impression on the people. Gifts to the head tribesman seemed the best method.

Nicol's most difficult moment with his photography occurred in the town of Nodoa. A crowd of people became upset with him when he began to take pictures on the street. Before he could escape, the ruckus attracted the attention of the local soldiers who contacted the chief of police. The chief presented himself to Reverend Melrose. The crux of the matter was they believed he was a White Russian and was in league with the Japanese. They thought Nicol was a spy. They forbid Nicol from taking pictures in the town as the military did not want any photographs of their fortifications to fall into the wrong hands. Ironically, there were no fortifications, but by not allowing any photographs no one would find out the secret of the Hainan military.[5]

Prior to Nicol's illness, the guide had brought him a pet. It was a funny little thing with the head of a fox and the body of a raccoon but without a tail. It was just a baby and was referred to by the natives as a fruit cat. Nicol immediately bought it for sixty cents Chinese and they became fast friends. It would sleep on his pillow or on cool nights it would burrow into his sleeping bag.

Nicol received another pet when he returned to the mission. A tiny reddish-brown monkey, he named Baxa, was given to him. The monkey and the fruit cat were both babies and got along famously. Devoted to Nicol, they followed him everywhere and seemed to view him as their parent. The two pets stayed with Nicol until he left for the mainland a month later.

Leonard emerged from the jungle with five coolies, the cook and the interpreter. During the two weeks after his recovery Nicol was hard at work filming the natives. He spent nights in fourteen different Lois villages. Leonard and Nicol spent the next few days recording their travels and cataloging the film that would be developed upon their return to the states.

Prior to the expedition undertaken by Nicol and Leonard, nothing was known about the interior of Hainan Island by either the Chinese or foreigners. The dangers of interior travel were noted when it became known that of the seventeen members comprising the exploratory party, only Leonard and two of the Chinese coolies succeeded in making the first crossing of the interior on three hundred miles of difficult and treacherous trails. There were deaths on the expedition and all the men leaving the expedition did so on account of the hardships and disease. Nicol completed more than one hundred miles of their original plan before he became ill. He then logged an additional one hundred miles while filming the Lois villages.

With their notes in order for the *National Geographic* article, the trio packed. The rumblings of war preparation were escalating. Nicol, Jean and Leonard found passage on a coastal freighter bound for Hong Kong. Two days later, Hoihow was bombarded by Japanese destroyers.

✒

The trip to Hong Kong on board the *Hai Ching*, was a sweltering excursion on a boat overloaded with passengers, including
eight hundred coolies, twelve hundred pigs and one hundred sixty
cows. One passenger died of cholera enroute and everyone was
quarantined for sixteen days on the boat when it arrived in port.

Fortunately Nicol and the Clarks had previously been vacci-
nated and were allowed to disembark in Hong Kong after several
hours of negotiations. After a week at the Flynn's home, the
Clarks and Nicol parted ways. Nicol continued by ship to
Haiphong and Hanoi where he boarded a train for Laokay on the
China frontier. The train ride was comfortable and cool compared to the boat travel. The train cars consisted of compart-
ments with two bunks in each one and an electric fan to keep it
cool. Nicol still did not sleep too well as the train made numerous starts and stops. It was his first train ride in several years.

At Laokay, the trading center on the Hanoi-Kunming railroad, Nicol changed trains to travel to the tin country of interior
China. The train ride amazed him. From an elevation of 230
feet to 6,600 feet, the track climbed, passing over 107 viaducts
and bridges and through 172 tunnels, whose total length was
more than fifteen miles, and finally reached the Yunnan Province and Kunming.

Nicol called on the American Consul, Paul Meyer, to whom
he had a letter of introduction from Anne Archbold. Paul had
previously been a secretary in Peking and he and Nicol hit it off
immediately. Nicol's destination was Kochiu, the leading tin-
mining center of China. It was the focal point for an area of
seven hundred square miles that was riddled with tin mines.
Traveling on the Michelin, the auto car on rails that journeyed to
the China border in half the time as the train, Nicol headed to
Kochiu.[6] There he found a region rich in ore which yielded twenty-
five million dollars a year, but provided only sheer misery and
poverty for the people.

The tragedy of Kochiu had been going on for three hundred
years. Only in recent years had rumors come whispering out of
the hills of the region. A few were so horrible that the League of
Nations sent an investigator to make a report. Even President
Chiang Kai-shek had attempted to probe the conditions, but both
were thwarted in their efforts. Between fifty to one hundred

thousand people mined the tin, more than half of them boys under the age of fifteen. Nearly a third of the miners died each year from deplorable conditions. Children, many of them sold into slavery by their parents, worked for a penny a day.

Even in the most advanced mines, Nicol found children carrying loads of ore weighing up to sixty pounds. During Nicol's visit, a rock slide in a mine trapped eight young boys. When no rescue attempt was made, Nicol inquired, demanding a reason. It was considered be too expensive, possibly upwards of fifty dollars. Even when Nicol offered to pay, the wealthy mine owner, ignoring Nicol's demands, ordered work to continue.

Appalled by the poverty and slavery of the Chinese people, held in the hands of less than a dozen wealthy Chinese owners, Nicol returned to Kunming. He kept a careful daily diary, recording the atrocities of the tin region. He knew the story would be of interest to the American press.

The story of Kochiu did attract interest when Nicol returned home. He befriended a wealthy mine owner who facilitated his tours of the region. Previous visitors, and investigators' efforts were thwarted by the opulent owners who did not want publicity. It might lead to a change in the conditions which would likely increase their expenses in mining the ore. But Nicol managed what no one before him was able to do and he learned the horrors of the secrets of Kochiu. He wrote numerous newspaper articles. These experiences were also recorded in his first book. Nicol would incorporate his first travels on mainland China with his later trip across the Burma Road into one book. Nicol had finally reached China where he experienced its beauty and witnessed its secret horror of child slavery.

↵づ

12

MOIRA

Nicol settled into the bungalow after his return from Hainan Island and China. Developing the material from his detailed diary and his photographs, he began to work on a new lecture series.

It was difficult to keep his mind on his work. Instead his thoughts wandered to Washington, D.C., where he last visited Moira Archbold, John's younger sister. During his stay, they had secretly planned a trip together and it was quickly approaching. The excursion would be to Mexico and it would either bring them both closer or turn them apart.

John had married Elizabeth Brown the previous year. Since John's marriage, Nicol now must approach Moira on his own and heard very little about her through her brother. Nicol worried about Moira and knew that her older brother had often been responsible for her well-being. Now all her siblings had left Hillandale and she remained there, living quietly with her mother, Anne, and the servants.

Nicol's popularity was unprecedented. He had friends or made friends wherever he was. He enjoyed the company of friends and often he was the center of attention. His social life was complete with the Bachelor's Club, the coming-out balls and the Burlingame Country Club which he had recently joined. He had many friends, but his thoughts were turning to marriage.

He often wondered who would marry a man who traveled and talked for a living. He really didn't think of any one place as home but preferred packing his bags and setting off to another country, another adventure. With many of his friends married, Nicol hoped to marry also. His times at the bungalow were lonely and it was too small for entertaining. He hoped for a fine home, no financial worries, and a wife who would love to travel as he did.

At the age of twenty-seven, he had met many young women but only three interested him as far as marriage was concerned. The first occurred during his late teenage years, but she unexpectedly moved away from the area with her family. They remained fast friends. In fact, he had written John a letter of introduction to meet Barbara Cates. The next affair of heart took a more drastic turn. After his interest became apparent, Dale King had married someone else while he was away. He had been hurt when he learned of her marriage.

Then there was last spring at Hillandale. He and Moira had known each other for years. He had enjoyed her company since their first meeting at Lake Geneva in 1929 where they went canoeing together. He wrote her faithfully over the years and each visit to Hillandale brought them closer.

After John's wedding, Nicol felt all his friends were betrothed. Suddenly, that spring he asked Moira if she would consider a long-term engagement to him. She had been so surprised she turned him down. Weeks later, she telephoned from Hillandale in Georgetown and asked Nicol if she could think about his proposal. She felt unsure.

Nicol, feeling rejected, decided he could wait for her answer. But an answer never came. His several visits to Hillandale during the year had not helped Moira decide. Then when they last saw each other, they secretly planned a trip to Mexico.

Nicol's upbringing had been lonely. He had no siblings and had little contact with his parents. The responsibilities for his needs had been turned over to his nanny, then his governess and later a tutor. His home life had never known the closeness a family can share. Moira also had a lonely upbringing, even with three older siblings very close in age. Moira had been born in Montecito, California on July 9, 1911.[1] Within a few months, her mother Anne and she returned to their home in England.

Moira's mother, Anne Archbold Saunderson, was the second child of John Dustin and Ann Eliza Archbold. Anne's father,

John, was a noted oilman and later became John D. Rockefeller's business partner. John Dustin Archbold had an enthusiasm for his work in the oil regions around Titusville, Pennsylvania. He was an activist and became the secretary of the Titusville Oil Exchange. During the Oil War of 1872, Rockefeller and the railroads attempted to monopolize control over the output of oil in the region.[2] John emerged as a leader in the outcome and Rockefeller had recognized the man's abilities. In 1875, Rockefeller asked John to join his organization and he accepted. A mere two years later, Rockefeller turned all the administrative leadership of Standard Oil over to John Dustin Archbold,[3] while Rockefeller retained the title of president.

John's daughter, Anne, married Armar Dayrolles Saunderson of Castle Saunderson, County Caven, Ireland in 1906.[4] In the next five years they had four children, Lydia, Armar, John and Moira. All except the eldest were born on American soil. Anne would travel to the states for the birth of each child and then rejoin her husband in England. Within a few years their marriage had dissolved. Anne determined to return to the states to make a new beginning for herself and her children. Being a feminist, she was afraid a divorce in England would be opposed. Concerned that her husband, Armar Saunderson, would not allow her to leave to live in the states, and knowing English law would not provide her with many rights as a divorced woman, she began to devise a plan for their departure.

She contacted her father, John. He arranged for an oil tanker, the Saranac, to provide them transport from England to Baton Rouge. The difficult part of the journey was arranging to meet the tanker without her husband's knowledge. The four children, their mother and their nurse, Eva Bennet, drove to the wharf and under cover of darkness, they boarded the waiting tanker. For three weeks they lived in the captain's quarters as they crossed the Atlantic. When they landed in Baton Rouge, Uncle Jack,[5] Anne's younger brother, had his private rail car meet them. Traveling by rail to Thomasville, Georgia, they stayed with their uncle and his family.

Anne resumed her maiden name of Archbold and the children's surname was changed from Saunderson to Archbold. The first winter was spent in Portland, Maine, followed by summer in the home Anne already owned in Bar Harbor, Maine.[6] Anne was considering where her children should be raised. Settling on Washington, D.C., she purchased forty acres in Georgetown. Anne began planning their new home while the older children were enrolled in school. John was sent to a Quaker day school. Moira was kept at home.

Moira had been severely ill with pneumonia the winter before their departure from England. She lingered for several weeks, her family afraid she might not recover. Each day her sister Lydia and her two brothers, Armar and John, made a present to cheer their ailing sister. Since her recovery, Moira had been inattentive and frequently ill. Eva, the nanny, who escaped from England with Anne and her children, now took care of Moira tirelessly.

Anne feared that Moira's illness may have had a lasting effect on her. Protecting her at home seemed to be the best course. Eva became Moira's constant companion and a strong influence in her life.

~

Moira's health improved over the next few years. Still Anne and Eva felt she was quite fragile and constantly protected her from overexertion. Infrequently a tutor was employed to help Moira stay abreast of studies for her age group, but each year found her falling further behind her peers.

John became responsible for Moira on many occasions. When he was enrolled in the Dalton School in New York, Moira begged to go. She would be the only child at home now that all her siblings were at boarding school. Finally Anne relented. John and Moira could both attend the school, but they would be required to return home each weekend on the train.

All winter they commuted each Sunday to New York and back to Hillandale on the following Friday. Moira's education began to advance with the year of formal education. She was enrolled for the following year while John went on to St. George's School in Newport, Rhode Island.

After completing her studies in New York, Moira remained at home until 1929. She was even left behind during the summer of 1925 when Anne took her other three children to China. Finally, as John completed the Odyssey tour, Moira was allowed to travel with her mother to Lake Geneva in Switzerland to meet

John. It was here that Nicol visited John and first met Moira. Although Nicol had met Anne on her regular visits to Choate, Moira had never been along.

John was enrolled at the University of Geneva for one year, while Moira lived nearby with a family and attended school at a local convent. During the year, Moira began to take violin lessons and enjoyed the companionship offered by nuns at their school. Shortly after Christmas, Moira confided to John she intended to join the convent. Hurriedly, John wrote to his mother explaining there was nothing he could do to stop Moira. Her mind was made up. Moira had previously made hasty choices and John rarely could rationalize with her about the implications of her decisions. He knew Moira was headstrong and determined.

Within a week of receiving the letter from John, Anne had intervened. Moira would not be joining the convent. If any further discussion ensued, she would be booked for the trip home immediately. Moira was chagrined. The situation had embarrassed her at school. She wanted to make her own decisions and felt she was entirely capable. It would be eight years before she again attempted to make a decision of consequence about her life.

Moira liked Nicol when they met at Lake Geneva. He had even taken time to write her after he returned home. Nicol made her feel special with his undivided attention and witty stories. She hoped to meet him again, but felt she was unimportant and unattractive. Nicol had many friends according to the information John told her. Maybe she would not hear from him again.

The year came to an end, and Moira returned to Hillandale and her previous life within the mansion. Eva still worked there even though the children were all grown. With Moira gone for the past year, Eva had time to herself and made a new friend. Once Moira returned, Eva again felt responsible for her welfare. Eva had cared for her charge all of Moira's life and in some ways she felt the young lady would always need her.

Moira's social life was quiet. Her best friend was Ky Bell who was often invited on the summer pack trips and spent many hours at Hillandale with Moira. Each trip east, Nicol stopped to visit John and often learned the latest news about Moira. When John first became occupied with his invention in Pennsylvania and later when he married, Nicol still stopped in Georgetown to visit at Hillandale.

Nicol was unable to describe how he felt about Moira. He repeatedly felt empathy for the young woman, as she could sometimes seem helpless and fragile. At the same time she was determined and knew what she wanted. She liked to travel but infrequently left Hillandale except for the family camping trips or the family Christmas in St. Moritz. She would invite herself along whenever Eva left the house and was unhappy if Eva made plans that did not include her.

Nicol and Moira spent hours together. Nicol told his stories of adventure while Moira listened enraptured, wondering what made her brother's friend seek such wild places.

ᕬ

One afternoon Moira learned Eva was leaving for a visit with a friend in Virginia. Inquiring how long she would be gone, Moira wanted to accompany Eva rather than remain behind. Quickly, Eva rang up Bex, asking if her charge, Moira, could join them for the afternoon visit. Eva's friend willingly agreed, although she was surprised that the Archbold girl would enjoy listening to Eva and her converse.

Rebecca McBride lived in Arlington with her husband, John. A well-educated woman, she and Eva had met several years before in 1930 while she attended graduate school in Washington. Moira had been in Switzerland at the convent school that year, and Eva and Bex, a nickname her husband had given her, became fast friends during Eva's free time.

Bex had married John McBride and left Washington, only to return during the Depression years. She found Eva busy with her responsibilities at Hillandale. The introduction of Moira and Bex was the beginning of a lifelong friendship. The following day, Eva again rang up Bex to inquire whether Moira could return on her own to visit. Moira admired Bex. Quickly Bex became her confidant. Her friendship provided an escape from Moira's routine life at Hillandale. Within days, Moira asked Bex to help her. Her education had shortcomings and she felt her responsibilities would soon outdistance her abilities. Moira and each of her siblings had inherited fortunes from their grandfather's Standard Oil holdings.

Immediately the two women set to work. Moira would arrive in her chauffeured car each day. The afternoon was spent learning basic arithmetic to enable her to manage money, along with typing lessons and letter writing. Moira included the letter writing as a part of the lessons since a young man from California was writing frequent letters to her. She hoped to improve her writing skills so they would not be an embarrassment to her.

As the friendship blossomed, Moira confided to Bex that Nicol had asked her to consider marriage. She had told him no and then reconsidered. He was still waiting for an answer. Moira felt the decision was overwhelming. She liked Nicol and admired his lifestyle. She wondered aloud if they could travel together. She wanted a release from the influences of Hillandale. Her life seemed dull in comparison.

Bex was reluctant to influence Moira. Eva had confided to Bex that Moira's childhood illness had left her weak for several years. Yes, her education had been lacking, but the youngster hadn't the stamina of a normal child. The entire family and Eva had protected her. Now Moira found it difficult to do the things her brothers and sister were doing. They were no longer at home to help her or include her in their activities. Moira was left under the protection of Eva and infrequently made her own decisions.

When Moira asked to telephone Nicol from the McBride's, Bex encouraged her. Knowing Moira, she felt the stronger the friendship between Moira and Nicol, the more Moira would be able to make a decision about the engagement.

The telephone calls started. Each day at noon, Moira dialed California and she and Nicol spoke. Sitting side by side on the hall steps, Moira conversed with Nicol as Bex kept her ear close to the telephone receiver and listened to every word. Each month Moira paid the McBride's for the use of their telephone. Month after month the telephone bill escalated until John was notified at work by the telephone company. They wanted to know if he was aware of the size of his telephone bill. Amused, he assured them it was fine. He knew about the calls to California and they were all being paid.

Moira and Ky left for California by train in early November of 1937. Moira's cousin, Adrian Archbold, was marrying in San Diego on November 25. Nicol was going to meet the women

164

and they planned to travel to Mexico, then back to California for a visit to Hollywood before returning to Washington.

Nicol and Moira had a fabulous time. Adrian's wedding was grand and their sneaky escapade to Mexico was wonderful. Nicol let Moira do the driving. He felt she was a wonderful driver compared to him as the Smiths were notoriously poor drivers. Ky was a delightful companion. Nicol toured them around Hollywood and introduced them to his acquaintances. Nicol, a wandering social register, had friends wherever he went.

As they parted to return to their homes for the holidays, Moira consented. She would marry Nicol if he still wanted her. She apologized for her shock the spring before and for the time her decision had taken. Nicol assured her he understood. They agreed to keep their engagement a secret. No wedding plans were made. No announcement date was pending. Ky was not even privy to their secret.

✦

The letters began to fly between Nicol's bungalow and the typewriter on Third Street in Arlington. Moira let Bex in on their secret and couldn't wait until Nicol met the McBrides. The first unexpected event occurred at The Crossroads. In December, Moira wrote to Nicol apologizing for the telephone call on the previous Saturday night:

> I feel I must write to you now to explain why I called. When Armar told me, it was such a shock and my first reaction was to call because I always like to hear things directly rather than indirectly. But I realize from what you said over the phone it has nothing to do with you. But you know I like your whole family.... It's a shame it had to happen a second time but what delights is that you are independent financially....[7]

R.H. was broke, flat broke. He had nothing left to invest in oil and he had lost the last of his real estate in foreclosures. Capitola was gone along with Mr. Rispin. The Stanislaus River property was in foreclosure. He had borrowed money from several of his closest business associates, many of whom could ill-afford the loan during the Depression years.

Their secret barely made it to the new year. The next uproar began when Eva discovered that Moira, her lifelong charge, was secretly engaged. Once Eva knew, Anne, who was wintering at her home in Nassau, Bahamas, was immediately informed. Moira was angry. When Eva confronted her, she made her promise not to tell her mother. Needless to say, Eva did not keep her promise.

Nicol decided to go east after his twenty-eighth birthday. He had several lectures pending but thought he could be there by mid-March. Receiving a telegraph from Moira he completed his plans:

> Eva heard from mother. Mother is quite amazed and wonders if anything can be done about it. She may plan to be here when you come east. I have not heard from her myself. Everyone believed we made the decision while I was in Nassau, so let them continue to think so. Lots of Love, Moira.[8]

Again, Moira sent the telegraph from Arlington where Bex lived. Moira conducted all of her correspondence with Nicol from the McBride's home. She was afraid her mother or Eva would intercept the letters and forbid the telephone calls, if she conducted the courtship from Hillandale. They might even attempt to prevent her from marrying Nicol. Never had she been so happy as when she told Nicol she had made up her mind. Now she didn't want her lifelong authority figures to intervene. She had made up her mind. Her decision was final.

Moira felt the only way she would get what she desired was to do as much as possible in secret. Bex was her support and constant friend. Moira had never felt the warmth of friendship as she did at the McBride's home.

Finally Nicol arrived. Anne had decided to remain in Nassau, requesting they visit her there. She planned to put Nicol through his paces.

Meanwhile Bex planned a wonderful dinner for the young couple. She and John anticipated meeting Nicol. Her neighbor insisted she hire a maid. The couple were accustomed to being waited on and Bex must provide the same service.

Nicol immediately felt welcome in the two-story brick home. Dinner began without a hitch. Each course arrived as Bex tapped the bell under the table with her foot. Everything continued smoothly until she could no longer ring the bell. Bex remained calm as she continued to tap and search for the bell with her toe, praying it would ring. There was a pause between courses. Finally Bex found the bell and tapped it. It would not ring. Finally she stomped on it as hard as possible without appearing the least bit ruffled. Politely Nicol turned to Bex. To her mortification, he smiled, his eyes twinkling, and asked her to please stop playing footsy under the table.[9] Nicol was amused by Bex's misguided foot.

The dinner ended without another hitch. Nicol liked the McBrides. He felt Bex's influence was building confidence in Moira, who was proud of what she had achieved with Bex's help. The McBride's home was Moira's haven.

The McBrides remained friends with Moira and Nicol for the remainder of their lives. Their eldest son, David, became Nicol and Moira's first godchild. The youngest son became Nicol's namesake, Howard Nicol McBride.

~

The difficulties arising from the engagement were taxing for Moira. Having led a carefully protected childhood and young adulthood, she was not prepared for the tumultuous events that led to her marriage. Every letter to Nicol told of the strain she was under:

> I feel so worn out from this whole tiring affair that I want to scream. You have no idea what a terrible strain it has been for me. If I didn't have Mrs. McBride to talk to, I don't know what I would do and her husband has been wonderful to me too....[10]

A week later she continued to inform Nicol of her trials:

> Eva is still trying to quiz me about everything so I don't know where I stand with her and she tried to get me to change my mind. Nicol, nothing on earth could make me do this for I LOVE YOU so much that I couldn't live without you.... I haven't heard from Mother yet.... I dread hearing and yet I want to hear, but I know I am going to go ahead with our plans no matter what she says. Whatever she thinks or says won't matter to us because I will not have my life destroyed by her....[11]

For possibly only the second time in her life, Moira had made up her mind. No one was going to change her plans this time. She was not an eighteen-year-old girl at a school run by nuns, but a woman of twenty-six. Her mother and her childhood nanny were not going to make her decisions any longer.

On March 16, before Nicol left Burlingame, he sat down and wrote a heart-to-heart letter to his old friend, John. It seemed odd to be writing to John now as the brother of his future wife:

> It seems strange to be writing you, one of my oldest, and certainly my best friend about his own sister. But it is a letter that I write with real feeling.[12]

Nicol's letter was a moving composition of honesty. He truly felt he was the luckiest man in the world. Moira had asked John to give her away and John had agreed. Nicol wrote his emotions, his caring, and his financial concerns with the freshness of a young man in love:

> Well, John, there is nothing in the world you could lend me that would be one tenth as precious as your sister and I will always do my best for you not to regret such an action.
>
> I know that I am the luckiest boy in the world to have anyone so good, sweet, and wonderful as Moira interested in me and it all seems like a dream. Moira is to me completely different from any girl I have ever met. She is by far the most considerate and understanding, that goes without question but than [sic] she is unspoilt and always so appreciative. We have never had a cross word nor an argument. True, when I first asked her to marry me more than a year ago, she was a little stunned and upset. But from that day to the present moment there has been gradual acceptance that has developed into what I know is her feeling for me today.
>
> We have seen each other under many conditions and in many situations, in New York, Washington, Burlingame, Hollywood and deep down in Mexico.
>
> I know that she will love to go on long expeditions with me and that the type of work that has been and will be my life will interest her enormously....
>
> I wrote your mother also several weeks ago, a long letter asking for her permission and she has since been kind enough

to answer it. At the time that I wrote your mother, I told her
the truth as I have always done with Moira. I do not have a
great deal in a worldly way to offer her. My own private fortune,
with but a small exception, I had to put up as security for
father whose great losses you have known about....

Out of my newspaper stories, school, lecture tours and
radio work I earn a comfortable living of several hundred a
month....

I guess I am not much of a catch but I love your sister and
I will do my best to make her happy. I think you know me well
enough for that.

We have known each other a very long time John, and I
guess I have a lot of faults but I am not fickle. Marriage for me
to Moira will be forever and I will devote my life to making her
just as happy as I possibly can and that will be one hundred
per cent....[13]

Nicol honestly and sincerely expressed his feelings. Con-
trary to gossip, he was not seeking his fortune from Moira. The
young man who had a lonely childhood was in love with a young
woman who also had a lonely childhood. From their perspec-
tive, the couple knew no hurdles. At that time his lifestyle and
her inheritance were not a consideration. Only love, honesty
and forthrightness were needed to start their union, along with
Anne's approval from Nassau. She had requested that Nicol provide her with a private lecture, no movies, just his speaking. Then
she would decide.

~

Nicol and Moira traveled to Nassau in late March of 1938.
Both were nervous about the outcome of their visit. Anne had
made herself clear. If she liked what Nicol had to present, then
the engagement would be announced. No mention was made
about what would happen if she didn't like the lecture. The in-
ference was clear.

Anne met them when they docked after an overnight trip by
ship from Florida. They went first to her home for the travelers
to bathe and change. From there they drove to her friend Lord
Duveen's spacious winter home where twenty-four guests were
assembled for lunch. After lunch, the entire group retired to a
large room to listen to Nicol's lecture. Nicol had primarily given

lectures with his motion picture films, except for his early ones. This one he had to do without props.

Anne sat in the center of the front row next to Lord Duveen. A woman of small stature, she nonetheless presented an imposing image directly in front of the nervous young man. She gave Nicol her full attention. Within five minutes, Nicol felt his tension slip. Now completely at ease, he talked for nearly an hour. He abandoned his usual prepared lecture and instead told stories of curiosity from around the world. At the end of the hour, he stopped, bowed and walked over to Anne and the host. By the time he reached them they were both on their feet clapping and Anne was smiling. She said, "Nicol, that was fine."[14]

Nothing more was said. A few days later the engagement was announced.

Nicol and Moira married in a simple ceremony on June 2, 1938, at Hillandale in Georgetown. John gave Moira away while Armar was Nicol's best man. Ky Bell was Moira's maid of honor. The only guests present were Anne, Nicol's mother, Sue, and John's wife. R.H., completely broke, did not have the means to make the trip. Neither Sue nor Nicol offered to pay for his train fare. The marriage began ostentatiously for the young couple during the depths of the Depression. Nicol gave Moira a lovely full-length fur coat. In return Moira bought Nicol a new 1938 Cadillac sedan.

13

BVRMA ROAD

Departing from New York, Nicol and Moira headed to Europe for the summer to spend the remainder of their honeymoon. Both were relieved to leave their families behind and begin their own life together. Fortunately, Nicol won enough money in a poker game with Elsa Maxwell, his mother's good friend, a few weeks before his wedding to finance the honeymoon to Europe.

The Atlantic crossing was rough and Nicol spent most of the time in his bunk, seasick. Moira survived the trip without any sign of seasickness but became seriously ill after disembarking at Cherbourg, France. Arriving in Paris, Nicol checked them into the hotel and immediately put Moira to bed. The next morning Moira had taken a turn for the worse and Nicol decided to call an ambulance. She was unable to eat or keep down any liquids. When they arrived at the hospital, the doctor informed them Moira's appendix had ruptured and she must be operated on immediately.

For five weeks Moira recovered in the hospital while Nicol traveled between the hospital and the hotel. The telephone calls and telegrams between the states and Paris were constant. Never before had Moira been so far from her mother and Eva at such a critical time. After this initial, trying period of their honeymoon, Nicol wrote to John of Moira's bravery:

The old girl was magnificent throughout all the ether and ambulance period. We thought for a minute it was curtains, but she never said a word and took it in her stride. She certainly has the

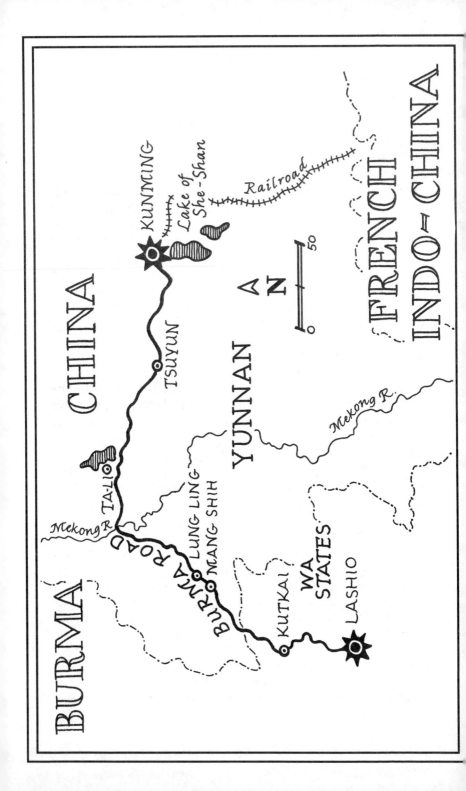

disposition of an angel and I am glad she is right down here and not up in heaven.[1]

Moira regained her health quickly and the honeymoon progressed as planned.

Their personalities seemed to compliment each other. Nicol was outgoing, the center of attention and cheerful. Moira was comfortable as the quiet, retiring companion. Her disposition was sweet and only occasionally outspoken. She liked Nicol's stories and wanted to be a part of his adventures. When her moments of stubbornness provoked a disagreement, Nicol was willing to let the issue at hand settle itself. Nicol had never been comfortable with conflict and avoided it whenever possible. With Moira, he just tried to keep her happy and side-stepped any issue that might create a problem.

Many of Nicol's friends felt he had married a woman who was demanding of him yet too simple to satisfy him. Friends discussed among themselves why he married the Archbold girl. What did she bring to the marriage besides her wealth?

Nicol's letters to family and friends never mentioned that he was aware of the gossip among his social circle. It is conceivable he chose to ignore any comments that were made to him and never acknowledged those he overheard. Money would always be a factor with Nicol's marriage to Moira. It was insinuated that Nicol was a fortune seeker and he had married Moira for this reason only. How little friends knew of Nicol. A sincere and honest man, he and Moira had joined their two lonely lives. Nicol may have had many friends, but as an adult even the loneliness of friendship can be too much. Where was there any better choice for Nicol?

Moira probably suffered the most from the remarks of their friends and acquaintances. Not a becoming woman, she was as tall as Nicol and taller in pumps. She was big-boned, her front teeth protruded slightly and horn-rimmed glasses did not improve her appearance. Her clothing was not stylish and fit awkwardly. Her fair complexion and thick, wavy hair were redeeming features, but still Moira was an ugly duckling as a mature woman. One time someone asked Nicol what attracted him to Moira. Nicol's honest, if evasive, reply was he was not much of a catch himself.

Nicol was an attractive man in an odd sort of way. His clothes fit his five foot nine inch, pear-shaped body well. He was neat and always immaculately groomed with his hair trim and combed back, tie pin and watch fob in place and shoes shined. His personality outshone any shortcomings in looks and build. Now he carefully assisted Moira in improving her image.

In Nicol's business, appearance was important. He offered to purchase her any clothing she desired as she recovered in Paris. He had hats designed for her, had her hair done every few days and bought her a jacket of blue fox. By the time they returned to the states she was, in Nicol's words, the "smartest" dresser in Paris.

The two were a match of proportions unrecognizable to anyone else. They were happy. They were together. They planned to travel the world. Nicol was generous with any income he could provide. Moira had the wealth to allow them to live in the style to which she was accustomed. She assisted Nicol in funding his travels. Their situation never was understood among Nicol's friends.

Anne Archbold was probably the most influential person in the young couple's lives. Once she decided that Moira and Nicol could marry, she supported them in absolutely anything they desired to do. Being an adventurer herself, she brought two lion cubs back from an African safari when her eldest daughter, Lydia, was a baby. She was the first American woman to travel in Tibet. She had traveled the world seeking adventures unknown to women of her generation. She loved to hear Nicol's stories. His presentations for the National Geographic Society at Constitution Hall in Washington, D.C., were always followed by a reception hosted by Anne at Hillandale.

She truly admired the honest, strictly social-drinking, young man. Her relationship with Nicol often seemed closer than with her own sons. For years she sent Nicol a few thousand dollars to buy film for his travels. Each check was accompanied by a note from her financial manager at Rockefeller Plaza in New York. One that remains from 1948 said, "Mrs. Archbold was in yesterday. She said to send you the enclosed check. Mrs. Archbold said you still believe in Santa Claus."[2]

Nicol always wrote kind letters of thanks. Wherever he was in the world he would sit down and write to his mother-in-law. Nicol wrote letters generously. Sometimes Anne would receive daily letters, recounting every step of his trip. He always promised that Moira would write, but whether she did is not known. The correspondence written by Moira either never occurred, or the letters received by Nicol from Moira in the year of their courtship are the only ones that still exist.

Anne shared her longing for adventure with Nicol during his visits at Hillandale. At breakfast one morning in the expansive dining room, Anne was reading the morning paper at the table. It contained an article on the disappearance of the noted adventurer, Richard Haliburton. He had been sailing a Chinese junk across the Pacific Ocean when he was caught in a terrible storm at sea. All on board had been lost. The article inferred the junk was not a seaworthy vessel. Anne vehemently disagreed with the newspaper account of the abilities of a junk. After some discussion with Nicol about her sailing trip along the China coast in 1925, she immediately decided to have one built. Within hours she had contacted her financial manager, Joe Mulholland, in New York and started the search for an engineer. The junk was to be built at the Ah King shipyard in Hong Kong and Nicol was instructed to look in on its construction when he arrived there enroute to China.

Nicol was frequently amazed at the rapidity and finality of his mother-in-law's decisions. He had witnessed her first decision following his presentation in Nassau before his engagement to Moira was announced. He was dumbfounded. Anne knew what she wanted. Many times he mused that Moira also wasted no time in voicing her strong opinions and decisions. He could see similarities between the two women that the family members often overlooked.

Nicol's insatiable curiosity was the fodder for his adventuresome spirit. He had nothing to prove nor anyone to out do. Money was Nicol's only inhibitor. Money did not inhibit the Archbolds. He wanted to spend his life looking for the next unknown piece of road, the mysterious occurrence, the unusual lifestyle. Moira concurred. Marriage to Nicol was the most exciting event in her life since the sea voyage aboard the Saranac when she was eight-years-old. Their first trip together became the most noted of Nicol's life's travels. Even more than fifty years later Nicol would be remembered as the first American to cross the Burma Road.

～

Nicol and Moira left for China in late April of 1939. The preparations for their first trip together took six weeks of planning and packing, followed by a month-long ocean voyage, via Manila to Hong

Kong. They were accompanied by Mary Carter, a family friend, who assisted Moira throughout the trip.

The next stop was at the shipyard to view the building of the junk, Cheng Ho. Nicol wrote to Anne and John to inform each of them the construction of the junk was progressing. He forwarded to Anne the pictures he took, impressed by the dimensions of the vessel. The Cheng Ho was a Foochow type of junk, measuring eighty-five feet in length with a breadth of twenty-four feet. Among her accessories were a motor-driven and sail whale boat, a motor sampan and a non-powered, glass-bottom boat. Twelve Chinese would form the crew on its first expedition which would take place later that year.[3] When she set sail the following December, a two-year course around the world was planned for researching tropical plants. It would be conducted by Dr. David Fairchild, Director of the Fairchild Tropical Garden, Coconut Grove, Florida. Anne planned to be aboard for only certain parts of the journey.

From here Nicol and Moira journeyed three days on a Chinese freighter to Haiphong in French Indo-China. They stopped briefly at Pakhoi, the southernmost port of China. Along the way, Nicol visited each acquaintance from his travels two years earlier. Nicol forgot no one and all remembered him with great fondness.

At Pakhoi[4] Nicol obtained permission to visit the leper colony. Not many travelers visited Pakhoi and Nicol found the residents most accommodating. Captain Spencer, the harbormaster and a Texan who hadn't left China in thirty years, was Nicol's host. He found a British guide, Major Wright, for Nicol and loaned him his new Ford car.

The leper colony was ten miles inland from the sprawling coastal city. Nicol was interested in all aspects of the colony. He wanted to know how the disease was spread and what hope did its victims have. He found a modern development supported by the Church Mission Society of London.

Upon his arrival, he was greeted by a young man who was to be his guide. Nicol involuntarily stepped forward to shake hands and just as quickly stepped back. He embarrassed himself by offering to shake hands with the young man whose limbs were afflicted with the dreaded disease. The leper was gracious and simply bowed when introduced.

Nicol toured the facilities and listened to personal stories and superstitions. The people warmly welcomed the visitors. Nicol knew

*Above: William Smith, Jr.,
circa 1880.*

*Above right: Charlotte
Mathilda Gelvin Smith,
circa 1890.*

*Right: Robert Smith in
1900, the year he
graduated from law school
at Dickinson.*

Above: Adelaide Louise Dodge Nicol in 1894.

Above right: Frank D. Nicol, circa 1890.

Right: Judge George Woodburn Nicol, circa 1900.

Nicol and his nanny, Henrietta Lincoln Washington Alfred in 1910.

Susan Smith posing for the San Francisco Call in 1906. Photograph was on the front page of the society section on September 30, 1906.

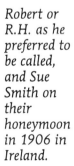

Robert or R.H. as he preferred to be called, and Sue Smith on their honeymoon in 1906 in Ireland.

Nicol and his mother, Sue.

Rudolph Spreckles, "Uncle
Ruddy" to Nicol.

Nicol seated
on the wicker
chair with
his friends
and their
nanny,
governess
and butler.

Nicol's fourth birday party in 1914. He is in the center
back, standing and looking toward the camera between
strands of flowing crepe paper.

Nicol, six, poses with his dance class. From left, the other
children are, John Drum, Sally Jenkins, Frank West,
Harriet Holbrook, Nicol Smith, Patricia Tobin, Larry
Harris, Noriaua Averali and Peter McBean.

Nicol and his governess, Miss Linette Whitman.

Nicol, five, poses for the camera in 1915.

Sue and her chauffeur.

R.H., front row, second from left, at Bohemian Grove in 1915.

From left,
Moira, John,
Armar and
Lydia Archbold
with their
nanny in
England in
1916.

Moira Archbold at
age five in 1916.

Left: Nicol and Aunt Myrtle in Pennsylvania, circa 1932.

Below: Nicol's Stanford graduation picture in 1933.

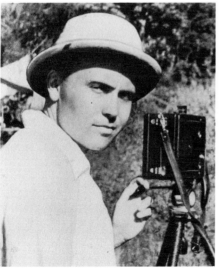

Nicol's first photograph for lecture promotion material in 1935.

Above: Nicol in the South Sea Islands during the summer of 1930.

Left: Nicol's second promotional photograph for lectures taken after his return from the Guianas in 1941.

*Above: Nicol
interviews
Governor Chot
of French
Guiana in 1938.*

*Right: Nicol and
Lo-Bo, a
Surinam
bushdog in
Dutch Guiana.*

*Below: Nicol
riding on a train
car in Dutch
Guiana in 1935.*

Above: Moira Archbold at Bex McBride's in 1938.

Left: Nicol and Moira on their wedding day at Hillandale in 1938.

Below: Nicol and Moira.

R.H., Moira, Sue and Nicol.

R.H. and Nicol.

Colonel Nicol Smith receives the Legion of Merit from General Donovan, head of the OSS, after the conclusion of WW II in 1945.

Colonel Nicol Smith in a newspaper interview for the OSS in August of 1945.

Left: Art Hall and Nicol.

Below: Nicol, his photographer and a companion.

Bottom: Nicol with the king of Ladakh in 1947.

Nicol's picture of Angel Falls, Venezuela.

Nicol at his typewriter in Kashmir in 1947. Rajah observes.

Nicol and Moira's retreat at Lashio Lodge on the Stanislaus River.

Above: Anne Archbold on her boat in Nassau shortly before her death in 1968.

Nicol waves from the deck of Lashio Lodge in 1965.

Above left: Art Hall at Lashio Lodge.

Above: Nicol's last photograph for lecture promotional material.

Left: Art and Nicol in Malta.

Nicol attends a welcome ceremony near Escaldes in ancient Andorra.

Nicol and Elvira, a seven-day-old musk ox, the star of his film Alaska Journey. This film, made in 1975, was the last of Nicol's career.

that every traveler to the Orient brought home souvenirs of their travels. He planned to bring home the stories. Leper colonies were viewed with distaste and superstition by the American people. Nicol planned to enlighten the public through his experiences.

The tour lasted all day. Nicol's heart went out to the innocent victims of leprosy. Their plight saddened him. It was only a few short months after his visit, on November 15, 1939, that Japan landed armed forces at Pakhoi and began their plans to overtake China. Nicol later wondered how his warm recipients at the colony fared in the takeover.

Leaving Paikoi, Nicol continued to Haiphong. This port had previously been a quiet town but now bustled with activity. It was the only gateway left on the east coast of Asia through which entrance could be gained to the interior of China. Japan controlled all the other ports to China.

With twenty-seven pieces of luggage, including movie cameras, thousands of feet of film, clothing, camping equipment and seven packing cases of tinned food, they made their way through customs to the hotel. Traveling by train, they stopped next at Hanoi. Another overnight stay gave the couple some free time. They saw the movie *Borneo*, by Martin and Osa Johnson. Nicol admired the Johnsons who were travelers much as himself. They filmed their own moving picture footage, organized their expeditions and returned to the states to conduct lecture circuits. Their film was about the native people and animals of Borneo, a place Nicol had not visited.

May was a time of heat and humidity. Everything was hot and steaming. Nicol and Moira dressed in fresh, cool khaki shorts and shirts, sporting broad-brimmed hats, damp scarves around their necks and light-weight tennis shoes each morning, only to find themselves sticky and sweaty within ten minutes. The rainy season was about to begin and perhaps it would offer some relief. The Hotel Metropole in Hanoi was an oasis in the sweltering city. It had been Charlie Chaplin, no less, who had advised Nicol before leaving California to stay at this establishment if he could. Nicol welcomed the gracious service of the immaculate hotel. He hated to leave, but the Burma Road beckoned him. Within minutes on their trip northward, a rain storm deluged the train. The downpour made it impossible to view the countryside for the next thirty miles.

Crossing the Red River into China at Laikai, the train stopped for the customs inspection.[5] Nicol personally carried three cameras and the one thousand feet of film with him at all times. He would not entrust all of his camera equipment to the porters in the baggage car. Even though he paid them extra to guard his luggage, he felt reassured only when he carried equipment with him in the passenger car. The customs officials debated among themselves if he should be allowed to take the equipment into their country. With Japan overrunning China, every foreigner was suspicious. Finally, Nicol was allowed to continue.

The trip by rail continued to Kunming, the city Nicol visited two years earlier when traveling to the tin mines of the Yunnan province of China. They arrived with all their luggage on June 2 amidst a torrential downpour. Kunming was just as Nicol had described it to Moira. It was located on the north shore of Lake of She-Shan at an altitude of 6,299 feet. The climate was more pleasant than the sweltering tropics they had just left. The city was a leading commercial and cultural center of southwest China. It was at the junction of important transportation routes; the terminus of the railroad from Hanoi from which they had just disembarked and of the Burma Road. The city consisted of the old walled portion, a modern commercial suburb and a residential and university section.

After settling in at the hotel, they left in a rickshaw for dinner with the American Consular, Paul Meyer, and his wife, Harriet. Paul was in his late thirties, was shy and level-headed. He had proven himself as an able diplomat, first in Peking and now in Kunming. Two years earlier on his trip to China following the Hainan expedition, Nicol had met Paul and Harriet. Paul and Nicol discussed traveling the Burma Road during that visit. Nicol had promised to return if Paul could arrange the trip. Paul felt he had obtained the necessary permission for the two of them to make the trip. Moira planned to stay at the hotel with her companion, Mary, while Harriet planned short excursions for them around the city until the men returned.

The Burma Road was approximately 725 breathtaking miles of new highway that climbed above the clouds and plunged into vast gorges to join Kunming, the capital of Yunnan Province of China, with Lashio, the railhead in Burma. The great road was born out of necessity by war. China had been steadily driven inland from her ports by the Japanese and depended upon getting supplies through her western gateway, the Burma Road. From far-off Rangoon, the Burmese seaport, a railway snaked its way northward through Burma to the hamlet of Lashio. Here the road began that stretched all the way to Kunming in China. The road was finished in 1938 and had been built by two hundred thousand workmen. Completed, it became the direct route for military supplies to the beleaguered China.

Approval for the trip needed to be granted by the Chinese Governor of Yunnan Province, Lung Yun, or his secretary, Mr. Wang. Then they waited for the Southwest Transportation Company to issue the gasoline ration card for the trip. Additional permission must be granted from the head of the military, Generalissimo Chiang Kai-shek. The question would then become would the rain, alone, make the trip impossible?

Nicol's prolonged wait in Kunming put him in one more interesting, although unusual, position. Attending a dinner party one evening at a Frenchman's home, he was introduced to his first opium party. Two years before Nicol had hoped to witness an opium den. Now as soon as the coffee was served after dinner, the host and several guests retired to the fumerie or smoking room. Nicol declined the invitation to indulge in opium smoking, but he found it interesting to watch the guests as they partook of the pipe. He observed that opium smoking was not conducive to brilliant conversation.[6] Nicol's curiosity was quickly satisfied.

～

Paul and Nicol's departure was delayed. Permission to take moving pictures was creating red tape. They would not be able to leave for another week. While waiting, Nicol and Moira familiarized themselves with the city. They spent one afternoon visiting the School for Blind Girls. The school was run by the German Sisters of Charity, led by Sister Anna, a wonderfully warm woman.

Attending the singing class, Nicol listened to the children as the headmistress told him individual stories of young girls sold into slavery for money. Often it was disease or mistreatment that had caused their blindness.

Learning that the girls knitted to support the school, Nicol asked what it was they made. Informed that socks were their specialty, he pulled up his trouser leg, requesting wool socks like the ones he wore. Picking out the colors, he ordered a dozen pair for ten dollars. They would be ready when he returned from his trip.

Two days later, he returned to the school to leave a pair of socks as a sample. On his first visit, Nicol's heart went out to the young girls, particularly to a five-year-old with a captivating smile. Nicol asked to be introduced to her. He adored the little girl and asked what it would take to support her. When he learned that ten American dollars a year would provide two dresses, two pairs of shoes, a woolen blanket and candy and fruit, he adopted her on the spot. Paying fifteen dollars, he hoped she could have a special year. As he was leaving, Nicol mused that he had planned to visit only and now he had ordered a dozen pair of socks and was an American uncle to a Chinese girl. Nicol continued to support Chen Hsiu-lien and visited her again when he was in China in 1943.

Finally, Nelson Johnson, the American Ambassador to China, obtained permission from Generalissimo Chiang Kai-shek for Nicol to take motion pictures along the Burma Road. Permission had not previously been granted to any foreigner. Apparently Nicol's offer to photograph the Governor himself had aided their decision.

Before departing, with two government censors accompanying him, Nicol would be allowed to photograph the north gate of the Burma Road in Kunming. The day with the censors permitted Nicol to get started on his moving picture. He was prohibited from filming any military attachment, crowded streets or citizens in native dress.

The day arrived but proved frustrating. Nicol felt his day of filming was not accomplishing anything. At noon he met a Chinese acquaintance for a picnic lunch with her two children. She solved his difficulties by amusing the two censors. They paid less attention to Nicol and he was able to film nearly everything he saw. They spent the afternoon touring Lake of She-Shan from aboard a hired junk. Consuming the lunch packed by Harriet, Nicol completed shooting five hundred feet of film.

With permissions secured, the packing began. The Ford was loaded with their supplies with room left for their newly hired assistant, Old Family, who rode in the rumble seat between the tent and the shovels. He rarely lifted a hand the entire trip.

Paul and Nicol started off in the 1937 Ford coupé. It had poured daily since the beginning of June and Paul was concerned how the rains had affected the road.

They left through the north gate of the city, turning west upon the Burma Road. The Ford bumped its way along the road outside the city wall, passing truck gardens, irrigation ditches and men, women and children toiling in their plots as they had for centuries.[7]

The journey across the Burma Road to Lashio and back to Kunming would take two weeks to complete. The first five days it drizzled constantly while they covered from 120 to 200 miles a day. Each night they lodged and fueled at stations of the Southwest Transportation Company. The road was rough and anything from 50 to 150 miles in six hours could be considered a good distance.

Old Family proved to be a worthless addition to their load. Hired at the last minute, he was given the responsibilities of preparing food, loading and unloading the Ford and other necessities such as changing a flat tire. But Old Family, who was a young man of eighteen from one of the oldest families in Szechwan, groaned at each pothole, moaned when it rained on him and posed for a photograph by the car as Paul changed their first flat tire. As far as Nicol was concerned, posing for pictures was the extent of Old Family's usefulness.

Along each leg of the journey, Nicol visited every sight or place of interest. The first day brought an introduction to a young man who had been brought to China to aid the government in the building of airplanes. The plant was constructed and began operating in 1934. When Japan first invaded China, the airplane factory was among the first places bombed. The workers dismantled the plant and moved it by rail to another location. The plant was moved four times before it was reassembled in an area deemed safe and with adequate transportation facilities.

Nicol met Colonel Claire Chennault, the noted instructor of Army pilots in Yunnanfu. He paid several visits and they became friends. This acquaintance would prove invaluable. Nicol's next trip to China would be during World War II and then he would need Channault's assistance.

The Ford continued to roll along the Burma Road accompanied by an endless drizzle. As uncomfortable as the persistent dampness was, the men knew they were lucky to escape the torrential downpours so common during that season. They crossed mountain passes of eight to nine thousand feet and suspension bridges hanging over canyons. Villages lay quietly along the road and the natives seemed uninterested in the passing vehicles.

The second day brought the first encounter with military vehicles. From that point on, military trucks were sighted regularly. It appeared to Nicol that the entire military was traveling over the Burma Road in order to protect it from the Japanese.

They arrived in the village of Kutkai during their first downpour on the fifth day. Now in Burma, they would have to pay cash for fuel and find their own lodging. Finding both in Kutkai, they decided to stop for the night. The British Political Officer, Norman Blaquiere, soon learned of their arrival and invited the men to dinner and hoped they would stay for a few days. Three days later the rains let up and Paul and Nicol made a dash for Lashio, less than fifty miles distant. The same evening they returned to Kutkai to spend another night.

Arriving in Lashio, the head of the Burma Road and the terminus point of the railroad from Rangoon, Nicol felt sorry for Old Family and gave him five rupees to cheer him up after the drenching he had received while riding in the rumble seat. Their woebegone servant vanished. Hours later he returned. Smirking he showed Nicol and Paul his new tennis shoes and a huge pole-like parcel clasped under his arm. He removed the wrapping paper to proudly display a huge black umbrella. Stepping outside he opened the umbrella and swaggered across the street.

As Nicol explored the village, the police approached him. Demanding that he turn over his cameras, Nicol was escorted to their station house in a newer section of the village. Nicol did not have the appropriate permissions to take moving pictures in the Burmese village. After careful questioning, Nicol was led to a jail cell. At the precise moment the cell door swung open, Paul appeared having heard an American, which he correctly assumed was Nicol, was detained at the police station. Straightening out the misunderstanding, Paul and Nicol prepared to depart. One last request was made. The police chief wanted to be in the moving picture along with all of his children.

After driving back to Kutkai, they were again hosted by Norman. He introduced Nicol to Kachin tribesmen and their culture. He shared stories of Palaung women, Naga Hills tribesman and the Wa people. Nicol was fascinated with the tales of Wa headhunters and the ferocity of the Naga Hills tribesmen. Along the road, he had seen three Palaung women with their filed, pointed teeth. Among the native groups, only the Kachin were local and Norman arranged an assemblage of natives in full costume doing their sword dance.

Fortunately the next day dawned clear and sunny. Norman's houseboy was a Kachin. He was sent to fetch representatives of his tribe. Nicol set up his camera and began grinding. He obtained ample footage before the heavens opened up. Moving indoors, he proceeded to barter with the Kachins and purchased ornaments. He felt the date was 939 instead of 1939.[8]

On the eighth day, they continued their return trip. Crossing the border from Burma to China, the deluge began afresh. Within minutes the road seemed a waterfall as the Ford crept along. Thirteen miles took an hour. Between the ruts were potholes and between the potholes was a sea of mud. Nicol donned his hip boots, which Old Family found for him without changing his position in the rumble seat, and stepped out to locate solid bits of roadbed to help Paul guide the automobile forward.

At Mang Shih they were told a landslide had covered the road. Twenty miles outside of town they reached the long line of military trucks stopped by the landslide. They were last in line. Not wanting to turn back to the last village, since it was in a malarial area, they hung the tarpaulin as a lean-to from the side of the car and set up camp. No one knew when the road would be cleared. It could be a day, a week or a month.

The next morning they decided to break camp and push past all the trucks to position themselves as close to the slide as possible. For five miles they snaked along the road to find a slide seventy-five feet wide and thirty feet high. Sixteen men with four shovels were picking away at the debris. In the two days since the slide they had made little headway.

Finally a group of men crossed from the other side of the slide and informed Nicol and Paul that it was passable on foot. Hiring all the coolies they could, they divided the remaining supplies and began the hike over the landslide, with Old Family carrying only his trustworthy umbrella.

Once across, a truck provided the twenty-minute ride to the village of Lung Ling. There they were offered respite from the rain in the compound of the Southwest Transportation Company.

Shortly after they ate dinner, a man arrived who was bound for Burma. Hearing there had been a break in the Burma Road, he inquired of Paul and Nicol if it was true he would have to spend the night. Sharing the misfortune with him, they forewarned him it could be much longer.

When Paul learned the man had arrived in a Ford, he inquired what year it was. Learning it was a 1938, he offered to trade his 1937 Coupe for the 1938. The man seemed unsure. Nicol, in his most convincing manner, confirmed he could be in Lung Ling for up to a month. Finally the man was persuaded. The next morning they drove him and his automobile as close to the slide as possible, where he departed with his baggage, walking over the mud and boulders.

Paul and Nicol loaded everything into their new automobile and were bound for Kunming.

14

THE GUIANAS

Adventure and photography, followed by the creation and editing of a moving picture to accompany his lectures, became an annual cycle for Nicol. Each spring he began plans for the next adventure. During the summer, he traveled abroad and enjoyed the experiences of a new place and new people. During the ensuing winter, a moving picture and a narration were developed by Nicol. Then began the travel circuit that lasted until spring.

It was a life of continuous movement. Nicol felt at home on the road as much as he did in his bungalow at the club. His audiences were intrigued by his stories of adventure. Each year he returned to lecture at locations from his previous circuits. He was developing a following. Nicol had a gift for his career. He was making a moving picture nearly every year while other explorers made new pictures every two or three years. He memorized the narration and practiced until the timing with the picture was perfect. He stood on the stage sharing his adventures with the enthusiasm of a newly returned traveler and delivered every lecture with the same fervor as the first one, even after dozens of presentations on the same topic.

As exciting as his career was, and Nicol did enjoy all aspects of it, it was not as lucrative as a traditional professional life might have been. His traveling expenses, supplies, photography equipment and lecture circuits accounted for nearly all of Nicol's income. He was accustomed to a lavish lifestyle. His early years had not wanted for anything. During the Depression, Nicol fared well compared to his parents, but the capital needed to buy real estate or settle in a home had not been available. Neither was it a priority. The winter season of lectures provided the means to a summer of travel. Nicol was content, but the means for earning additional income would have been welcome.

While on the lecture circuit in 1937, he met Alvin Hamer of Hamer's Book Service in Detroit, Michigan. After attending Nicol's lecture about the river expedition in Dutch Guiana, Mr. Hamer approached Nicol in the receiving line during the guest reception. He inquired whether Nicol had considered writing any travel books about his adventures. Nicol was interested. He had spent many hours working on articles for publication. Only two, the Madame Duez story and the Nudist Colony story, had been published so far. He hoped for more. Several newspapers had interviewed him, but nothing else had been forthcoming.

Mr. Hamer offered to represent him as his literary agent and he promised to find a book publisher for Nicol.

Nicol signed a contract with the Bobbs-Merrill Company of Indianapolis, Indiana. This initial contract[1] specified the topic, the proposed title and the length of the book. Apparently Nicol had already started writing a book called *Who's Who in the Guianas*. The agreement specified the manuscript be completed no later than December 1. It should total at least eighty thousand words and include pictures he took during his trip. The book would retail at three dollars apiece. Nicol would receive royalties based upon this price and number of books sold, receiving a total of three thousand dollars on the first ten thousand books sold. Of this amount, ninety percent would go to Nicol and ten percent to Alvin Hamer, his agent. The expectation was that a book on the Guianas would interest many Americans and there would be a foreign market as well. Special conditions were stated in the agreement with Bobbs-Merrill that allowed for alternative pricing on all exported books.

Nicol spent hours working on various manuscripts. He began to diligently pursue writing when he was teaching at Miss MacAleer's. The young lady, Lois Ferguson, had meticulously typed page after page for him. The following year Nicol had hired another student to come to his bungalow and type. He had mounds of material. Now he had to decide what was bookworthy.

Appended at the end of this first contract is a handwritten paragraph stating that Nicol had previously submitted his material on French Guiana to Metro-Goldwyn-Mayer. Again Nicol must have hoped to have a movie produced about French Guiana. Perhaps it was another attempt to find a producer for the Duez story. There is no record, however, of Nicol ever profiting from the purchase of movie rights.

The next correspondence that exists between Bobbs-Merrill and Nicol was dated more than two-and-a-half years later.[2] The letter, dated December 11, 1939, first referred to the initial contract:

> I suppose we should consider that the contract of April 6, 1937 is in full force and effect for this book, though it is about the Burma Road and not about the Guianas.[3]

Nicol never published a book entitled *Who's Who in the Guianas.* What happened to his first effort and how Bobbs-Merrill reacted is not known. From the context of the above quoted correspondence, Nicol had not turned in a manuscript prior to the Burma Road submission. Apparently they still expected to see something on his Guiana experiences.

The letter also refers to another agreement dated December 28, 1937. It can be assumed that Nicol did not complete the first book by the designated date and a new agreement was signed. This agreement does not exist in either Nicol's files or the remaining files of the late Bobbs-Merrill Publishing Company.

Regardless of the order of events, Bobbs-Merrill was pleased with the book about the Burma Road. Nicol's difficulties in producing a first book may have stemmed from naiveté. Writing pages upon pages in his diary, creating short stories from personal experiences and the occasional publication of an article in a magazine or newspaper had not prepared him for writing a book. In addition, 1937 and the following two years had been busy. The trip to Hainan Island was followed by the courtship between Nicol and Moira. Then the next year was the honeymoon summer abroad in Europe and then to China in 1939.

Guiana memories had faded. Now Nicol planned another trip to French and Dutch Guiana via Martinique.

⌒

The "New York Times Book Review" in March of 1940 ran a half page review of Nicol Smith's *Burma Road*. Three newly published travel books were reviewed, but the *Burma Road* made other travel books look dull in comparison:

> Compared with Nicol Smith's account of what he saw and experienced on the Burma Road, the average travel book seems tedious and drab. He collected tales instead of curios, and, as he seems to be not only intelligent but also a most engaging young man, he heard plenty of them, tales of opium smuggling, and pirates, of poison, magic, romance and murder....[4]

The illustrated book totaled 333 pages and cost $3.50. Immediately it became a best-seller. Overnight, Nicol became a noted authority on the China-Burma connection. Bobbs-Merrill was thrilled and pushed Nicol to start another travel book. *Burma Road* was selling as quickly as it was placed on bookstore shelves. Garden City Publishing Company and Star Books were allowed to print subsequent editions. These later editions were reduced in price and the book continued to outsell all other travel publications. *Burma Road* remained on the nonfiction best-seller list for over a year.

Nicol's lecture sponsor, now W. Colston Leigh of New York, capitalized upon his success. Lecture brochures and announcements were reprinted. Bookings were growing each season. New places, such as the Harvard Club in Boston and the National Geographic Society in Washington, D.C., were included in 1940. Appearances for the Burma Road lectures were presented in Washington at Constitution Hall and attracted thirty-two hundred people.

Nicol's writing career was off to an auspicious start. Producing the first manuscript had been more difficult than he anticipated. Sam McCoy, an editor found by Bobbs-Merrill, facilitated the completion of the first book. Both were encouraged by its initial success and soon they sat down to work together again.

Nicol put aside his travel plans for the summer of 1940 and began working diligently on his next book. Sam moved to San

Francisco and leased an apartment to be close to Nicol. Still Nicol felt he did not have the correct material for a book on the Guianas and wished to return to South America to collect more stories. But Sam thought otherwise. The writing began to flow. By December, a manuscript named *Bush Master* was in the hands of the publisher.

Chambers, the president of Bobbs-Merrill in Indianapolis, wired Nicol his congratulations on completing the manuscript. A week later Chambers wrote Nicol that he had just finished reading *Bush Master* that afternoon:

> It is a grand yarn, full of excitement, of suspense, of color, of fun. I enjoyed every page. This is the realization of all our long held hopes for the Dutch Guiana book, complete success after the several false starts.[5]

It was not until January of 1942 that *Bush Master, Into the Jungles of Dutch Guiana* was published. Meanwhile, Nicol had taken an advance of $350 on the book to subsidize his and Sam's living expenses during the writing of the book. The advance was based on projected sales with a royalty of ten percent on each book sold. The amount he received meant no other money would be forthcoming until more than one thousand books were sold.

Bush Master was a moderate success compared to *Burma Road*. Probably *Bush Master* would have seemed more successful if it had not been viewed in the aftermath of the earlier bestseller. Again Bobbs-Merrill allowed the second edition to be produced by another company. Blue Ribbon Books published the later edition under the title *The Jungles of Dutch Guiana*.

No contract exists specifically for *Burma Road* or *Bush Master*. The initial agreement in 1937 sufficed for the first book and the letter dated December 19, 1940 became the agreement for the second book.

↵

Throughout the writing of his second book, Nicol wanted to return to the Guianas to obtain more material. Sam discouraged the need for another expedition, afraid the interruption would prevent Nicol from capitalizing on the rapid succession of a bestseller immediately followed by another book. Moira was eager to travel again and Nicol needed new lecture material. Hainan

Island and Burma Road had been his topics for two consecutive seasons. He was anxious for a new adventure.

Nicol wanted to try new types of filming on his next trip. He needed to purchase new equipment and learn the techniques involved with color film. He decided to hire Loren Tutell to travel with him and Moira. He had met Tutell during his lecture circuit and decided to engage him as a technical photographer. Loren was a superb photographer and had experience producing color, moving pictures. Nicol repeatedly introduced Loren as an "ace color photographer." With four hundred pounds of camera equipment, they were prepared to produce a new film.

The two men left New York enroute to Dutch and French Guiana via Martinique. Moira and her companion, Mary Carter, were scheduled to join them when they reached Dutch Guiana. Each had his work cut out for him. Moira planned to record native music for the Library of Congress. Nicol prepared to find enough adventures to fill another book and a lecture season. Loren's photography would create a feature-length, color movie.

Before departing, Nicol's mother-in-law, Anne, provided the young man with several letters of introduction. Included was a letter from Dr. Fairchild, the noted explorer, and Dr. Staehel, a noted medical researcher. Nicol had briefly met the doctor on a previous expedition and hoped the man would remember him. Another letter presented Nicol to Governor Chot of French Guiana. Letters of introduction were a way of life for Nicol. For years his mother used letters as a means to further her social acquaintances. Nicol was accustomed to presenting himself to strangers. He never had a problem with this type of introduction.

Permission to visit Martinique was not easy to obtain. Late in April, a week prior to departure, found Nicol still in Washington, D.C., trying to obtain permission for his photographer to accompany him. Permission for Nicol had been granted from the consulate in San Francisco.

He was informed that no unofficial American travelers had been permitted to enter Martinique since the Germans seized France almost a year before. For five days cables went back and forth between Washington and Fort-de-France, the capitol of Martinique, before approval was granted.

This trip Nicol left the East Coast flying on a Pan American Clipper, rather than taking the lengthy boat ride from New York to South America. This was only Nicol's second experience with air travel. Pan American Airlines had placed three of the Boeing Clippers in service on their Atlantic routes in 1939. The Boeing Clipper represented a big step forward in air transportation. Long-range capabilities of 3,100 miles and the high standard of comfort allowed for forty passengers. Two days later, after an overnight stay in San Juan, Puerto Rico, Nicol and Loren arrived in Fort-de-France.

While encountering difficulties for the approval of Loren's proposed filming, Nicol overlooked lodging reservations. Finally a room was found when a Negro couple offered to vacate the quarters above their cafe for fifty cents a day. Mosquito netting made from bridal-veil tulle was purchased to surround the beds. Using Nicol's neckties and handkerchiefs, the veil was hung from the makeshift line.

Martinique, a French possession, was suffering from the effects of the German occupation in France. Supply ships had ceased to arrive and tourists had been stranded on the island for weeks. This precipitated the difficulty of obtaining a room, purchasing mosquito netting or even the cord to hang the veil from the ceiling.

Nicol spent two weeks on the island, hearing again and again the hopeful plea that a ship was due to leave for America. Refugees from France and Germany flooded the island, hoping to buy passage to the states. Accosted on the street, people begged Nicol to exchange money through them instead of at the bank. Dollars were needed to obtain the coveted passage.

Never attempting to exchange his money on the street, he soon asked a luncheon acquaintance about the desire for American money. He was informed that the exchange of American money on the streets of Martinique was forbidden. Occasionally a German refugee turned out to be an agent of the Gestapo. The agent then sent the coveted Yankee dollars to the Germans, who believed the dollar would buy supplies from America.

Filming of fishing villages, rum plantations and the workings of a cane processing plant proceeded smoothly. These would be the first indoor shots taken for Nicol's moving picture. Using flash bulbs and heavy lighting equipment, the cameras were able to record the processing of rum from the field to the bottle.

Receiving permission to continue to French Guiana after a two-week stay in Dutch Guiana, Nicol was informed the country had been closed to travelers for more than a year. He and Loren were going to be the only exception. The only condition that would affect their filming was they must be escorted by an aide while they toured the penal colony and Nicol must present his pictures before the French Embassy in Washington, D.C., upon his return.

Interest in the French colonies was at a peak with the American public. Rarely did news from Martinique or French Guiana reach the states. Other islands in the Caribbean were dotted with new air bases. Pan-American Airways had built landing fields in British and Dutch Guiana and in Brazil, but nothing in the French colony. There was not one American consular in all French Guiana. Nicol felt America knew more about France than her French colonies that were so much closer.

Leaving Martinique, they continued on to Dutch Guiana where Moira and Mary joined the two men. Writing to Anne at Hillandale, Nicol thanked her for obtaining the letter of introduction to Dr. Staehel, who took them into the jungle to a native village. The Indians had never been photographed before and performed ritual dances for the travelers. Moira busily recorded the native music as Nicol and Loren filmed the dances.

Moira worked hard at creating a collection of native music for the Library of Congress. Writing to Anne about Moira's work, Nicol said:

> Moira is in the next room recording music. She works like a dog all day and is getting some grand stuff for the Library of Congress. This morning we filmed a Koto Misies dance and Moira made the records of the music and singing. When she played it back the natives went wild with joy. They just couldn't believe it possible.[6]

Nicol and Loren left for two weeks to French Guiana, leaving Moira behind to work on her music. The French government had refused Moira a visa. Their reasons were the food shortages and the general conditions of the country, which were not conducive to travelers.

The plane made a water landing and taxied across a wide stream. Stopping at a shed on the pier, they climbed out to learn the out-building was the Pan-American Airways station. Next, their passports were taken from them and they would have to call at the police station to retrieve them.

French Guiana was to be made available to them by Governor Chot. Nicol sent his letter of introduction to the governor's palace and waited for a response. Governor Robert Chot, a dynamic personality, wiry and athletic, proved invaluable to the travelers. Currently he served as Governor of French Guiana for France, but he had previously served in the colonial administration of the French colonies of Madagascar and Pondichéry.

Providing the two men with a personal guide, Governor Chot saw no reason to inhibit the filming of his country. Captain Richards, the governor's right-hand man, accompanied the travelers. He arranged tours of places Nicol missed on his first trip. They toured the Pasteur Institute, founded in 1938, where a doctor was making tremendous inroads improving the sanitation and health of the country. The doctor escorted Nicol to the Rocks of Kourou, a seaside point thirty miles west of Cayenne. This site was to become a planned colony for lepers in French Guiana, where one of every twenty had leprosy.

The governor took them on a cruise up the Cayenne River on his yacht through uninhabited jungle. Stopping at a penal camp, he found the convicts all were from French Indo-China. Logging the timber-rich jungle was their occupation day after day.

French penal law had been modified since Nicol's previous trip. In 1938, France decreed that no more prisoners were to be sent to the colony. It was hoped that the colony would be emptied of convicts over the years. Nicol found this hard to believe, since the libérés had no money to ever leave the colony.

It was during this trip that Nicol attempted to locate Madame Duez to obtain a permission letter for Warner Brothers He had first met her in 1934 in Cayenne. Unable to learn of her whereabouts, Nicol, accompanied by Loren, traveled to her deserted home on the island of LeMére. Three of the convicts who had been her servants still lived on the little island and were glad to give the travelers a tour, filling them in on the life they had led with Mr. and Mrs. Duez.

Returning to Dutch Guiana, Loren left for the states, while Moira and Nicol remained for another month. Becoming acquainted with the animal catcher, their hotel room was home to a variety of pets. A small monkey they named Jo-Jo, who slept in Moira's slipper, was their favorite.

Moira succeeded in recording five native forms of music, including a voodoo fire dance. Few local white residents had ever witnessed the voodoo ceremonies.

Their last visit was to the colony's mine fields of bauxite ore. This was the chief export commodity from which aluminum was made. Traveling upstream fifty-five miles from Paramaribo, they were given a tour by the Netherlander who directed the mine. To reach the mine they skirted the hull of the German freighter Goslar. When Germany invaded the Netherlands, the Nazis simultaneously tried to sink the freighter in the channel of the Cottica River, thus attempting to block all exports of bauxite to the United States. Nicol realized that an important share of United States' requirements of this ore was imported from the mines in Dutch Guiana. The Dutch only had a small garrison to protect the mines and the equipment. Later that year the United States sent a contingent of its own troops to protect the interests of the Dutch mine.

Returning to Washington, Moira and Nicol both worked on their respective projects. Moira was busy with the Library of Congress, completing the recordings, conducting interviews and cataloging the music that she had worked diligently to record.

Nicol began to work on his next book, *Black Martinique, Red Guiana* and an article for *National Geographic Magazine*. Sam McCoy, his previous editor, again collaborated with Nicol to help him write the manuscript.

Nicol worked alone on the article for *National Geographic*. "Color Glows in the Guianas, French and Dutch" was published in April, 1943.[7] Accompanied by color and black and white photographs, only two were selected from the hundreds Loren had taken, while the others in the article were provided by a staff photographer from the magazine. Nicol was satisfied, nevertheless, to have his first solely authored article published in the renowned magazine.

Fortunately, Nicol kept careful daily notes in his diary and had typed manuscripts from his earlier trip to French Guiana. The contract for his book was not finalized until February of the following year. The Madame Duez story became a copyright nightmare. Without the Duez story, Bobbs-Merrill felt the book did not have enough human interest. Warner Brothers and Bobbs-Merrill ironed out details for several months. The book contained three sections: ninety-four pages on Martinique; one-hundred-sixty pages on French Guiana; and culminated with fifty-six pages about Madame Duez.

Nicol gathered the material that completed this third book over the course of two trips to French Guiana. The book, published in 1942, was not widely received. Americans no longer had travel or the nearby French colonies on their minds. World War II enveloped the next three years for Americans. Nicol's civilian adventures were placed on hold for nearly five years.

৸৶

15

LASHIO LODGE ON THE STANISLAUS

Following their honeymoon abroad, Moira persuaded Nicol to end his lease of the bungalow at the Burlingame Country Club. Their new residence became the St. Francis Hotel in San Francisco. On the East Coast they also maintained a residence at the Hampshire House on Central Park in New York City. With an apartment in two large cities, the couple considered a location where they could have a home to call their own.

Since Nicol's childhood, his father, R.H., had taken him on fishing trips along the Stanislaus River in the Sierra Nevada Mountains of central California. Nicol was never an avid fisherman like his father, but he enjoyed the beauty of the mountain property.

Since the purchase of the 160-acre parcel by Nicol's grandfather, Frank Nicol, ownership had been transferred among various family members. Frank Nicol died in March of 1910,[1] only two months after Nicol's birth. His death from Graves Disease, a thyroid disorder, occurred during his fifty-first year. Concerned about the welfare of his wife and family, he had willed the river property to his wife, Adelaide. The co-owner of the property, Dr. Wallace of Stockton, sold his share to Adelaide for $1,000 later that same year.[2] Before Frank passed away, he told Adelaide to sell the river property for a good price if money became scarce. The money from the property would help support her and her mother, Eliza. It was not too many years before she decided to sell the land and the buyer was her son-in-law, R.H.

The river property held fond memories for R.H. and he didn't want to lose what he thought might become valuable land. The trips to the mountains with Frank Nicol, the nights in the old, shake homesteader's cabin, fishing the Stanislaus River and visiting the families camped along the river front were experiences he had hoped to repeat with his family.

Camping along the river on the old Board's property had become a tradition. Frank Nicol and Wallace led many a group from Stockton to their property. Tents were pitched and children played together in the river while the fathers fished for trout. As the years passed, the children brought their families. Tents were left for the summer season, with the campers returning for weekends and vacations.

The Depression brought hard times even to the remote river property. Although R.H. purchased the land with cash from his mother-in-law in 1917, he leveraged the land during the mid-thirties. When Nicol brought Moira to the property in May of 1939, Wells Fargo Bank & Union Trust Company had repossessed the land nearly three years earlier.

Moira fell in love with the quiet and solitude of the mountains. Here she dreamed of freedom, away from the social constraints and expectations of her family, her friends and life at the country club. She could ride, swim and fish. She could be a tomboy and no one could ridicule her. Above all else she and Nicol could be alone together.

Before leaving the banks of the Stanislaus, Moira turned to Nicol and vehemently announced that this is where their home would be built.

∽

Purchasing the land from Wells Fargo Bank was not as easy as Nicol and Moira hoped. R.H.'s financial situation was worse than Nicol had ever dared to admit.

The couple were saddened when Nicol's father could not attend their wedding the previous summer at Hillandale in Georgetown. Moira liked her quietly eccentric father-in-law and hoped to get to know him. She also liked Sue, her mother-in-law, but frequently felt intimidated by Sue's vivacious personality and renowned social circle.

Sue had taken her personal financial matters into her own hands. Undaunted by R.H.'s misfortunes, she earned her own income. Sue now wrote for the *San Francisco Examiner*. Her daily column entitled "Sue Smith Says," was published in the society section. She got her car back after paying off the bills that had accumulated before its repossession. She paid for her own chauffeur. The luncheon several years earlier with William Hearst provided the opportunity she needed and for the next twenty years she wrote about society news in her column.

Nicol and his mother had always painted a rosy picture to family and friends of the situation at The Crossroads and they continued to do so. Moira was skeptical of the financial outlook but preferred to remain on the sidelines, afraid that Sue might be planning for her to rescue their dire situation.

Purchasing the 160 acres of river property became a nightmare of financial entanglements. Not only did the bank have to be paid off, but other institutions had placed liens against the property before its repossession by Well's Fargo Bank. R.H. attempted to prevent foreclosure on the property in 1935 when he sold eighty acres containing the Board's homestead cabin and the meadow to Louis Wetmore, who had spent summers camping on the property since 1913. Then, the couple learned R.H. sold the lumber rights to Pickering Lumber Company in 1927. The lumber company had the right to log the land unless the timber rights could be purchased back. Nicol earned a fair income, but it was limited. Moira was able to clear the title and purchase the land from the bank. The trees remained with Pickering Lumber Company until 1971, when Nicol paid $9,084 to prevent timber harvesting on his land.

Now Nicol had no misunderstanding of his father's situation. Neither did any of the rest of the Smith family. During rainstorms, Sue would lie in bed holding an open umbrella to protect herself from the leaks in the roof. The husband of a cousin in Pennsylvania traveled to California hoping to find employment. Visiting the Smiths at The Crossroads, he also learned of their desperate financial situation. Being a truthful young man, he wrote home, stating that R.H. was definitely and completely broke, his investments were bad and his credit rating was absolutely zero. This came as a surprise to the members of the Pennsylvania family. They had always heard only the "rosy" picture depicted by Nicol and his mother. Still the truth was best kept a secret from Aunt Myrtle and Billy Smith, R.H.'s younger brother who had worked in the oil fields for his opportunistic older brother before the 1906 earthquake. They were allowed to believe the California relatives survived the Depression unscathed.

After purchasing the river property, Moira was even more determined that she wouldn't help Sue or R.H. R.H. had a mind of his own when it came to investments and was easily persuaded by other rich men's poor dealings. At The Crossroads the phone was disconnected and the gas and light company were threatening the same. All the help was gone, except their faithful cook, Polly Khill, to whom R.H. owed six thousand dollars in back wages. R.H.'s car was in the shop for repairs and there it had sat for three months since he could not pay the repair bill. Moira also felt that Sue hoped her new daughter-in-law could fix the situation at The Crossroads. It had been insinuated that the marriage to Moira would put the family back in the money again. Moira knew differently. Nicol remained silent on the matter.

꒰

Moira dreamed of the home she and Nicol would have along the Stanislaus River some day. But who could they hire to build a house? Access to the property was a dirt road and it was several miles to the closest general store. Building materials were miles away. Nicol had an idea. A couple of years earlier, Art Hall unexpectedly visited The Crossroads. At the time of Art's arrival Nicol was on his way out with his mother, Sue. He hurriedly inquired what Art was doing. Nicol was in need of a chauffeur for his lecture season. The new circuit required he be in Chicago by the following week. Art quickly accepted the opportunity to drive Nicol from city to city that winter since he had just sold the last crop from his Patterson ranch and he had no employment plans on his horizon at the moment.

Now Nicol again wondered what trade his old friend was pursuing. Locating Art, he learned that he and Virginia now had a small daughter, Patricia. Art, a lanky man with seemingly few worries and a perpetually cheerful expression, was pleased to hear from his friend. Art was confident he could build a house to the specifications provided by Moira and Nicol and they moved to the property. They spent the summer living in a tent while Art began construction on the new house.

Collecting river rock for the foundation and fireplace, Art ordered the first load of supplies from the Manuel Lumber Company office in Angels Camp. Building progressed during the summer and the lumber truck delivered material each week from the mill at White Pines. Occasionally, when the load was small enough, Art and his family drove to the mill and hauled the supplies to the river in his own truck.

Fortunately the dirt road to the top of the hill at Dorrington had improved over the years. When the Board brothers had herded their cattle to the river, a narrow trail worn by the hooves of the livestock, wound its way to the Stanislaus River from the town of Dorrington. The cattle forded the river at the location that became known as Board's Crossing. The steep canyons of the Stanislaus River afforded few suitable crossings. It was the only location for miles where cattle were able to ford the river and the Board brothers may have charged a toll to the other ranchers who used their crossing. Then in 1925, the trail widened and became a dirt road when a building crew set up camp at Board's Crossing. That summer a bridge was constructed and appropriately named Board's Crossing Bridge. The Stanislaus River, dividing Calaveras and Tuolumne County, was miles from the closest town but could now be crossed by automobiles and log trucks in the heart of the Sierra.

Returning from the trip to China and the Burma Road, Moira and Nicol, drove to the mountains. Excited about their new home, they arrived to find a beautiful two-story, stone and timber lodge perched at the foot of a hill and facing the only quiet pools on the Stanislaus River. The ground floor was built of river rock, rounded from centuries of water cascading toward the valley below, while the second floor was constructed from pine, painted a pleasing green that blended with the forested hill behind the lodge. The lower floor contained quarters for the hired help and a garage for their Cadillac with a storage area under the stairway. The second floor consisted of three bedrooms, two of which faced the river, two full bathrooms, a living and dining area and a large, farm-style kitchen with a generator for electricity and propane for cooking and heating water. All the rooms were finished in a highly polished knotty pine with a soft, golden grain. The main room was balanced with a large, river-rock fireplace and chimney at one end, while the other end was entirely windows with double doors leading to the wooden decking that overlooked the river. The house was more than Moira had dared to dream. Turning to Nicol, her eyes brimming with tears of happiness, she smiled and said, "This is home at last." The bubbling river and the gentle sigh of the wind in the pine trees surrounded them in their mountain retreat.

It was too late in the season to begin to move to the river place. Winters could be severe in the Sierra Nevada Mountains. Their property lay above the snow line and often five feet or more could block the dirt road from Dorrington. Plans were laid for the following year and the new home was christened. They named their home Lashio Lodge in memory of Nicol's fond recollections of the last village on the Burma Road.

*

A new decade and new beginnings at Lashio Lodge began in 1940. Nicol entertained his first guests and campers along the river had guaranteed campsites for the summer season. The previous fall Nicol and Moira agreed with Art and Virginia that the campsites along the river needed to be organized. Many of the campers knew they were on private land and had spent summers along the Stanislaus for years. With the Smiths planning to live at Lashio Lodge, the campers wondered if they would be permitted to remain for the following summers.

Art and Virginia met most of the campers during the summer when they built Nicol and Moira's lodge. Art was quick to point out the benefits of the campers to Nicol. With campsites nearby, the new home would be safe. It was agreed the campers could stay. Organized by family groups, campsites were laid out along the river. Annual fees were assessed for each campsite and structures could be built by the campers but strictly at their own expense.

Art located a spring that provided ample water for Lashio Lodge. Extending the system to the campsites was his next project. Fees were assessed for each site to cover the supplies needed to build the water system. A few campsites were relocated so that Nicol and Moira would have privacy and an uninterrupted view of the river.

The first guest was to be Moira's mother, Anne. Skeptical about the information they had shared with her about their home, she was surprisingly delighted with the scenery and the remote location. Sitting on the front porch, she looked out on the huge ponderosa and sugar pines that covered the property. Directly in front of the lodge, the river formed a large pool and then broke into tiny rapids, bubbling over rocks a short distance away. Gazing across the river, Anne remarked how lucky they were to be surrounded by such beauty. During her dialog with Nicol, Anne learned that although Nicol and Moira's land extended across the river to Tuolumne County further downstream, it did not include the acreage directly across from Lashio Lodge.

Adamant, she sent Nicol to town to find out who owned the land. It must be purchased immediately. If the land fell into the wrong hands, she felt Nicol's entire location would be ruined. Surely someone would log the beautiful trees and the view would be destroyed. Anne was sure that for the right price they could purchase the land.

Knowing his mother-in-law's determination, Nicol agreed and by the next day he learned the land was owned by a local man, Frank Solinsky. Three days later, Mr. Solinsky was seated for dinner at Lashio Lodge. Before the cook served dessert, Anne purchased the land for $250 an acre. She turned to Nicol and informed him to rest easy now that his mountain retreat was protected by their private border of timbered land. The land became Nicol's the following Christmas when Anne deeded it to him as a gift.

BOOK FIVE:

WORLD WAR 11

I am glad I have been on so many
expeditions. All this is not as new for
me as some of the other officers, who
feel rather lost in such an
environment. We all would like to
see the war finished tomorrow.
Home will certainly look good to
me....

Nicol Smith
Letter to his parents
Written from
Szemao, China, 1943

16

THE OSS

Nicol's expeditions to Hainan Island in 1937, then across the Burma Road in 1939, followed by the Guianas and Martinique in 1941 brought him to the brink of the war brewing on the European and Asian continents. The Japanese invasion of Hainan Island occurred just four days after his departure. His photographs from Burma Road revealed lines of munitions trucks carrying supplies to China. In Martinique and French Guiana he discussed the occupation of France with acquaintances and witnessed the influx of French expatriates fleeing their homeland.

The American people no more wanted a part in the second World War than they had desired in the first war. Now the time came when national interest and the interest of humanity forced the country's entrance. From the time President Roosevelt announced the nation's neutrality[1] in September of 1939 until the American intervention in December of 1941, the American public's interest in the war was apparent to Nicol.

His opinion on war conditions in other countries was frequently sought. Nicol's exposure to people and places where the war was progressing made him a knowledgeable resource. He was questioned by his friends, at newspaper interviews and during lectures about the effects of the war in far-off countries.

Then on December 6, 1941, at a poker party, Nicol bet eight friends twenty-five dollars each that the Americans wouldn't be at war with the Japanese for at least another year. Nicol lost $200 the following morning.

↩

Pearl Harbor precipitated the American involvement in World War II. Five months before the Japanese attack, President Roosevelt designated a mysterious new agency called the COI, the Office of the Coordinator of Information. It was directed by Roosevelt to guide America's first full-scale venture into espionage, sabotage and other subversive forms of warfare. Heading this new agency was William J. Donovan, a World War I hero who held America's three highest military decorations[2] and was a millionaire Wall Street lawyer.

The new organization was not particularly popular among the senior governmental departments, such as the War Department and the State Department. Even the newspapers scoffed at the idea of an agency that attracted wealthy civilians for duty in a world war.

Six months after America's entry into the war, the COI divided into two branches. Donovan's organization became the OSS, Office of Strategic Services.[3] Its purpose was to plan and operate any special services necessitated by the American involvement in the war. It would be directed by the United States Joint Chiefs of Staff.[4]

General Donovan drew up a simple selection standard to recruit personnel for behind-the-lines duty. The foremost requirement was strength of character. Americans who could best lead a double-life in enemy territory were men who had never led a double-life before.[5] It took an unusual type of person for service in the OSS. People who thrived on danger and excitement, with an appetite for intrigue, were attracted to the OSS. By the end of the war more than thirteen thousand would join the ranks of the newly formed department.

Among the numerous recruits and volunteers were the children of notoriously wealthy and famous Americans. Andrew Mellon's son Paul, cousin to Nicol's classmate Larry Mellon, served in London and Luxembourg. A Vanderbilt worked in Washington. Ilya Tolstoy, grandson of the Russian novelist, Leo Tolstoy, and a friend of Nicol's, were among the many who served their country in the OSS.

John Archbold presented his curriculum vitae to the OSS in November just before Pearl Harbor.[6] Sharing his plans with no one, he hoped to escape his loneliness from the sudden death of his wife. While Nicol was traveling the Burma Road in China, John's wife had died in June of 1939. John had been considering a career to occupy his time. The OSS provided that opportunity. Because of circumstances that neither John nor Nicol could have predicted, their careers in the OSS brought about an unexpected reunion abroad.

Nicol's parents were acquaintances of Bill and Ruth Donovan. It was possibly through this connection that Nicol first became interested in joining the OSS. The earliest existing documentation proving Nicol's intent to serve in the OSS is a letter from the Eleventh Naval District in Los Angeles written just two days after Christmas. Apparently Nicol previously sent a lengthy report on his Martinique film to Lieutenant Commander Alfred Bolton in the Los Angeles office of the United States Navy. A return letter confirmed the information on Martinique had reached the District Intelligence Officer. The reply suggested that Nicol contact the Office of Naval Intelligence during his pending visit to Washington.

Why the interest in Martinique and why Nicol prepared and mailed a report is not apparent, but this was not the only avenue he was pursuing. A letter on War Department stationery, dated December 29, from Major Carroll T. Harris of the Military Intelligence Division in the San Francisco office was sent to Nicol at his St. Francis Hotel apartment. Harris, a friend of the Smith family, stated he should contact the Assistant Chief of Staff of the War Department upon arriving in Washington.

When Nicol visited the office of Major Harris, an Army officer, another officer stopped in to meet him. When he returned to his own office, Colonel Joseph Rogers immediately penned a letter to General Raymond Lee and sent a copy to Nicol:

> Mr. Smith is not only a man of unusual mentality, a graduate of Stanford, and a traveler and an explorer for a number of years now. With his partner he made explorations of the Island of Hainan and the Kwang Chowan Peninsula of China. He has some very useful information with reference to this country, having flown in and landed on fields unknown. Recently he has been in Martinique and French Guiana.
>
> I am sure you will find him very interesting and with considerable useful knowledge of value at this time, and I know

you will be quite happy to have seen him on conclusion of his
visit.

I write this letter not in Mr. Smith's interest, but in the
interest of the War Department and with the hope that our
former association may cause you to feel the information contained herein of use.[7]

Two days later, on New Year's Eve, Nicol was given a letter of
introduction from the San Francisco Naval Intelligence Office:

I am pleased to vouch for the integrity and high standing
of Mr. Smith in this community.

His past experiences and plans for the future, I feel certain, are of interest to Naval Intelligence.

Any advice you can give Mr. Smith will be appreciated.[8]

Nothing but positive and persuasive letters were presented on
Nicol's behalf to the various federal departments. Though highly
recommended, his wait would be lengthy before induction into
the OSS.

Nicol's trip to Washington was an auspicious beginning. He
and Moira left San Francisco during the first week of January.
Nicol fulfilled speaking engagements while traveling across the
country, finally presenting his lecture and colored motion pictures of Martinique and the Guianas at Constitution Hall before
the National Geographic Society on January 28.

Unknown to Moira, her family and her brother John, was
Nicol's interest and diligent pursuit of an opportunity in the OSS.
The correspondence from his recent contacts appeared to display
a genuine regard for Nicol's qualifications.

Among the basic requirements were, of course, experience
abroad and knowledge of foreign lands and languages. The principal asset for an agent was ingenuity. Nicol possessed this characteristic and all the necessary qualifications. His travel experience
spoke for itself. He was fluent in French and ingenuity was a
mainstay of Nicol's character.

During the early stages of America's involvement abroad, the
objectives of OSS operations fell into two categories. The first
was to establish agents in neutral territories to report on local
conditions, on Axis activities and to penetrate adjacent enemy

and enemy-occupied territory through native contacts and sub-agents. The second was to establish bases in friendly territories from which penetration of enemy and enemy-occupied territory could be organized and directed.[9] Nicol's OSS career would be influenced by both of these objectives.

～

Finishing the lecture circuit during March of 1942, Nicol began to wonder what he should plan for the summer. He had not proceeded with plans to explore Tibet since he hoped to be employed by the OSS shortly.

Ambiguous answers to his repeated inquiries left Nicol doubting he would ever be allowed to complete the induction process. Unknown to Nicol, several questions had arisen about his character. Overall he received a favorable letter from the Office of Naval Intelligence in Los Angeles, yet two officers there attempted to besmirch his character.

The State Department constructed a written resume of Nicol from his letter, meetings and the letters of introduction. Penned in longhand at the bottom of the one-page profile is a note stating:

> Cleared by P. D., but attention called to report from ONI that Smith is 'undependable and a consummate liar.'[10]

P. D. must stand for the personnel department while ONI is the Office of Naval Intelligence. The resume, presented on April 23, did not originally contain the longhand note at the bottom with the date of May 11, which included a signature consisting of four illegible capital letters. Obviously when Nicol was presented to the State Department the note had not yet been written. Although exonerated by the personnel department, the investigation continued. Nine days later a memorandum was sent to Colonel Goodfellow of the OSS again from the District Office in Los Angeles. The subject was Nicol Smith:

> ONI reports that they have no further information regarding subject but that there are two officers in the District Intelligence Office in Los Angeles who know subject to be unreliable.[11]

The names of the two officers did not appear on the memorandum. Documentation does not exist from the District Office of Naval Intelligence so it is impossible to determine who Nicol's opponents were. If Nicol had been aware of the problem at that time, he probably would have found the words "undependable," a "consummate liar" and "unreliable" disconcerting. His character would have been accurately described by the words dependable, reliable and a man of his word. A liar he was not. A storyteller or a spinner of adventuresome yarns more accurately described the skills necessary for his profession.

Little did the slander matter. Plans were being laid to send Nicol to Vichy, France, the locale of the displaced French government.

17

MISSION TO VICHY

A strange succession of events during the spring of 1942 propelled Nicol into a new career. It was a career for which he never prepared but for which he was inherently suited. In April, a British intelligence staff officer paid a visit to the War Department in Washington, D.C. Following the visit, a search began for a suitable agent to send into France. The British government was requesting assistance for a project to send secret agents into unoccupied France. This person would aid the organizing of the French underground resistance by handling the funds that must be regularly placed into the hands of the agents. The British wanted an American in this position who would not be suspected by the Pétain-Laval government in Vichy, France, or by the Germans. But where could such a person be found?

On May 9, 1942, the Special Operations branch of the COI approved mission SO-5.[1] The task was to develop adequate communications and organization of resistance units within unoccupied France. The status of SO-5 was suspended pending further arrangements with the British, specifically, locating an agent. The State Department could not permit any regular member of the embassy staff to engage in such a mission. The problem was referred to General Donovan, head of the OSS and a search began for a qualified agent.

The United States did not sever relations with the Vichy government, but instead moved its embassy to each new location of the displaced French government. American diplomats, who worked in the United States Embassy in Paris, also made numerous moves. The Embassy maintained relations with the French government even after Marshal Pétain, the hero of the World War I Battle of Verdun, signed the German armistice terms.

Marshal Pétain had become the new premier of France in a closed session on June 17. His first act was to ask the Germans for an armistice.[2] The armistice specified the French fleet was to be demobilized, the French were to turn over to the Nazis all the German and Austrian Jews who had fled persecution and the country was split into two territories. Essentially France had surrendered to the Germans.

A former premier, Senator Pierre Laval, was named the chief of government by Premier Pétain. Laval, a Nazi puppet, did not bother to hide the fact he was Hitler's man. Issuing decrees, Pétain's government became a fascist French State.[3]

On July 1, 1940, the French government made its final move after the German occupation of Paris to the resort town of Vichy, site of the famous spa and the world-renowned Vichy water.[4] Since June 10, the French ministries and officials had been on the road after fleeing Paris as the Germans entered the capital. The French government moved first to Tours, then a few days later further south to Bordeaux, then to Clermont-Ferrand in central France. The last move to Vichy was necessary because the numerous hotels in the resort town, all of them empty because of the war, provided lodging for the displaced government.

France had been divided into two zones with a line running from the east to west. The northern part was occupied by the Germans and the southern portion was the unoccupied or French zone. A French citizen traveling from one zone to another needed a German pass. Any individual trying to cross without a pass was severely punished.

The American diplomats in Vichy were convinced it would become an important place for espionage. William Donovan left to report on the situation at Vichy. His report was prepared for President Roosevelt, who decided it would be useful to establish and maintain diplomatic relations with the Vichy government. He hoped the American diplomats could work with the French underground and pass vital military secrets on to the British.[5] Roosevelt appointed Admiral William Leahy, a personal friend, as the United States ambassador. Vichy was then recognized as the legitimate government of France by the United States.

↩

As Nicol waited for an assignment, a number of people were suggested for OSS duty in Vichy. None were acceptable because they lacked a valid excuse for visiting France.

Nicol's resume, prepared from information gathered by the OSS Personnel Department, was impressive. It described his education, published books, his journeys to unknown areas, marriage to a descendant of a Standard Oil founder and included a narrative of his colored, motion pictures of Martinique and Dutch Guiana. It concluded with, "He has many contacts today in both Occupied and Unoccupied France."

The groundwork was set. Nicol spoke French fluently, he had visited the country only four years earlier and he had contacts. Finally on May 9, 1942, General Donovan sent a letter to G. Howland Shaw, the Assistant Secretary of State:

> In connection with the work of this office, we should appreciate the appointment of Mr. Nicol Smith as Special Assistant at the American Embassy, Vichy, France.[6]

General Donovan continued the letter to the State Department requesting that Nicol be permitted to authorize cables and request money through the officials at the U.S. Embassy and the State Department. He also asked that the proper people be notified of Nicol's status and the approximate date of his arrival. The letter stated his salary would be $4,800 annually with an additional allowance of a six dollar per diem.

Nicol was assigned as a Special Assistant to Admiral Leahy, the American Ambassador. It wasn't until June 22 that a telegram was sent by the State Department to the Embassy in Vichy explaining Nicol's designation and duties:

> Smith is an author and lecturer of some repute and has friendly sentiments toward the French people. Should the Foreign Office make inquiry concerning him in connection with authorization for issuance of a French visa you may say that he is being assigned to assist in the work of political reporting.[7]

Again, a few weeks later, another cable was sent requesting the expediting of a French visa for Nicol. Finally a reply returned confirming that instructions had been issued to the French Embassy in Washington authorizing the visa.

Meanwhile, Nicol had been notified of his assignment by the Office of the Coordinator of Information, which had become the new Office of Strategic Services. His assignment was reissued by the new department, the OSS. Nicol would leave New York for France via Lisbon.

While Nicol had waited for his assignment, he told Moira he would be sent to France by the OSS. She was alarmed. She had no idea Nicol might become involved in the war. She pleaded with him to remain at home and was confident her mother could help prevent Nicol from serving. After several days of talking and calming her fears, Moira acquiesced. Nicol assured her he would not be near any fighting and would probably never be near a battle zone. He felt the war would not last much longer now that the United States was involved. Moira planned to split her time between Hillandale and their San Francisco apartment.

Before telling Moira of his impending departure, Nicol contemplated what he could use for a cover among his family members and friends. The OSS had been quite clear that its war-time assignments were not to be shared with anyone. The civilian population was not privy to the actions of the new organization. Nicol did not ponder this problem for long. He concocted a plausible cover. Since he was going to France and his status was as an assistant to the ambassador, Nicol could use his own name and background instead of a fictitious front. He only needed a reason for his appointment in Vichy. Nicol devised the pretext that he was traveling to Vichy as the bearer of the motion pictures of Martinique and French Guiana. He was to present the pictures to Pétain and Laval as a friendly gift to France. Permission would be requested for him to gather material for another lecture, also designed to promote friendship between France and the United States. The color motion picture of Martinique and French Guiana offered Nicol an odd introduction to service in the OSS, but his family and friends found the reason plausible. Stranger things had happened to Nicol and this looked like another opportunity for a rare adventure.

Even a reason for leaving Moira behind was simple to come by. Their travels to the Guianas only allowed her to meet him in Dutch Guiana. Because of the situation in French Guiana at that time she had not been granted a visa for that part of the trip. Since she had never been to French Guiana, there would be no reason for her to accompany him to France.

"Cultural attaché" was Nicol's term for the credible front he contrived. The term caught on. His mother even wrote about her son's connections in France in her newspaper column. The word was out among his friends and associates. Letters of introduction and letters to families stranded in France were sent to Nicol for him to deliver. His potential for contacts in France quickly grew.

On July 10, the visa required to enter France arrived. Plans for his departure were put into action. New film cases were bought for transporting the motion picture, clothing was bought and packed and good-byes were said. Just days before heading to New York for his scheduled departure, a large farewell luncheon was given for Nicol.

Events took a dramatic turn near the end of lunch, when an acquaintance drew Nicol aside. The young man knew nearly as much as Nicol did about his mission. Alarmed, Nicol managed to maintain his composure and repeated his story of "cultural attaché." The acquaintance smugly walked away.

Afraid to telephone the OSS headquarters from Hillandale, Nicol hurried into the city from Georgetown that afternoon. A State Department official had virtually admitted to the French Embassy in Washington that Nicol would be functioning in Vichy as a spy. Decisions were made quickly after Nicol told about his encounter. It was possible the acquaintance was planted at the luncheon to try and trip up Nicol in order to learn more about his assignment. He would be sent to France regardless. It was too late to back out since a change of plans would appear suspicious and could jeopardize any future placements in Vichy. All too often the State Department resented and mistrusted the OSS agents using their diplomatic posts as a cover. Someone had undercut Nicol's mission.

Nicol's revised instructions allowed him to collect new lecture material, to do what he pleased, go wherever he was allowed and keep his eyes open. Any information or contacts he made would be helpful to the OSS. But a new paymaster would have to be found for the clandestine agents.

The next morning, Nicol and Moira prepared to leave for New York where he would board the Pan American Clipper. As he finished packing an urgent messenger arrived at Hillandale's front gate and refused to leave his message with Fred Cousins, the head groundskeeper. Eva rang for the couple, obviously agitated at the disruption. Nicol requested the messenger be sent to the back door. Without a word, the boy handed a typed message to Nicol. He was needed at OSS headquarters for a short briefing. Then he could return to Hillandale to continue his preparations for departure.

Neglecting to explain, Nicol called the chauffeur and requested an automobile for a trip into town. By the time Moira came downstairs to see what the fuss was about, Nicol was gone and the chauffeur was left standing in the doorway to the servants' quarters.

Moira was upset. She dreaded having Nicol leave and wondered how she would cope. She did not enjoy Hillandale where she felt she was treated as a child. Her husband and her friend, Bex, in Arlington, were the only people that respected her wishes and treated her as an adult. Now Nicol was running off, not explaining what was happening. Until his assignment with the OSS, they had always been open and honest with each other. Heartbroken, Moira went upstairs to cry alone. She didn't understand what was happening. Even Nicol's explanations and comforting had not filled the emptiness she felt. How long would he be gone?

౿

Boarding the Clipper for Lisbon on August 4, Nicol left behind his wife and the adventure and lecture circuit indefinitely. Excitement and apprehension gripped him. Only the unknown lay ahead. From New York the Pan American Clipper headed to the Bahamas and then the Azores, refueling at the island stopovers. The next stop was Lisbon, Portugal and the last airborne leg concluded in Madrid, Spain.

By the time General Donovan wrote the letter to the State Department clarifying the arrangements for his assignment, Nicol was already enroute. To complicate Nicol's mission Ambassador Leahy had returned to the states. Although he was Special Assistant to the ambassador, there now was no ambassador to assist. The situation became more complex when Nicol's films were seized in Madrid. Not only was he now an assistant to an absent ambassador, the films he was using as a cover were delayed for weeks in Spanish customs.

The remainder of the trip was made by train from Madrid to Barcelona, an area Nicol compared to Bakersfield, California, where he always found the parched and barren country distasteful. He changed trains at Cerbère, France, the rail and custom station on the Spanish border, which was a smuggling center between the two countries. The small town clung to the sides of hills over the Mediterranean. He boarded his final train in Valence enroute to Vichy and arrived five days after his departure from New York.

Nicol's diary entries began on the fourth day of his travels. The trip was long and tiring and he found the scenery dull throughout Spain. He complained in his writings of the poor food and the lack of meat. Dinner cost him eight dollars and when he finished eating he was not satisfied. He had not seen people in such poor conditions since his trip to Russia in 1931. Nicol offered three young girls some money for candy at a train station. The solemn children informed him there was no candy, cookies or cakes available. He wondered if further food shortages could be expected in Vichy.

Nicol met a self-proclaimed Swiss banker on the Clipper. When he boarded the train in Madrid, the banker appeared on the same train. The man invited himself to join Nicol for nearly every meal. The last night, Nicol planned to turn in early since he would be changing trains at 4:00 A.M. in Valence. He had doubts about the banker because the man spoke vehemently against the Germans when they talked on the Clipper, but suddenly the evening before, Nicol observed the banker talking to a German lady on the train platform after he slipped away from the dinner table.

Now, as Nicol turned in, the Swiss man asked him to come to his sleeping compartment. The banker boldly asked Nicol to come to Paris. He promised to provide the necessary papers.

Confused, Nicol did not understand what the man was requesting, but quickly he realized the so-called Swiss banker was probably enticing him into a dangerous situation. Managing to claim ignorance and exhaustion, Nicol excused himself, spending a sleepless night worrying in his own compartment. The next morning while waiting at Valence for the connecting train to Vichy, Nicol wrote in his diary, "I began to see the point of the whole business. I was going to be touched."[8] Without the special visa required for Paris, travel to the German occupied city was very dangerous. Nicol could have disappeared, never to be heard from again.

The first day in Vichy was spent finding lodging and locating old acquaintances. He telephoned the MacArthurs and dined with them that evening in the country at a tiny, black-market restaurant. Douglas MacArthur II, the nephew of General MacArthur, was one of the third secretaries at the U.S. Embassy. Nicol knew him through Page Huffty, the husband of Moira's cousin, Frances Archbold. He wrote:

> Doug MacArthur appears to be most alert and very well informed. He has been over here for four years and is a part of the original Paris staff. He has a friendly manner and is yet suave at the same time, carries himself well and is a gentleman. Mrs. MacArthur has a radiant personality. The young lady has a southern dash which only her own blue grass [sic] state of Kentucky can produce and is a woman of definite ideas. She is the daughter of U.S. Senator Alben W. Barkley. She is hospitable and one can see that nothing is too much trouble for her if she likes you.[9]

The MacArthurs became invaluable to Nicol, helping him with his accommodations, directing him to the best restaurants and including him in their social activities.

The following day was Monday and Nicol's activities began in earnest, although his instructions essentially directed him to lay low and observe. After a lunch given by Tyler Thompson, another secretary at the U.S. Embassy, and his wife Ruth, Nicol delivered a package that had traveled from Washington to Vichy in his briefcase.

The last minute message that arrived at Hillandale before his departure informed Nicol he was needed in Washington to pick up supplies for Vichy. The hasty exodus when he left Moira upstairs and the chauffeur standing in the doorway had been to OSS headquarters. A small, nondescript package weighing thirty-some pounds was handed to Nicol and carefully stowed in his briefcase. Nicol memorized the delivery instructions consisting of an address and a man's description before he returned to Hillandale to continue packing. He was not informed what the package contained or why he must deliver it. Orders were not to be questioned.

Borrowing a bicycle, he easily found the memorized address. Entering the dark building, he climbed a stairway that led to a second floor office. At the counter he asked for Henri. A man appeared who fit the description Nicol remembered, right down to the faint birthmark on his temple. Handing over the package, Nicol heard the man mutter, "thank you," and then he quickly shuffled back into the room from which he had come. Nicol left, wondering if he would ever know what he had just delivered.

Time did not reveal the contents of the package nor the identity of the man receiving it. Speculation, based on recent research, led to the conclusion that the package contained either ciphers or badly needed radio equipment. The smuggling of contraband into Vichy was strictly prohibited. The possession of a short-wave transmitter could bring one before a firing squad. Nicol's delivery was a twofold success.

The need for radios was becoming critical. By the following year, General Donovan issued a special order whereby every OSS officer enroute to the theaters would deliver an SSTR-1.[10] This was one of the first models of the radios developed as lightweight portable transmitters suitable for clandestine activities. Labeled during development as the Strategic Services Transmitter-Receiver, it became commonly known as the SSTR-1. It became the standard OSS radio for undercover operations and was widely known as the "suitcase radio"[11] because it fit easily into a small suitcase.

Changes were also occurring in the use of cipher equipment. At the outset of the war the only cipher equipment in use was a commercial product available for purchase by anyone. By 1942, the OSS was expanding rapidly and additional communication equipment was needed to handle the message traffic. An electric model of a cipher machine called "Betty"[12] began to appear in OSS code rooms during that year. On a regular schedule the ciphers or codes had to be changed to maintain security for wartime communications.

On August 4, Lisbon was notified that two new cipher strips would arrive by the next air flight. Madrid received a similar message and on August 6, Vichy was also informed of the pending change. Since ciphers were regularly changed, they normally were delivered through a set of standard procedures. Although Nicol's special delivery might have been ciphers, it is more likely that he carried a radio transmitter or transmitter parts into unoccupied France.

After his arrival on August 10, Nicol sent a telegram to Moira. She did not receive it until four days later. The message was brief:

> Arrived Vichy safely. Notify mother. Unable cash dollar bills. Please deposit Manufactures Trust Company, 513 Fifth Avenue $350. Drawing check. Next month salary starts by check. Cable me Embassy Vichy. Love.[13]

Moira cabled his parents in California. She was relieved to know Nicol had reached Vichy without a mishap. The days of waiting were miserable ones for Moira, but waiting for Nicol had barely begun.

Nicol began his work through Count de Seguin, the husband of Pétain's supposedly illegitimate daughter. He was a slender man with a vague and rather distraught personality. Nicol wrote:

> I understand that aside from his marital connection he is of relatively little importance. He looks as if he had the cares of the world on his shoulders. I think he has an inkling of why I have come to France. He let it slip out and then tried to cover up. I don't think he has all the information but at least a small part. I believe he is a man who likes intrigue without being aware of the personal complications one can embroil oneself in when following such a road. He is the logical person for me to work through in regard to my pictures.[14]

After several ineffective dealings with Count de Seguin, Nicol labeled the man "a rimless zero" in his diary.

Colonel Bob Schow, the Military Attaché at the embassy soon became a valuable resource along with Captain Curtis Davison, his assistant, whom Nicol had connections to through Lydia, Moira's older sister. Next he looked up Governor Chot whom he had met on his last trip to French Guiana. The Chots, enroute from their home in French Guiana to Paris, planned to be with their son for four months. The Governor had been having political difficulties in Guiana because of his membership in the Masons. Strangely enough the Masonic order had been blamed for a number of the travails of the French.

Name after name appears in Nicol's diary. He seemed to have had connections to everyone in Vichy. He delivered the letters he carried from the states, presented gifts from distant relatives and shared news of the war effort at home. His social contacts reached all segments of the population. He even attempted to deliver a message he had brought from Washington to Laval's daughter. Unfortunately Laval was not accepting any telephone calls or messages.

Nicol's activities occupied every waking minute. The hotel servants that he found so willing to help he began to suspect as Gestapo agents. The telephone operator annoyed him by breaking in on his every conversation. He used the sink in his bathroom to burn papers he felt should not fall into anyone's hands.

Nicol had a natural ability to talk with people, and his OSS responsibilities required garnering information from people. Coveted information included indications of political sentiments, loyalties, and underground functionings. One day an anonymous note was left at the hotel office for him. The carefully worded message, written in French, spoke of badly needed munitions and where they should be dropped. During that same morning the telephone operator knocked unannounced at Nicol's door requesting American medication for her cold. Nicol doubted her flimsy excuse but provided the remedy. He suspected she really wanted to know what he looked like.

While retying his shoe in the hotel lobby, a slip of paper fluttered to the floor next to his hand. It invited Nicol to dinner at a certain time and location. Intrigued, he decided to accept the anonymous invitation. He met a large man who professed to have contacts with the underground. Suspicious, Nicol denied any involvement with clandestine operations but he committed the man's dinner conversation to memory.

The following afternoon Colonel Schow stopped in to warn Nicol that his previous evening's dinner companion was a suspected German spy. Somewhat rattled, Nicol vowed to be careful as he prepared for his first trip since his arrival. Borrowing Doug MacArthur's car, Nicol and Pierre Cafeau, the nephew of Governor Chot, proceeded to explore the region. Their first stop was a black-market butcher shop where Nicol purchased a ham. Over lunch Nicol and Pierre discussed the threat of Russia. At this time Nicol felt the German propaganda machine had turned the French away from the Russians. "I attempted to tell them that Russia is swinging away from her earlier ideals and back toward capitalism," Nicol wrote, "but they would not believe me."[15]

The next man Nicol met had traveled to the interior of Hainan Island. Only three men besides Nicol had ever made the trip and Nicol met this one in a French restaurant. They exchanged stories and reveled in their past adventures.

A bicycle became Nicol's mode of transportation. Everyone in Vichy wanted a bicycle because petrol was rationed and difficult to obtain for civilian automobiles. Bicycle tires were more difficult to obtain than petrol, so every object that might flatten a tire was avoided at all possible costs. Cigarettes were also a valuable commodity and when Nicol won twenty packs of Camels in a poker game he traded them for a bicycle the following morning.

The same afternoon he bicycled to Laura Corrigan's two-room apartment. In Nicol's estimate Laura was one of the world's wealthiest women as she was an heiress of a Pittsburgh steel mill family. She was also his mother's friend and Nicol had met her in Paris during a previous trip. The war had frozen her assets in the states and she was living in Vichy by selling her jewelry. When Nicol left New York, Laura's sister asked him to take a message to Vichy. Laura needed to know the sum of her money in a New York bank even though she was unable to access it from beleaguered France.

Nicol, with the letter in his pocket, arrived with fresh roses. Flowers were the only item that he found in abundance in unoccupied France. Nicol purchased and gave them as gifts liberally. Laura gave Nicol two rolls of toilet paper in return of his thoughtfulness. An item, in contrast, that was difficult to obtain.

Laura was selling her jewels to feed not only herself but to buy supplies for the local hospital. She visited twice a week and presented gifts of fruit juice, chocolate and cigarettes to each of the young French soldiers. Nicol accompanied her to the hospital several times and assisted her in handing out the supplies to the soldiers. Laura's efforts at relief were recognized and rewarded at the end of the war when she was decorated by the French for her valor and heroic relief efforts.[16]

꒰꒱

Nicol's responsibilities were clearly defined when he left New York. Now in Vichy, he wondered how he would "do what he pleased, go where the French would let him, keep his eyes open, but don't get mixed up in anything!" The purpose of Nicol's mission before his cover was blown was to be the financial officer for an underground movement. He would be responsible for finding representatives of the Free French, locating operational facilities especially for communications, and providing transportation resources[17] to aid contact between the British and the French.

Nicol's social connections facilitated most of his meetings. Prince Andre Poniatowski, whose mother was a Californian and whom Nicol had known when they were children, was able to fill Nicol in on French affairs. The man was intimately involved with French politics and was eager to assist his American acquaintance. Nicol and Andre visited the family chateau near the demarcation zone between occupied and unoccupied France.

He reported on the conditions of war-torn France in the frequent accounts he provided the OSS. He submitted reports on English agents in unoccupied France, the food and fuel situation, the French underground movement, his knowledge of Laval and numerous other topics. Nicol's reports provided complete and accurate information to the OSS. Although the embassy officials frequently reported on identical topics, their information reached the State Department but remained there. The OSS needed its own reliable source.

As Nicol traveled in France, he observed and listened keenly. Gathering information for the reports was similar to story collecting during his expeditions. The difference was that he must suspect every contact who might perhaps be a German spy.

While traveling, Nicol used every opportunity to shop for antiques or art items. Often it was easier to buy a work of art than to obtain meat. On his visit with Andre to the demarcation border, the Countess had shown Nicol through the art gallery at the chateau. Pointing to a small painting by Whistler, the famed American artist who had kept studios in both London and Paris, she told him to take it. She believed the Americans would rescue France and she wanted to thank Nicol for his efforts, whatever they might be. Whistler's *Seated Lady* was her token of gratitude.[18] Nicol was astonished. He and Moira collected art and Whistler was a favorite of both of them.

Nicol was welcomed by the French who hoped his presence meant the Americans would soon be involved in protecting their country from the Nazis. Everywhere people asked him when the second front would begin. Initially the repeated inquiries about a second front took him completely by surprise. He found it difficult to believe the French thought his arrival implied the imminent coming of U.S. troops. Nicol tried to explain, using his carefully constructed cover. No one believed him or they did not want to believe him. Soon he tired of explaining his position and preferred to remain silent on the subject by simply agreeing with the French people. Surely the American soldiers would arrive soon.

Andre continued to prove to be a valuable contact. He managed the family steel mills in Saint Étienne. He invited Nicol to visit the mills later that month. Nicol suspected that more might be in store when he traveled south to the Loire district of France. But he was eager to travel and determined to learn what he could in the industrial city. It was a leading coal-mining area with iron foundries, smelters, forges and steel-rolling mills. Among its output of heavy durable goods were machines, automotive supplies and armaments.

Bob Schow proved to be an invaluable asset to Nicol. A small man with gray hair and shrewd, penetrating eyes, he was well informed on French affairs. Nicol had a lot to learn and Schow was an asset. He forewarned Nicol of suspicious individuals, drove him to clandestine introductions and helped him with office protocol. He warned Nicol to burn all notes and his secret code. Security was a foremost issue. When Admiral Leahy left Vichy, the embassy staff breathed easier, knowing Leahy's diary was no longer available for the enemy to capture.

Keeping a diary was not a "safe" habit for an OSS agent. Yet Nicol kept a daily diary from the moment he arrived until he departed Vichy the following November. Unfortunately the security of the embassy officials and his underground contacts were jeopardized by his journal. Many events were not recorded, but he carefully included people's names and described his travels. He wrote about advice offered by Schow and conversations with people. Fortunately Nicol's diary survived and was never confiscated. His fate and that of others might have been very different had his writings fallen into the wrong hands. Why he kept a diary while he burned papers he deemed important in the bathroom sink is a mystery.

Letters from Nicol to his family left out details, but he did not attempt to cover up his movements:

> I have been wanting to write you for several weeks and at last an excellent opportunity presents itself. Mrs. Douglas MacArthur, the daughter of Senator Barkley, is returning to Washington tomorrow and has told me she will take several letters over for me. When we mail them here we are never quite sure just how long it will be before they arrive.
>
> I have been in France for ten weeks now and the time has passed so quickly it has seemed more like ten minutes. I have been on many little trips all over the country. I have just made a short journey to the Occupied line and at times was not more than thirty feet away from the Germans. The line is completely guarded with men and machine guns and men with blood hounds who move back and forth....
>
> The Jews have suffered terribly. They were paying as high as fifty thousand francs a car to take them from Marseilles to Monte Carlo when the great drive against the foreign Jews started....

225

> There is a lack of everything here.... I travel a great deal and have met many intensely interesting people. I am in Vichy about half my time and have varied in my travels from coal mines to great castles....[19]

The individuals he maintained frequent contact with were Stash Osterog, Gilbert de Chambrun and Jacques Tine. These three Frenchmen were convinced that Nicol was their link to the American involvement in France. Among the techniques Nicol used to start a conversation with his contacts was presenting a pack of American cigarettes. Although he did not smoke, he found the simple gift stimulated conversation.

A three-day bicycle trip led Nicol to more contacts. Ostensibly touring to work on his new movie, Nicol rendezvoused with several contacts made through Gilbert de Chambrun. Making arrangements to meet in southern France, Nicol pedaled back to Vichy and packed to leave at 3:00 A.M. the following morning. At the only transfer during the train trip, Nicol managed to board the wrong train. At the first stop he realized his error. Now he felt assured the man who repeatedly passed his compartment was following him. At the last moment before the train pulled away from the station, Nicol crawled on hands and knees past the strange man's compartment door. As he jumped to the station platform with his overnight bag and the camera equipment he used for cover, the train departed. Watching the cars roll past as they gained speed, Nicol saw the man with his face pressed against the glass as the train sped out of sight. Relieved Nicol entered the station to inquire when a train would return in the other direction.

Nicol spent four nights with Gilbert at the de Chambrun Chateau in Marvejols, a town on the slopes of the Monts d'Aubrac in Southern France. There Nicol met with eight men who offered to help the U.S. obtain any information it needed.

From what he learned, the Lozere district, the area of France where Marvejols was located, was well honeycombed with groups like these eight underground agents. Nicol observed from their vehement insistence of U.S. involvement that they were well prepared for contact with American representatives such as himself. They provided him with a report concerning fifty-five cases of agent sabotage for the month of July in occupied territory alone.

What Nicol provided to the French underground is not known. Whether he was able to disseminate the information he obtained from his contacts to the OSS is not known either. Due to his blown cover, it was at best difficult for him to work safely among French contacts and relay pertinent information to the OSS. From all appearances, it seems the French contacts were not as concerned about Nicol's compromised status as they were with their assumption that he represented the future involvement of the U.S.

Nicol did provide numerous reports of his observations. Among the reports that had previously reached the OSS, several had proven to be highly inaccurate. Author David Shoenbrun in his book, *Soldiers of the Night*, best captured Nicol's work in Vichy:

> There were, however, some sophisticated and reliable observers among the woolly-headed. One was an attractive, cultured young American writer, lecturer, and world traveler, thirty-two-year-old Colonel Nicol Smith of the OSS....
>
> Smith reported back that Vichy was "mad," a kind of "Graustark" or other fabled kingdom. On all sides he saw Gestapo agents, at bars, restaurants, at the opera. "You expect to find them in your bed and perhaps you would not be wrong." He soon observed that hotel servants were busy eavesdropping and were paid spies. He received anonymous letters telling him to blow up various places. Traps were opened before him everywhere. "Foreign ladies of a type never to have noticed me in the past now find me irresistible."
>
> Smith found considerable pro-Allied sentiment in the unoccupied zone and learned soon enough to appreciate the force that the Resistance movements represented. But since he was in Vichy, he also discovered a hard-core fascist minority and was alert enough to realize that it was, for the most part, an opportunistic minority and in no way representative of France.[20]

Meanwhile thoughts of Moira were never far off. At every opportunity he shopped, perusing art or other treasures for Lashio Lodge. Recording the purchases in his diary, just as he did during the Odyssey Tour years before, he mused on Moira's reactions. He hoped to please her with the gifts from France. In addition to the Whistler painting, he collected a portrait by Boilly, the prolific painter who captured Parisian scenes during the French Revolution, and several others.

Nicol's mission in Vichy ended abruptly. On November 3, he quickly departed from Vichy to return to the U.S. The Allied landings in North Africa were projected for the night of November 7. It was feared that once the Germans learned of the invasion they would capture all Americans in unoccupied France. The OSS cabled the embassy to recall Nicol to Washington headquarters.

Prior to the North African invasion, Nicol's return to Washington was probably already in the planning stages. The October OSS Special Operations mission report possibly precipitated his return:

> S.O. now has one representative in unoccupied France. It is not believed that this representative can be of any real service to the organization by reason of the fact that his association with us was disclosed prior to departure. He should be recalled and another chief representative substituted. Plans looking toward this are being considered and a new agent will be sent out as soon as the appropriate man and adequate cover can be found. Time is of the essence, of course.[21]

By this time, a replacement was impossible for Vichy. As was suspected, the Germans immediately overran the resort town and the unoccupied portion of France after the North African invasion on November 7. The Americans remaining at the embassy were captured by the Germans. They were relocated to internment camps to await negotiations between the U.S. and Germany.

18

MISSION TO THAILAND

N icol conceived a plan for his next mission with the OSS as he departed from Lisbon. He was assigned to a desk and chair in the Q Building, OSS headquarters in Washington, D.C., and had barely accustomed himself to speaking English again when he plotted his re-entry to German-occupied territory. On his return from France he had been promoted from lieutenant to captain for his outstanding job in a compromised situation. No one even listened to his concocted plan. Dejected, Nicol worried he would spend the remainder of the war in Washington.

The work he accomplished in France agreed with Nicol. With his knowledge of many parts of the globe now at war, it was inevitable he would be sent on another mission for the OSS. Before his second assignment, Paul Meyer invited Nicol to a luncheon. He blithely assumed the engagement was strictly social. Upon arriving, he found not only Paul Meyer, whom he had traveled with over the Burma Road, but Leonard Clark, his partner from Hainan Island, and Sabin Chase, a State Department official. Unknown to Nicol, Leonard was now a lieutenant in the OSS.

The topic of discussion was Hainan Island. Nicol and Leonard were asked to write a report concerning the findings of their 1937 expedition. They were considered the foremost authorities in the world on Hainan Island. Chase referred to the island as "one of the most important places in the world today."[1] Little was known about Hainan Island and it was considered a possible location for a base in the Pacific, but more information was

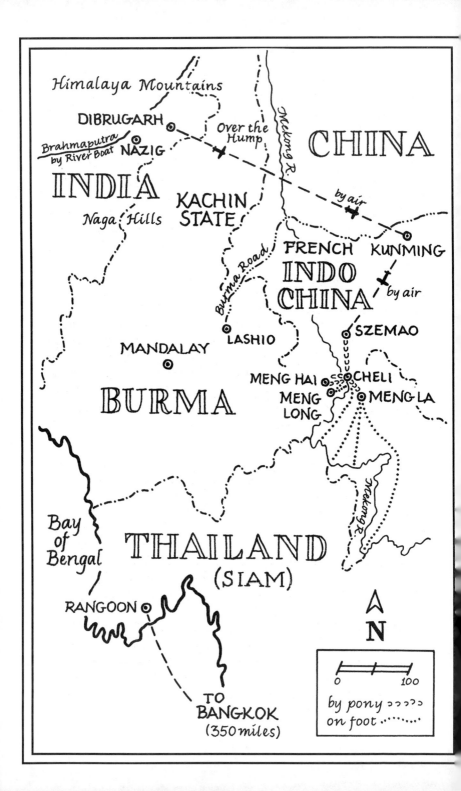

needed. With Japan conquering the Pacific and the Asian countries, the U.S. was looking for additional footholds in the region.

Following lunch, the group went to the office of Mr. Grosvenor of the National Geographic Society. There they obtained a copy of the article written by Leonard for the magazine several years earlier. They learned that Chase was gathering information for a detailed report that would be available to the State Department but not to the OSS. His comment was a cause of concern for Nicol and Leonard. Each of the men advised Chase that they were connected to OSS and would have to consult with their superiors. They received an affirmative reply. The report was needed.

As they prepared their extensive report, with approximately five hundred pages of written material and 750 photographs, Nicol's second mission began in earnest and his efforts on the report were short lived. Leonard continued gathering the material on Hainan Island and completed his work in August of 1943. Incorporating Nicol's preliminary work, Captain Carl O. Hoffman of OSS later forwarded the information to Captain Milton Miles of the U.S. Navy. Nicol's duties demanded his attention on the China-Burma border, however, and thoughts of the Hainan report were far from his mind.

✍

Nicol's next mission had been approved before his return from France. Fully expecting to be sent into a German-occupied territory of Western Europe, he was surprised by the plan that was presented to him. Major Frank Devlin summoned him to his office. He needed a quartermaster and finance officer for a mission to Thailand, a country Nicol had not even considered for an expedition, let alone OSS duty. His knowledge of Thailand was zero, but his experience with outfitting expeditions, managing expenses and traveling in the Far East qualified him for the job.

The OSS Detachment 101 commissioned a Special Operations mission, FE-3, to send a group of Thailand nationals into their country to make contact with any underground organization, if it existed. If not, an underground must be organized. The country, under Japanese influence since the occupation on December 8, 1941, had declared war on the Allies. Little was known about the situation in Thailand, but at the time it declared war on the U.S., officials of the Thai Legation in Washington D.C. declared themselves independent of their home country and the State Department recognized the legation.

Thailand was a blind spot in the intelligence of the Far East. The OSS wanted to put Allied agents there to assess Japanese control of the country. The need for information was critical. General Stilwell wanted to know how many Japanese soldiers were in Thailand, how many Thais were under arms and whether they really wanted to fight. The Air Force lacked knowledge about the locations of important Japanese installations. General Chennault, who Nicol had met during his Burma Road expedition, required information about prison camps and whether any of his fliers downed over Thailand could be rescued. With agents and a transmitter slipped into Thailand, possibly a wealth of information could be made available to the Allies.

Twenty-one Thai men had been hand-picked for the operation. They were Thai nationals who were in the U.S. on scholarships. They attended the leading American universities, including Harvard and the Massachusetts Institute of Technology. They had completed their OSS training and were prepared to head for Thailand. Nicol was briefed on his responsibilities and sent to Area B in the Catoctin Mountains of Maryland, now known as Camp David, the weekend presidential retreat, to begin his training. He began the rigorous daily regimen with the earliest recruits of OSS Detachment 101 which was the first class to be trained at the newly established school.

Detachment 101, the first U.S. unit of its kind, was officially activated in April 1942. It was an organization very different from the resistance efforts in Western Europe that was trained to conduct a wide variety of clandestine operations. It would conduct a warfare that knew no rules, with a wide variety of operations, including espionage, sabotage, guerrilla warfare, propaganda, escape, evasion and assassination. Its area of operation was the Far East. The men recruited had to show extraordinary enthusiasm and ingenuity. Their duties and responsibilities required an abundance of both.

The first people Nicol met after arriving for his intensive training were the three instructors who spent the next two weeks with him, Lieutenants Frank Gleason, Leopold Karwaski and Joseph Lazarsky, otherwise known as the three "Ski" brothers. All were experts with dynamite. They had learned their skills in the anthracite mines around Hazelton, Pennsylvania, where they were raised.

Lieutenant Joe Lazarsky ran Nicol through a variety of exercises including the handling of a number of explosives. Nicol was a little frightened as he worked with the demolitions using booby-traps, Composition C (a new plastic explosive), dynamite, TNT, delaying devices, caps and fuses. The "Ski" brothers always wondered if Nicol was soldier material, but trained him to the best of their ability.[2] Nicol's true identity was not revealed during training camp nor was anyone else's. He was given GI fatigues to wear, a nickname and no reference could be made to his civilian occupation or status.

Nicol's skills grew as he trained in areas introduced to him in his earlier experiences in France. Cryptography, secret writing, methods of agent operations and searching for downed air crews were agent responsibilities in which he excelled.

Graduation exercises brought out Nicol's true colors. He and Ray Peers, who Nicol recognized as an exceptional leader during training camp, were instructed to gain entry into the Fairchild Aircraft Division plant near Hagerstown, Maryland. The plant made primary and advanced trainers and cargo planes. It was carefully guarded against enemy sabotage and espionage. Their mission was to study the plant and determine where bombs should be placed to cause the most destruction.

Nicol had friends everywhere and one was a Fairchild executive who had previously been a high school principal at a school at which Nicol lectured during his annual circuits. Calling his friend from a hotel lobby, after changing from scruffy fatigues into presentable clothing, Nicol made the necessary arrangements for a lunch meeting.

During lunch, the executive offered to take Nicol and Ray on a tour of the factory. For an hour and a half, Nicol amused the Fairchild executive with his stories, as Ray made mental notes of everything he saw. The tour turned out better than they ever expected and needless to say their Area B instructors were impressed with the information they gathered.

The procedure used by Nicol and Ray Peers may not have been in close accordance to the rules of the exercise. With only a short period of time to accomplish the task, Nicol knew every shortcut available to employ. His experience in France educated him on the time it could take to finish the simplest assignment. Besides, Nicol's methods were proven. Everywhere he went he knew people or met those of influence whose assistance could later be called upon.

Finished with his training, Nicol now needed to complete his remaining responsibilities to coordinate the Thai agents for departure. He was in charge of purchasing all necessary supplies and equipment and responsible for all monies spent on the mission. The officer in charge of special funds, Douglas Diamond, made out ten checks to Nicol. Each was for the amount of fifty thousand dollars.

The funds were drawn on Thai money unfrozen by the State Department (Thai assets had been frozen when the country declared war on the U.S.) for the purpose of the mission. The Thais wanted to pay their own expenses wherever possible.

Nicol decided to deposit the money one check at a time in the Bank of New York. Having banked there for some time, his own checking account rarely ran over three figures. Meeting with the bank manager, a personal friend of his, he opened a new, personal account with the first of the checks. The manager was inquisitive and Nicol carefully skirted his prying questions. The remaining nine checks he deposited one a day for the next two weeks at a different teller window each time. Nicol was sure his sudden wealth raised questions among the bank employees.

With money in hand his shopping led him from secondhand Army-Navy stores to big sporting goods shops and finally to Abernathy & Finch, the upscale expedition supplier in New York City that he frequented for his own expeditions. He bought each man a forty-five pistol knowing each had been trained in its use. For protection against the tropical diseases with which they would be plagued, he bought quantities of quinine and other drugs, including eight thousand sulfa pills. To combat vitamin deficiency he obtained special tablets so potent that each one contained a ten-day supply. They were almost too big for the men to swallow. Knowing how agents whose lives were in constant danger need to relax their tense nerves, he purchased fifty pocket-sized books, as well as seventy-five packs of playing cards, six pairs of dice and a small roulette wheel.

The young men were enthusiastic and eager to begin their duties. Eighty-seven days after departing from Baltimore, Maryland, on the liberty ship, *Abraham Clark*, they disembarked at Bombay, India, the port city on the Arabian Sea. Morale had flagged as the twenty-one men suffered numerous delays before leaving the states. Then the days at sea crept along as a myriad of problems arose onboard the ship.

Nicol's relationship with the men developed during this lengthy and critical period. On board the liberty ship the "Ski" brothers held training classes for the Thai nationals, while Nicol organized their duties. Nicol's success in establishing a rapport with them was apparent when they began. He was rewarded when the Thai men began calling him "Lung Nick." Lung meant "honorable uncle" in Thai. This new title was used with respect by his Thai charges during the two and a half years they spent together in China, Ceylon and Thailand.

Travel, illness and additional training in the Naga Hills of the Indian state of Assam with Colonel Carl Eifler's organization prolonged their journey. During the stay, General Donovan arrived to inspect the accomplishments of his Detachment 101. Colonel Eifler would fly Donovan behind Japanese lines in what Nicol thought was an extremely dangerous mission. Nicol's roommate that night turned out to be General Donovan himself. Nicol voiced his fears to Donovan, questioning the consequences if the Japanese should catch the director of America's secret service organization. He handed over his wallet and identification papers for safekeeping with Nicol in order to travel incognito in case the plane went down. Donovan assured him that his men risked their lives daily and they deserved his personal evaluation and recognition when necessary. All the men in the camp in the Naga Hills were on edge until the Tiger Moth, piloted by Eifler, touched down on the strip. By that trip, General Donovan earned the devout loyalty of everyone in the North Burma jungle. It gave the Thai group a tremendous boost in morale to feel that a man was working for them in Washington who understood exactly what they were going through and was doing all he could to help.

Finally after Nicol's lengthy recovery from malaria, which he contracted after reaching India, he and the Thai men arrived in Friendship Valley, ten miles from Chungking, China, homebase of Rear Admiral Milton Miles, head of the Navy Intelligence Group and OSS in China. Now located at the headquarters of Detachment 101, the next weeks were spent in more precise planning.

Colonel Kharb Kunjara, the Thai Military Attaché who was in charge of the group, had flown in ahead to greet them as he had not accompanied them on the trip aboard the liberty ship. He had strange news. Before Kunjara left Washington, the Thai Legation received a perplexing message from Chungking. It was from a man named Balankura requesting funds to bring him to the United States. No one at the legation had previously heard of this person. When Kunjara reached China, he set out to find Balankura and discover whether or not he was a true patriot escaped from Thailand. Possibly the man might be a point of contact inside the country. Unfortunately, Kunjara had no luck before Nicol and the Thai men arrived. Balankura could not be produced for questioning. Delays occurred and Kunjara did not meet with the man from Thailand for a couple more weeks.

While Kunjara negotiated for a base in South China with General Tai Li, head of China's incredible secret-service organization and reputed to have an agent in every railroad station and post office in most parts of China, Nicol went to Calcutta for additional supplies and to replace radio equipment that had failed to arrive. At the OSS Security Office, Nicol met Harry Little who had trained at Area B with him. To his surprise his brother-in-law, John Archbold, walked in. Neither knew the other one was associated with the OSS in the China-Burma-India Theater. They enjoyed the impromptu reunion and shared news from home during every spare moment they spent together.

When Nicol returned two weeks later, he was informed by Kunjara that an underground existed within Thailand. The news excited Nicol. He had feared that each agent would have been forced once inside Thailand to build up an intelligence network of his own among his trusted friends. By this tedious and dangerous method, months could elapse before there would be much hope for information on a large scale. The news was splendid—if true.

During Nicol's absence, Tai Li's men informed Admiral Miles that two more Siamese, Tularak and Tilaka, had also arrived in Chungking. When the men were questioned Tularak assured them that a loyal group was well organized into an underground within Thailand. In 1942, the head of the Thai underground had sent a mission to China which mysteriously disappeared. Then in 1943 Balankura was dispatched. He had been picked up by Tai Li's men. When no word had come from Balankura, the underground head back in Bangkok tried a third time with Tularak and Tilaka. The two men were sent to Washington to meet with Thai Minister M. R. Seni Pramoj, who had originally repudiated the Thai government's declaration of war on the United States. The two men wanted to establish a government-in-exile and use radio to rally patriots inside the country to join the Free Thai army.

After much delay, in accordance with plans made with General Tai Li and one of his regional assistants, General Tso, Nicol and his men established their base at Szemao. Originally plans had been made to locate at Cheli, a town on the bank of the Mckong River in the Yunnan Province near the border of China and Laos, but General Chennault had built an air strip at Szemao which facilitated their transportation to the new base. Nicol had bought horses to caravan to Cheli. With the change in location, he was able to work a deal with Chennault, whom he had met during his earlier Burma Road travels. Nicol arranged for Chennault to loan him two C-47's to transport his group and all of their equipment. In return Nicol was responsible for daily reports and the guarding of the fuel supply at the airstrip. Chennault forewarned Nicol that when the Thai men infiltrated Siam, he would need an additional favor.

They were located 250 miles south of Kunming, China, the equivalent of twenty-one days by caravan. The area was inaccessible by motor car. The trip by caravan would have been a grueling one. For some the C-47 trip provided plenty of hardship. Lieutenant Karwaski, six of the Thai men and Nicol left Kunming to arrive at Szemao only one hour and twenty minutes later. All of the Thais were violently ill for the greater part of the short journey. All but one of the remaining Thai men were transported the following day, while the other agent caravaned to their base with the twenty-three mounts Nicol had purchased.

Szemao, once a rich Chinese customs and trading center, had fallen to ruins. Located at an elevation of forty-three hundred feet, it overlooked a large valley surrounded by peaks from six to seven thousand feet. The climate was mild with cool nights. Pine trees surrounded the compound. It was big-game country with tigers and cobras. The area was known as one of the worst malaria regions in China. The group made their base headquarters in a boarding school in which they had eight bedrooms and a recreation area. Five minutes from headquarters was a three-story tile pagoda which they converted to a radio tower. It was the most powerful field station in China with a 100-watt transmitter. From here they were to slip the agents down to General Tso at Cheli. He was to arrange the rest, coordinating the movement of the Thai agents with his underground contacts on the border between Burma and Thailand.

Five of the men were selected to blaze the trail. Cary[3] had a B.S. from M.I.T. and a M.S. from Syracuse University. He was a splendid athlete and was also very resourceful. Sal,[4] who had been a student of pharmacy at Philadelphia College, was impetuous and afraid of nothing. Ian,[5] who had just obtained his M.S. degree in agriculture from the University of Iowa, was the most intellectual member of the group. Ken[6] had been a student of mechanical engineering at Miami University. He was the brother of Madame Bhakdi, wife of the first secretary of the Washington Legation. He was an extremely good-natured and hard-working youth. Paul,[7] the fifth member of the group, was in his middle thirties, financially well-to-do and was the ladies' man of the group.[8]

Tuesday, February 29, 1944 at 10:00 A.M., the five men, disguised as Chinese merchants, together with Colonel Kunjara and a guide, took the cobblestone trail to Cheli. The distance to Bangkok from Szemao was 650 to 700 miles. Ken and Sal had lived in their outfits for days and somehow looked more natural than the others. Ken had a tiny "cavity compass" which was actually small enough to carry in a hollow tooth that he inserted into a Buddhist talisman which hung about his neck. Sewn on each man's shirt was a button compass which looked like a duplicate of the buttons on their coolie outfits. Each one carried a square, silk scarf on which was printed a map of Indo-China and Thailand.

238

They also carried a tiny but complete escape kit. Each set contained a diminutive steel saw, a canteen, halazone tablets, Benzedrine, a bar of chocolate and a pack of chewing gum. Concealed in salt bags across the mule's back, each agent had an OSS-developed, demountable radio set. Power plant, transmitter and receiver made a package no bigger than six loaves of bread, but once assembled, it could send a message five hundred miles with ease.

Each man was well set with cash, carrying what amounted to a portable mint, considering the amounts concealed on their bodies. Two thousand dollars worth of gold was hidden somewhere on the body, usually in a small leather pouch secured to the belt or suspended from a cord around the neck. One-fourth of the amount was in the form of chains, rings, and bracelets. The rest was in gold Indian tolas specially made without markings so that no one who might receive them would have any inkling as to their place of origin. Also well hidden was a small sum of French Indo-China paper piastres and one hundred Yunnan silver dollars.

Thursday morning, Nicol and Captain Leo Karwaski took to the trail. They were to meet Kunjara at General Tso's headquarters in Cheli but were to see nothing more of the infiltrating agents for fear of endangering the mission.

A six-day journey over mountain trails brought them to the Mekong River. On the other side lay Cheli and the area of General Tso's command. There Nicol met the colonel who was to be directly in charge of Cary, Sal, Ken, Ian and Paul on the first lap of their journey to the Indo-China frontier and who then was to assume responsibility for getting them into Thailand. Although the Japanese guarded all main roads leading across the borders, the colonel and his agents had lived all their lives in this region and knew many unpatrolled back trails.

On Nicol's way back to Szemao from Cheli, he and Leo stopped at the headquarters of General Lu of the 93rd Army, where they met a most unusual man, who was a political advisor to the 93rd Division. He was a Chinese Catholic priest, Father Jean Tong, thirty-eight years old, one-time amateur boxing champion of China and educated by the French fathers in Shanghai. As a priest he worked among the people of all the border regions in that part of China, including the little-known headhunters of the remote Wa states. Nicol promised to get him a ride by plane to Kunming to see his bishop, to whom he had not reported in five years, if he came with them to Szemao. Nicol saw potential in the priest.

By the middle of April the men remaining at the Szemao base were at the radio every hour of every day desperately listening for word from the agents whom they expected by then to be inside Thailand. Washington was continually asking, "Why the delay? Where is the information we sent you to get?"

To Nicol's amazement, one morning Paul walked in. They had not even started on their infiltration. The promises made by Tai Li were not being fulfilled by his lieutenants. It was discouraging. Thousands of dollars and months of valuable time had been spent to get to the very edge of China, only to be stopped there by the agents of people whom they had most counted upon.

Father Tong, returning from his visit with the Catholic bishop in Kunming, became the answer to Nicol's prayers. Knowing the country as no one else did, he could get a group across the border if anyone could. Nicol offered him a thousand silver dollars with which to build a church for the reward of risking his life. Overjoyed, Father Tong agreed to assist the Thai mission.

Meanwhile, Lieutenant Charles[9] volunteered to go on his own into Indo-China and work back and forth between the Thai frontier and their subbase at Meng La. He was a logical choice as he had studied in France and spoke French fluently. He would attempt to set up a courier system over which extra radio parts and spare crystals could be moved. Alone, he set out on his mission.

Having secured additional pack animals, there was no reason to delay. Pow, Pete, Bunny and Sam,[10] guided by Father Tong, followed soon after. Their radio sets were wrapped in waterproof blankets and packed into the bottom of hampers lined with a layer of leaves and straw. On top of the blankets were their items of trade: safety pins and needles, small mirrors, spools of thread and blue cotton cloth, quinine pills and even a few sulfa tablets, stories of the tablets miraculous properties having reached even this remote corner of the world.

Again Nicol and Leo accompanied the party to Meng Long on China's Yunnan-Burma border. Climbing to a summit of the mountain, Nicol and Leo watched the sons of some of the oldest and wealthiest families of the Orient, looking exactly like impoverished peddlers as they went down the mountainside. That morning it began to rain, a pounding, continuous, drenching downpour. The monsoon season had started.

Back in Szemao, July 1 arrived and no messages. When the radio receiver was adjusted to the frequency assigned the young men, they heard nothing. Finally, nine days later, a message came in from Charles on the Indo-China border. It was startlingly clear, "Cary and Sal have been killed. More following."[11]

Charles told how Tai Li's men had faithfully guided Cary and Sal to the capital of Laos and into the hands of a merchant about to cross into Thailand. He in turn led them to a house believed safe, where someone working with the enemy tipped off pro-Japanese police. They arrested the agents, took them into the woods and murdered them for their gold.

All the more anxiously Nicol and the remaining young men listened at the radio ten times a day for the four men left at the border by Father Tong. The waiting continued. The interminable months of the monsoon wore on—July, August, September.

Each month Nicol wrote reports of his activities in letter form for Colonel John Coughlin who was now in charge of OSS activities in China. By July, Nicol was thoroughly discouraged. His last hope rested on Father Tong. The politics of the controlling Chinese organizations was exasperating Nicol. Working through General Tso, a Tai Li adjutant, Nicol and his men began to distrust Tso. Nicol learned that the Tso organization was in a nearly bankrupt situation and felt they were pressing him for inordinate sums of money. Each passing month he became less trusting. His use of Father Tong circumvented his group's dependence on General Tso's rank-and-file agents.

In July he wrote to Colonel John Coughlin of his daily difficulties and feelings about the Chinese he was depending upon:

> Lt. Charles no longer trusts the Chinese in the Tai Lee [sic] setup. He has informed me that the Chinese have tried to keep the news of Cary and Sal's death from him. He also believes they used our first group as an experiment and sent them to Thailand over a new untested route, keeping from them the established trail along which they had operated for

some time. He also feels they are in a semi-bankrupt condition and their own agents are not given sufficient food. Certainly General Tso's trying to get some 3,000,000 piastres out of me for a courier system through Indo-China to Thailand by the beginning of June was odd to say the least. I refused to do this as you know from my letters of that time. He said the money was to be in the nature of a loan to be paid back by the Chinese after the war.[12]

The problems persisted even in their daily lives at Szemao with the Chinese employed at the wilderness base:

> Here in Szemao we have met with one difficulty after another in regard to the Chinese. The soldiers whose food bill we pay and whom we use in connection with the construction of the house are always sick. To have thirty-three and a third per cent available in any one day is a miracle. We are squeezed on all sides. There are petty difficulties with the Chinese Colonel in command. I will not bother you with these troubles at this time. They are only incidental in the big picture but the net result is THE MEN HAVE LOST ALL FAITH IN THE THAI LI CHINESE.
>
> We have since found out Tai Li himself does not completely trust the TSO group in this area but has another group—a civilian unit to compete with it and report on the men in the rival section.[13]

Between listening schedules at the pagoda transmitter they passed the time as best they could. Nicol taught the men new poker tips. A garden was planted and provided fresh vegetables as a welcome change to their diet. Nicol collected several pets, Lucky and Happy, both dogs, Spooky, a monkey, and Teddy, a bear cub whom he fed with a bottle until he was nearly as large as a Great Dane.

Writing from Szemao to Colonel Coughlin, Nicol provided the latest information supplied by Ben[14] who had returned from their temporary radio station at Meng La:

> Our suspicions have been realized about the Chinese. The two officers definitely assure us, General Tso has kept the established route to Thailand through Indo China from our men and they were forced to journey over new experimental routes. The

general has not turned out the Rose I pictured him in earlier reports. I was mistaken.[15]

Nicol continued the report chronicling the deaths of Cary and Sal. He had received information that a Thai had turned them into the police. Paul and his two companions "disappeared into the blue"[16] and nothing was known about Father Tong's movements with Pow, Bunny, Pete and Sam. Nicol concluded with the latest information at Szemao:

> We have moved into our new house. The main building is four-fifths finished. The radio and cook houses are both completed. The toilet is in working order and the shower and servants shack are both under construction. The tension of waiting for news is sometimes difficult but everyone's health remains better than expected and the weather has been considerably less rainy than I thought possible. We all continue on the best of terms with each other and only wish our men could get through to THAILAND, so that we could send you daily messages of interest and complete our job.[17]

At this point he felt the mission was a failure. This letter revealed the lowest ebb of Nicol's emotions. The waiting was taking its toll on all of the men. Six days later the letter was forwarded to General Donovan at headquarters with an accompanying note:

> Please find enclosed copies to Colonel John Coughlin from Major Nicol Smith who has long been with the Thai Group.
>   It should be born in mind that Nicol is, at present, somewhat malarial and so may be unduly pessimistic.[18]

By October 5 they had nearly given up hope. That evening Nicol was playing what seemed like his ten thousandth game of seven-card stud. It was about 8:20 P.M. when the door flew open and in rushed Lieutenant Nick, the leading radio operator.[19]
Yelling excitedly, he announced that contact had been made. All at once Nicol and the men jumped up, their makeshift table crashed to the floor and they ran for the radio pagoda. The tap–tap–tap sounded over and over again. Ironically, because of an electrical storm the reception was the poorest it had been in all their months at Szemao.

Nick had arranged a special grouping of letters, different for each man, that would represent a "danger group." Its appearance at the beginning of his message would indicate that he was in the hands of the enemy or had revealed the location of the home station and was operating under duress. Nick quickly determined that the danger code was not there and handed the message to Jim.[20] In ten minutes, Jim had the translation.

It began by saying all four of the men were safe. It then confirmed the deaths of Cary and Sal, which had advertised to the enemy that there was a movement afoot for infiltration of agents with radio sets. The Japanese were on the alert everywhere along the frontier and patrolled areas never before guarded. The party had been forced off the already remote trails onto barely discernible jungle paths. Their provisions soon became exhausted and at times berries and roots were all that kept them alive. All five contracted malaria and Sam almost died of dysentery. It took them eighty-seven days to reach the Thai frontier. Father Tong left them once they were several miles across the border.

Fortunately, the word about agents with radio sets reached not only the Japanese but also the Thai underground. When they finally crossed the frontier border, the Thai police, whose leader General Adun Adundetcharat (code-named Betty), the number two man of the underground, secretly arrested and jailed them. They were transported to Bangkok, from where they were sending the message. Regular contact could be counted on. Their report confirmed the British operations were simultaneously attempting to infiltrate the Thai underground.

Within the hour, the news was sent to Kunming, Delhi, Chungking, Kandy and Washington. Contact had been made by the OSS agents within the borders of Thailand at Bangkok more than 650 miles to the south.

⌖

Requests for information from Allied posts began to pour in. General Wedemeyer wanted to know how many Japanese troops were in Thailand and whether any were moving from Indo-China across Thailand to Burma. The Air Force needed information on which side of the Don Muang airport, the closest airport to Bangkok, was used by Thais and which by the Japanese. General Chennault asked them to find one of his best fighter pilots, Bill

McGarry. Supposedly he was located in a Japanese-supervised Thai internment camp. The Air Force requested twenty-four-hour weather reports. From the pagoda they radioed the information as quickly as it was transmitted to their station.

The men inside Thailand discovered that "Ruth," (his OSS code name) head of the now extensive Thai underground, was none other than Luang Pradit Manudharm, brother-in-law of the agent, Arnold. He was also regent of the country in the absence of the Boy King Ananda Mahidol, who was in Switzerland studying when the war broke out and could not return home. While Luang Pradit was ostensibly cooperating with the Japanese, he was actually coordinating the underground and its contact with the Allied forces.

Daily information poured in over the airwaves from Bangkok. The infiltration of more OSS-trained agents was arranged. A short four months later, on January 28, 1945, the first Americans entered the Japanese-occupied country. Major Richard Greenlee and Major John Wester flew in from Kandy, Ceylon, by British seaplanes. They landed on the Gulf of Siam and were taken by motor launch up the coast and then by automobile through the streets of Bangkok to a mansion in the Japanese-occupied city.

Five days later, Greenlee slipped out of Bangkok on his way to Washington with the information he had learned about the plans of the Japanese Army in Thailand and a proposal for a Thai uprising.

Ruth was trying to persuade the State Department to agree to a supply of arms from the OSS to the Thai Army. Department officials were not in favor of dropping guns to the armed services of a country that had declared war on the U.S. It was agreed, however, to begin arming the guerrilla groups.

One by one, daring American OSS men parachuted in at night to train the guerrilla bands. By summer, twenty-eight Americans had armed and trained more than three thousand guerrillas now ready to fight. They were just waiting for the signal.

With the successful completion of mission FE-3, Nicol traveled to Washington in April 1945 for two months. In Washington State Department officials briefed him on the political complexities of the Allied planning for Thai guerrilla training and warfare. Colonel John Coughlin was hesitant to send him as he greatly valued Nicol's abilities to manage the men:

> As you know, Major Nicol Smith is located here at Kandy now and will be leaving for the States in about a week.... Nicol has been a big help down here and I am most anxious that he return. He has done more to weld the two groups into one than all the rest of us put together.... At the present time, Nicol says he wants to come back. I want to be sure that he doesn't change after he gets home. I think he is completely up-to-date right now on our plans and thinking Thai-wise. He should be helpful to you, but don't keep him. Nicol has agreed to come back after sixty days in the States. If you can see that he doesn't spend one day over sixty days back there, I will appreciate it too.
>
> Nicol is a great guy as we both know. Don't let him talk you into three months instead of two.[21]

Returning to the South East Asia Command (SEAC) headquarters at Kandy, where the Szemao base had relocated in order to remove themselves from Tai Li's territory and work more closely with OSS Detachment 404 and with Admiral Lord Louis Mountbatten and the British, Nicol was now going into Bangkok himself to meet with Ruth and to discuss certain problems. During Nicol's debriefing in Washington, his value during this critical period became apparent. A letter to Colonel John Coughlin re-emphasized Nicol's importance in the cooperation of operations between OSS and SEAC forces located at Kandy:

> We all know of Nick's special value to this particular situation at its critical period, and he is not only willing but anxious to go back and help in putting it through to a successful conclusion.... We are increasingly impressed with the value to the organization here of having men who have been long in the field help us with our problems in servicing our foreign operations.[22]

Nicol made his clandestine trip into Bangkok in mid-July 1945. Reaching Rangoon, Burma from Kandy he departed in a C-47 accompanied by Lloyd George, an intelligence specialist and Major Alex Griswold, an OSS agent, Dr. Chanai, and Les, a Thai radio operator.

The first stop was at Pukiew, one of the remoter districts of Thailand where Alex was to be left in charge of the secret airfield. The next stop was at Saraburi, another Thai-controlled airfield only half an hour's flight from the Don Muang airfield, a village fifteen miles north of Bangkok. Waiting for the cover of darkness, they continued their covert trip.

At Don Muang the pilot did not risk circling the field but instead made a quick landing on the Thai side of the airfield. Men quickly rolled the plane into an open hanger and the door was closed. Huddled on the floor, Nicol and Lloyd waited for the okay to disembark. Finally a car, an old Dodge, was at the side door, and Nicol and Lloyd ran through the pitch black hanger and cowered in the back seat of the automobile. After a short drive through dark streets they arrived safely at the palace of the late Prince Asdang. Known as the Criminal Investigation Department, it was actually OSS headquarters in Bangkok.

Operating a radio from the palace did not alarm the Japanese with their direction finding equipment. The Criminal Investigation Department had long had a radio operating in connection with their work. It was adequate cover for the operating of the OSS radio. The Japanese also wished to maintain their "friendly" relationship with the Thai and never fully investigated the suspicious radio signals emitting from Thai-controlled buildings.

Nicol's instructions included persuading the Thai underground to wait until the British were prepared before rising up against the Japanese. Ruth had already stated on several occasions that he was having difficulty in holding his people back and could not do so indefinitely. Now in Bangkok, Nicol could appreciate the tense situation. He found the days of inaction nearly unbearable. He and the other men were confined to the building. Meeting with Ruth, Nicol again heard the trouble he was having holding his people back. As instructed by his superiors in Washington, Nicol could only repeat they must wait. Both Washington and London were in agreement. They wanted to wait until Admiral Mountbatten, the Supreme Allied Commander for Southeast Asia, was ready and that certainly would not be before November.

Checking on his men, he was glad to see they were in good

form. They were equally relieved to see "Lung" Nick and provide him with any information they had.

Nicol's responsibilities included improving the productivity of communications coming from the Bangkok underground station. He obtained information on the Thai Navy and the location of Japanese troops within the country during his visit. While he was there he arranged to visit the British post. They were engaged in the same type of operations as the OSS.

Nicol's anticipation of the trip to visit the British was not without danger. It took some courage to accept their hospitality as it required traveling through Bangkok past numerous Japanese guards. An ancient automobile waited for the unnerving trip to the British headquarters. Timing was essential to catch the Japanese off guard so the car would not be stopped.

The trip went without a hitch, except once when the driver flooded and killed the engine. Quickly the point of the visit was reached and Nicol and Lloyd made the return trip after obtaining information about the British efforts in Thailand.

The next forty-eight hours seemed like as many days. The Japanese had discovered several of the clandestine airfields in northern Thailand. Then they began a search for ammunition and supply dumps. The situation was beginning to look bad because the air route from Burma might be cut off.

Preparing to leave, Nicol carried documents from Ruth to the State Department and the Free Thai Legation in Washington. As he said his good-byes, Ruth presented him with a pair of royal cuff links in a green velvet box. They were pure gold and red enamel made from pounded ruby dust. On one link were the initials "A.M.," for the boy king, Ananda Mahidol, and on the other a replica of his golden crown above the mark of his dynasty.

On Saturday, August 4, Nicol and Lloyd completed their responsibilities for OSS Operation Siren, their clandestine and highly successful trip to Bangkok. They started their return journey to the outside world two days before the atomic bomb was dropped on Japan.

∽

19

A PUBLIC IMAGE

Letters were Nicol's connection to the life he left behind in the states. He wrote a constant stream of letters, sharing the events of his life and his thoughts with his parents, his mother-in-law and his wife. In June of 1944, Nicol wrote to Anne Archbold and contemplated the pattern of his life. Sounding melancholy, he shared his ruminations with her:

> It's all really another world, Anne. The very nature of my work is so different from most of our other soldiers that sometimes it seems to me I am in a little war of my own. I travel over corduroy paths through corrugated mountains. I live in a land where the footprint of a tiger on the trail is as common as that of the house cat at home. I have wild flowers in my garden as different as the convolvulus and the orchid.... It's illusory to say man does not adapt himself to his surroundings no matter how strange they may be. I find in life that with time, anything is possible. Life must go on and man falls into this pattern willy nilly.[1]

Earlier that year Nicol wrote to his mother and emphasized the importance of letters in his daily routine. Again he seemed melancholy:

> Your wonderful letter of December 21st arrived yesterday and I cannot tell you how pleased I was to hear from you. Letters mean more and more to me as the months pass.... Without your letters Mother and the letters of my wife, my life would be a rather empty thing.[2]

He identified the letter as "LETTER 31" in the upper left corner of the first page. He continued to mark each letter to his mother or father in this manner, frequently writing letters to them singly, rather than addressing them together. Only a few of the numerous letters to his parents remain.

He wrote an equal number of letters to his mother-in-law, Anne Archbold, the majority of which survived.[3] It can be safely assumed that Nicol also wrote to Moira as regularly and possibly more often than to his parents and Anne. In letters to Moira's good friend, Ellen Dockery, Nicol mentioned he just wrote to his wife. The letters to Moira no longer exist. Neither do any of the letters that Nicol received while he was overseas with the OSS. Based on his numbering scheme, he probably wrote nearly a letter a day. Many of them were typed since he had access to a small typewriter in Vichy and a portable typewriter at his outpost in Szemao. They contained the events, the traumas, the waiting and the dreams of Nicol, a young man with his normal life on hold. He was serving his country faithfully and he looked for adventure in his OSS experiences.

Nicol kept a diary of his Vichy experiences and began to keep one while in China. With the tedium of the waiting for his men to radio from inside Thailand, Nicol skipped a day, then several days, and finally the diary remained untouched. Either the boredom of the routine at Szemao left him with nothing to write or his time was spent writing to his loved ones at home.

Nicol longed to hear from his family. In every letter he included the date of the last letter he had received, the number of weeks it had been and wondered if they had written again:

> Do write soon. The days when your letters come in are very special ones for me indeed. I think you would be pleased if you saw my pin up parade. It consists of all the snapshots you sent me. Any more you could find would be very welcome.... In two weeks I will have been overseas eighteen months on this job. When you think of the time spent in Vichy, it makes nearly two years in the army abroad. It is getting to be quite enough. I listen avidly to the news every night. It is good, exciting news and the world is certainly ready to hear it.[4]

The hours and days of waiting provided ample spare time to

contemplate his return to his previous lifestyle:

> After the war I shall make an expedition every four years. I will travel for eight months at that time and journey in the fall, winter and spring. I will visit four countries taking a photographer with me and make four different pictures enroute. It will be fun every fourth year to go away but that will be quite enough. The rest of the time I want to be at home. Moira has already agreed. We will spend our summers in California between the Burlingame Country Club and the lodge in the mountains. The fall we will be in New York at the apartment at Hampshire house and January, February and March I will lecture. In the fall each year for three months I will try my hand at fiction. If I am successful with it I will give up lecturing and expeditions completely. If not I will always have that to fall back on. In the late spring before coming to California for the summer we can go to Florida, Nassau or Europe for a month or two. Then if Moira is agreeable, and I think she will be, three or four years after the war is over and I am back in the swing of my work again we will build a house somewhere in the hills behind Burlingame.[5]

Nicol left for duty in China in March 1943 and he returned to the states in August 1945 with a leave of two months in the spring of 1945. When he wrote this letter to his mother, he still had another full year of duty before he would return home.

As the year progressed, Nicol continued to long for home and think more frequently of his friends, family and the lifestyle they all had previously enjoyed. Eating rations and sleeping in the jungle allowed Nicol ample time to contemplate his own feelings and values:

> We just never—any of us appreciated all the wonderful things we had before. The more we all got the more we wanted. I was the same as you and father and most of our friends. We wanted different things but we all WANTED. Some of us wanted power, others money or popularity or another car or more servants. Then the depression came and jolted us and afterwards the war and it all stopped—. How petty all those other worries seem now.
>
> I know you and father and Moira and my friends will mean a great deal more to me than ever before. I have always loved

you deeply but at times did not understand you. I would feel
you were being bossy that you had no right to say I could have
another cocktail or not. I would resent suggestions on your
part. All that is now changed.[6]

Along with his feelings of melancholy, the inward searching for
the value and importance of his life, he also felt the immense
responsibilities of his position:

> I have had immense responsibility in this war for one who
> never expected to have any at all. I have been given great sums
> of money to spend for certain purposes and at all times I have
> tried to follow this procedure. I am far from a regular army
> post. I have no standard to follow. I must make the decisions
> myself and as frequently men's lives depend on that decision I
> study the problem as thoroughly as possible before any deci-
> sion is made. I have just been through a crisis. We have survived
> it. There will be others. I do the best I can and when I fail, I
> feel it has been an honest failure.[7]

Letter after letter left Szemao. Nicol even had stationary printed
and shipped to him at the radio base in southwestern China.
The time at Szemao crept by, seeming to continue forever.

After Nicol sneaked out of Bangkok in the last fateful days
before the dropping of the atom bombs on Hiroshima and
Nagasaki, he soon traveled to Washington. The next role he
fulfilled was important. The new responsibilities were of consequence for the future of the OSS but also were a factor in determining his career after the war. Having already contemplated
discontinuing his regular expeditions and the extensive winter
lecture tours of the past, his OSS experiences were going to be
valuable.

On August 19, Nicol was promoted to lieutenant colonel and
dispatched to Washington. This was his third promotion since
he had entered the OSS three years earlier. Not only did Nicol
receive the promotion, but nine days earlier he had been awarded
the Legion of Merit for his outstanding duty in Thailand.

Publicity was Nicol's next assignment. The OSS wanted to
provide the country with positive information to facilitate the
continuation of the agency after the end of hostilities.

Nicol's wartime letters had already made the newspaper in the *San Francisco Examiner*, where his mother, Sue, published her column. Starting in mid-1943, each week the paper printed a letter that Nicol had written to his family. Sue capitalized on her son's war career and managed to generate a little additional income from Nicol's letters home. The paper never referred to Nicol's career with the OSS. They may not have known, although Sue was well aware of her son's position but not his mission. One such letter read:

> At last we have reached our final destination. The journey has been a long one and we have covered many thousands of miles.
> My little house is at the edge of a river. I am deep in primitive jungle. The rains have started and they never stop. My house is unbelievably primitive. The walls are of mud, and the roof of thatch. The floor is of dirt, the supporting beams of bamboo. We have woven mats over the dirt....
> I am glad I have been on so many expeditions. All this is not as new for me as some of the other officers, who feel rather lost in such an environment. We all would like to see the war finished tomorrow. Home will certainly look good to me. I have always appreciated it but I will 100 percent more in the future. From an eighteenth century English apartment to a mud hut in a jungle is quite a change. Well, it's all a part of life, and we must take things as we find them.
> I have a fascinating job in a section of the world that has always interested me and you can't have everything. Comfort and climate just does not go here. One must make the best of it. I am not so very military, but I am becoming more so every day. After a year of this, there should be quite an improvement.[8]

Besides writing letters and in his diary, Nicol had time on his hands at Szemao to begin work on additional stories. His first, "Baby Ma," was about a Thai doctor crossing the Hump, the section of Himalayas regarded as a barrier to air transportation during the war. The doctor made the trek with a Chinese couple and their baby. Completing the short story in November of 1943, he immediately began to work on another one. Nicol contemplated a book of short stories of human interest from his Asian experiences. Titling the manuscript "Long Red Peppers," he told tales of the orphanage where he visited Chen Hsiu-lien whom he adopted during his earlier Burma Road trip.

Then his writings took on a more serious tone. Documenting his experiences and knowledge of General Tai Li, Nicol wrote a fascinating, personal account of their meeting and of Tai Li's influence over his mission at Szemao. The majority of the fifty-some pages was later incorporated into his book of war experiences.

The next notable manuscript concerned Admiral (Lord) Mountbatten, the British Supreme Commander of SEAC. Nicol met Louis Mountbatten when his base at Szemao was relocated to Trincomalee, Ceylon, the chief British naval base in the Far East. Nicol admired the British Commander and became good friends with Mountbatten. He attended a July 4 party at his residence in India on a trip several years later.

Nicol understood that his return to Washington would launch him back into his lecturing and writing career. The OSS wanted to publicize its activities in Thailand and Nicol would be its spokesman. He was natural as a representative for the OSS which was focused on gaining public support for their efforts during the war.

The newspaper interviews began within days of Nicol's arrival in Washington. The *Washington Post* was first with a front page article that quoted Nicol about the locating of the survivors of the Houston crew, who had been lost in the Java Sea battle forty-two months prior. They were found in a Japanese prison camp in Thailand. The *Washington Evening Star*, the *Washington Times Herald* and the *Philadelphia Record* all followed suit with front-page articles. On August 29, the *New York Times* featured a cover article on Nicol's views of the Thai mission.

This was only the beginning of the interviews Nicol conducted. The *San Francisco Chronicle* published an "exclusive" account of their telephone interview hoping to capture the excitement of Nicol's announcement that he was connected with the OSS. In October, *Collier's* ran a four-part series on the OSS involvement during the war, which included an interview of Nicol in the first segment. Then in December, *Cosmopolitan* ran an extensive article previewing the forthcoming book by Nicol and his co-author, Blake Clark. The magazine cover displayed one of the fifty thousand dollar checks written to Nicol for the Thai mission.

Before his departure from Ceylon to Washington, he began planning his future. Lectures, books and movies of his experiences were bound to launch him back into his career. Because of the OSS desire for publicity, he was free to speak openly about his experiences.

Lloyd George, his companion on the clandestine trip to Bangkok, and Nicol agreed to work together to develop a story of their experiences in Bangkok. The contract read:

> The undersigned, Lloyd George and Nicol Smith, agree that they shall jointly prepare, write or develop the story of American clandestine operations in Thailand to be made into a motion picture, based on their knowledge and experience before, during and after their joint trip to Thailand in July and August 1945. They further agree that any income derived from above mentioned joint preparation of ideas and/or story for a motion picture shall be shared equally. Nothing in this agreement shall be construed to apply to any article, book, lecture, or radio program prepared or performed individually by either of the undersigned.[9]

Again Nicol hoped to make a movie from his personal experiences. He had tried with Madame Duez, the Burma Road and now he planned to try again with his OSS-Bangkok experiences. Nothing ever came of the agreement nor was a movie made. The only link Nicol possibly ever had to a movie was a tenuous one. During World War II, two movies were made about the Burma Road. Neither movie represented his book *Burma Road*, but possibly his bestseller sparked an idea or provided an occasional detail for the American movie industry during that period.

Once back in Washington, Nicol began to look for a collaborator to work with him on a book of his experiences. It was not until he met Blake Clark, a staffer from the Reports Section in OSS headquarters, that Nicol found a co-author. Clark had already written three books, including *Remember Pearl Harbor*.[10] Clark thought he had already arranged to work with another proven author on an OSS book. When that possibility fell through, he was receptive to Nicol's offer.

Nicol had been busy and had already obtained the permissions necessary during the month after his return to complete a fifteen thousand-word feature article for the December issue of

Cosmopolitan Magazine, with the complete story to be published at a later date by Bobbs-Merrill. In addition, he planned to write a book about his experiences in Vichy, France. All manuscripts were subject to approval by the OSS Reports Declassification Office before publication.

Nicol and Blake went to work. Blake had access to many of the reports needed to document and fill in the events in which Nicol had participated. But Nicol had a different view of the book he was about to write. An adventurer by spirit and profession, he set out to write a book of adventure, not war stories. Retelling events to Blake, he recaptured the highlights of his experiences in reaching the Thai underground which he termed as the "biggest blind spot in military history," an exaggeration on Nicol's part but probably an accurate description of how he felt as he waited for radio contact in Szemao.

With the manuscript completed by early December, Bobbs-Merrill published *Into Siam Underground Kingdom* the following May. Only three books were published about the OSS in 1945 with three more following in the next four years. Nicol and Blake should have found a curious and receptive market for their book.

Hoping for a success like *Burma Road*, Nicol and Blake were disappointed. The reviews were mixed, tending to view the book unfavorably. One reads:

> It takes the authors almost 200 pages to tell about it [OSS infiltration] in a loose, discursive narrative. The most dramatic incidents await the last 100 pages, and the conflicts of national interests, which dogged all our efforts in the Far East are barely mentioned....
>
> It is a pity that our policy, so intelligently conceived, became so vitiated in action that Siam is now back in a semi-colonial status, buffeted by both French and British interests. And our reservoir of good-will, once so full, is thereby further dehydrated. Of this the authors of *Into Siam* are scarcely conscious. They were too concerned with the adventure.[11]

Unfortunately this was to be the tone of reception for Nicol and Blake's book. Events, which took place after Nicol's departure and of which he had no involvement, concerned Thailand's postwar fate. The book was printed only once with a run of five thousand copies.

A book about Nicol's responsibilities in Vichy during 1942 never came to fruition. After writing an extensive outline for a twenty-three chapter book, he became discouraged by the lack of sales of *Into Siam* and decided there was not enough material to merit a full-length manuscript. Instead, he turned his work into a series of thirteen radio shows which aired in San Francisco. These were the last radio shows he performed.

Nicol also took his OSS adventures on the lecture circuit. Traveling the states by train during the winter of 1946, he retold the events of his induction, the Vichy mission and the Thai mission in town halls and school auditoriums. It was in this setting that he had the greatest success with his stories and escapades of his OSS career.

∽

Before Nicol's flight into Bangkok, memos were circulating asking that he be awarded the Legion of Merit. Nicol's service in Thailand had been exemplary and his superior, Coughlin, wanted him rewarded. In a memo to Major General Robert B. McClure on June 30, 1945, Coughlin pushed for recognition:

> He was frequently referred to in Kunming as "Fabulous" or "Fantastic" Nicol Smith, never as Major Smith. He is the son of wealthy parents, an author, world traveler, and lecturer in his own right, and married to a daughter of Dowager Archbold of Standard Oil Millions.[12]

After identifying Nicol, the memo went on to say:

> [At Szemao he] showed great patience and initiative, and finally achieved worthwhile results long after I had given up all hope of anything good coming of the venture. Major Smith is directly responsible for our present intelligence unit in Thailand, which, good or bad, is producing considerable intelligence from that area, including some worthwhile stuff from Japan itself.[13]

Finally, a summary report was written and included in Nicol's personnel file:

Not a military person, but possesses a remarkable personality; wins friends quickly on all levels. He is sincere, loyal, honest and hard working. Has done superior job on every assignment. Because he apparently enjoys every task, some people are prone to take him lightly. However, he is a careful planner, has ample courage and accomplishes superior results. In his field, he is one of the best, and has proven most useful in working with Asiatics on intelligence work.[14]

More than two years earlier the "Ski" brothers observed that Nicol was not of a military bearing and many people that Nicol met during his OSS career concurred. Regardless of this supposed shortcoming, he had proven himself in a role that seemed almost customized to his abilities. The report concluded by giving Nicol an overall rating of superior.

In a debriefing report of Nicol's service in Asia, he was credited with the overall success of his mission. More importantly, two additional factors were regarded as crucial to completing the job. First, Nicol operated well in the field of diplomacy. He exploited and continually built up a wider circle of useful and influential people, and secondly, he was also required to have considerable patience and tact to live with and direct the efforts of a group of Thais far away from a settlement. Never in the months of isolated camaraderie association could he afford for one minute to treat them as anything other than brothers-in-arms and full equals. He slept in the same rooms with them and ate the same food. Any hint or small suggestion evident in his words or behavior that he considered himself superior would have meant failure for his mission. Nicol had nothing but the deepest respect for the Thais. He called Thailand a gallant nation that deserved the utmost in respect and cooperation from the U.S.[15] Nicol was true to his men and himself. He had earned their esteemed regard and they in return gave him their honorable title of "Lung Nick."

After numerous delays and memos, Nicol was awarded the Legion of Merit before his promotion to Lieutenant Colonel. The citation presented to Nicol stated:

Major NICHOL[sic] SMITH, 0 914 632, Army of the United States, is awarded the LEGION OF MERIT for exceptionally meritorious service and distinguished service as Commanding Officer of the Free Thai Movement operating in the China Theater. Major Smith organized and established the Free Thai Movement and acted as sponsor, finance officer and liaison officer for the group. This group succeeded in penetrating Thailand, obtained most valuable information, exfiltrated important personalities from that country and established and maintained our relations on a most favorable plan. In order to accomplish the above it was necessary for Major SMITH to show unusual initiative, perseverance, good judgment, and above all an even temper and high morale. He encountered many trying and disappointing situations. Under difficult conditions, eight months of which were spent in the unexplored jungles of Burma and Yunnan country and with outstanding professional skill, unflagging zeal and great resourcefulness he supervised the Free Thai Movement to the stage at which is became an efficient operating organization. The morale of the Free Thais was frequently at the lowest ebb and doubtlessly this mission would have failed without Major SMITH. He accompanied the unit from the United States and made all arrangements for moving it in the China and India-Burma Theaters. He obtained necessary supplies and transportation from many sources, showing great initiative in this respect. He assisted in the planning, accompanied the first units into the jungle, established forward headquarters and remained with the unit until their success was definitely established. He created and organized an intelligence net which supplied the 14th Air Force, the State Department, and other U.S. agencies with exceedingly valuable information. His drive and perfect knowledge of the handling of the organization have won the confidence of the people under him and has materially strengthened the friendly relations existing between the Free Thai Government and the United States. A most important and difficult mission was successfully accomplished, reflecting the highest credit upon this officer and the Armed Forces of the United States. Entered service from Washington, D.C.[16]

Nicol's military career was over. When he was debriefed on August 17 the reason for his return to the U.S. was "In order to complete work he has been doing for two years and the release of story to the press."[17] He was recommended by the personnel officer filing the report for continued service with the OSS. Nicol also wanted to stay with the OSS. The officer wrote an additional note suggesting he be used as an observer in the course of his normal civilian occupation as a traveler and lecturer. Nicol's pre-war career provided a possibly adequate cover for future work.

He had served his country and his men well. Nicol's closest associate, Leopold Karwaski, credits Nicol with leading the mission, morally, tactically and financially to a successful conclusion.[18] Writing from Bangkok, Chok na Ranong, known as Charles, one of the twenty-one Free Thai, said in a letter dated February 1994:

> Believe it or not, you played the key role in the success of the Free Thai. Of all the Free Thais in Thailand at that time only your boys got the radio sets with them into Thailand and from them you got radio contact with Thailand.[19]

To this day Nicol's role is remembered among his men as a pivotal one in the success of the mission in Thailand. He came home after thirty months and never returned to Thailand, China, Burma or Ceylon where his successful mission took place.

BOOK SIX:

TRAVELOGS

Here I am seated on the ground at
the air strip—two days journey from
Angel Falls. As we landed, something
went wrong with the plane. Art and
the pilot are trying to fix it. If you
receive this letter—they have been
successful—I sure hope you receive it.

Nicol Smith
Letter to Anne Archbold
written from
Mayupa, Venezuela
April 6, 1950

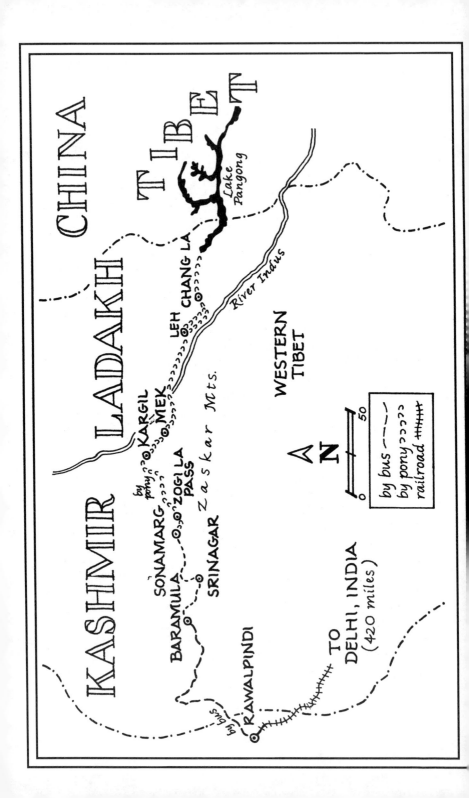

20

TRIP TO TIBET

Nicol and Moira's reunion was a happy one. Their nearly three-year separation during the war seemed interminable to Moira. During that period, they had been together in Washington after Nicol's return from Vichy until his departure for China. His sixty-day leave in the spring of 1945 was the only other opportunity they had together.

Moira lived between their apartments in San Francisco and New York. Lashio Lodge on the Stanislaus River in California remained closed since their last summer visit in 1941. Occasionally she joined her mother, Anne, traveling to her home in Bar Harbor, Maine, or in Nassau, the Bahamas.

While Nicol was in China, Moira felt compelled to contribute her time to the war effort. After considering several options, she found a job in South San Francisco. She became a welder. Each morning she left their St. Francis apartment dressed in her coveralls carrying her lunch to the car. Driving to work in the Cadillac she had given Nicol as a wedding gift in 1938, she stopped enroute to pick up an acquaintance whom she had met at her new job.

Welding agreed with Moira. For five months she worked diligently, and became an outstanding welder. It helped pass the time and kept her from worrying about Nicol. Since childhood, Moira's teachers and tutors remarked that the girl was mechanically inclined. She enjoyed the job and continued her war work until, unfortunately, a problem developed with her eyes. To her dismay a vision problem required her to discontinue the welding.

Writing to his mother-in-law, Nicol shared his concern about Moira:

> I hope you are hearing regularly from Moira and will be able to keep your eye on her. I worry a lot about her and am so afraid she will be lonely. It is too bad she had that trouble with her eyes. I know she enjoyed her work in the plant enormously. It helped so very much to pass the time. Perhaps she will be able to find a new job which she will be able to handle without impairing further her eyesight.[1]

Moira did not find further employment in the war effort. Possibly she did not pursue another job. If her enjoyment with the welding position was sincere, this alone might have fueled her desire to look. Seeking employment where she could use her limited skills was foreign to Moira. It would have been difficult for her to find a job.

Nicol knew his absences were hard on Moira since she was overly dependent upon him. Their short separations during his expeditions were long and Nicol always tried to include Moira whenever possible. But with the war this was impossible. As with so many other wives and girlfriends, Moira remained at home. Before his departure for China, Nicol reassured Moira and his mother, Sue, that he thought he would not be gone any longer than a year. When he wrote to Anne eight months after his departure, he didn't think he would be home for at least another year and possibly longer. He did not share this thought with Moira. Nicol kept in touch with Moira's closest friends and her family always encouraging them to look out for her. In every letter he thanked them for caring for his wife.

When Nicol returned, he sincerely expected to limit his travel career as he had written to his mother during the days at Szemao. The time apart was difficult for Moira and she dreaded his leaving more than ever before. Nicol hoped to honor her wishes and restrict their time apart.

However, his options were limited. Nicol did not know how he could earn an income. Regardless of Moira's wealth, he felt a responsibility for contributing a portion, however small it might be, of their finances. His only hope was to join his father, R.H., in managing his business investments. But R.H.'s financial situation never recovered to its pre-Depression status. R.H. was sixty-eight when Nicol returned from China and his business concerns involved only the invention in the garage and the land purchases he was making throughout California. There really wasn't anything for the ambitious young man to do.

Anne, meanwhile, felt Nicol's career suited him perfectly. The OSS publicity was in his favor. The four years since his last expedition was not a concern. He could capitalize on his OSS experiences and the publicity image they created for him. Now was the time to continue. Nicol concurred. Although hesitant because of Moira's wishes, Nicol's enthusiasm for his career was apparent. Moira couldn't see any options. Claiming she loved to travel, she decided to continue to accompany her husband. Nicol began booking lecture appearances based on his OSS experiences. For two winter lecture circuits he capitalized on his war stories. Finally the time came for new material. Plans for a trip began in 1947.

～

Locating Loren Tutell, the photographer who accompanied Nicol on his last trip to the Guianas before World War II, the planning began in earnest. Loren had served in the Army during the war in the Fifth Combat Camera Unit in the Pacific. He was eager to join Nicol on an expedition. Deciding where to venture was the first step.

Consulting Moira and Loren, Nicol narrowed his options. He looked toward the East for his next travels. India interested him. It was in the forefront of the news with British rule coming to an end in the two-centuries-old empire. Colonial rule came increasingly under fire since the end of the hostilities of World War II. During his tour of duty with OSS, Nicol had been granted a leave after twenty-one months and he had gone to India. From Delhi he had traveled by train to the city of Rawalpindi where he rented a car and drove to the northwestern province of Kashmir. Covering miles of the country, Nicol dreamed of making a color movie. He felt Kashmir was a paradise after the months in the jungles of China. Writing to Anne, his mother-in-law, Nicol shared his ideas about an expedition:

I want to bring Moira back with me after the war and go on an expedition through [Kashmir] to Yarkand....[2] If we made the journey in June, we would be able to film in color.... I believe Moira would get some very interesting recordings and I should have some beautiful pictures.[3]

Nicol's sentiments were very different in this letter to Anne than when he wrote his mother from the base at Szemao about limiting his expeditions to every four years. Realistically, he probably was never far from planning the next trip. Leaving for India in early May of 1947, Nicol was not to return for nearly six months. Only Loren accompanied him. Moira stayed at Hillandale, bracing herself for another bout of interminable waiting.

Traveling by ship, the first stop was Manila which Nicol found chaotic. The port was still filled with sunken ships. The war had destroyed the city and everything was outrageously expensive. The next stop was Hong Kong which he also found greatly changed. There was not the devastation as in Manila, but the old spirit of the island that he remembered so well was gone. The mansions that had belonged to the British were now in the hands of the Chinese and Nicol's favorite shop, known as the "Little Shop," had not reopened after the war. Its owner, Mrs. Boyd, had not returned. The great jade pieces he loved to shop for when in Hong Kong were no longer for sale.

Finally reaching Madras, India, he boarded a train for a fifty-one hour ride to Delhi. The long, hot ride wore on Nicol's already thin patience. Customs in Madras had been frightful with the twenty-six trunks and bags, six of which contained photography equipment. The officials wanted a thirty-six percent tax on everything which totaled several thousand rupees. Meanwhile the officials went out to lunch while Nicol waited. When they returned, he managed to get to the head customs officer. With some quick talking and presenting his letters of introduction, Nicol passed through customs without paying a penny.

Nicol's story-gathering began in earnest in the inferno of the summer season. The heat in Delhi was the worst it had been in seventy-five years. For all his suffering, Nicol did not miss a single social engagement. He attempted to remain cool while shooting endless footage of his social and political excursions.

Tea parties, dinner parties and meetings with political figures provided Nicol with interesting stories and personalities. One early story told to him at a tea party given by his old friend Esther Connally fascinated Nicol. It concerned the naming of Yale University in the states after a man named Elihu Yale whose generosity reached from India. Elihu was an Englishman working for the East India Company. His copious gifts to the fledgling school resulted in the renaming to Yale. Nicol delighted in the story and recorded every detail in his diary and in a letter to Anne. He thought his audiences would find it as interesting as he did. He planned to include it in his new movie to show Americans that from far away India came the influence of a man in the shaping of an American institution.[4]

Shortly after his arrival in the city, Lieutenant Colonel Peter Green of the Indian Army, who had also been on the ship coming over, invited Nicol and Loren to stay at his bungalow, which occupied a city block. It would be better than suffering the heat of Delhi. The location on the edge of the city suited the men and Nicol found himself across the street from the residence of Mohammed Ali Jinnah, chief founder of the new state of Pakistan, which would come into being on August 15.

The most glorious occasion was the Fourth of July party given by the American Ambassador, Dr. Henry Grady at the Viceroy and Viscount Mountbatten's home. With 138 guests and a waiter for each, Nicol thought it was a dinner party that could never be duplicated. Handed a seating chart upon entering, which contained the guest list and the menu, he saved it as a memento for many years. Louis Mountbatten, whom Nicol knew from his Ceylon days at the end of World War II, was an outstanding host. At the party Nicol met Edwina, Mounbatten's wife. She had joined her husband in Ceylon after Nicol returned to Washington, D.C. with the OSS. Mountbatten, whose great-grandmother had been Queen Victoria of England, and Nicol became good friends. He generously assisted Nicol with political introductions. Their friendship continued for many years. They exchanged letters until Mountbatten's assassination off the coast of Ireland in 1979. Today these letters can be found framed and hung on the wall of Lashio Lodge.

The next day he held audience with Mohandus Gandhi, the Hindu nationalist and spiritual leader who was assassinated the following year. They discussed the heated political situation in the country briefly, but Gandhi's interests focused on Nicol's photography equipment.

Nicol continued to meet the most important leaders of India during that time of political upheaval. He filmed Jawaharlal Nehru, the Indian Nationalist leader and the first prime minister. Next he met Mohammed Ali Jinnah, the Moslem leader and the first governor of Pakistan, who spent time with him in his office and then allowed fifteen minutes of filming in his garden.

He looked forward to the relief Kashmir would offer from the oppressive heat. Except for the dinner party at the Mountbatten's, Nicol felt it had been stifling hot since he left the ship in Madras. Spending one day in Rawalpindi, in the western region of Pakistan, they continued onto the home of their next host, the head of the Snatan Sikhs. Filming continued for the next fifteen days as they worked on footage of Kashmir.

The following part of their journey would be quite different from the last month of house parties and social visits. The main objective of the new movie was to be Kashmir. Their travels would take them from the state's western end to Lake Pangong in the east on the border of Tibet. The scenery of Kashmir would offer a distinct variation from the filming already completed in India. The region was almost wholly mountainous and dominated by some of the world's highest peaks and largest alpine glaciers. The rugged beauty of the country and the relatively little information that reached the U.S. would provide ample material for their movie.

As no railway entered Kashmir, they continued by a bus to Srinagar with their luggage lashed to the roof. At the border they were searched by the inspectors for beef. Importation of any kind was not allowed. Nicol was unaware that their supplies contained tin cans of dried beef soup, which fortunately the inspectors overlooked. Later in the trip they would cause consternation among their hired assistants until Nicol finally stripped the paper wrappers from the cans. Their sealed cases of motion-picture film, containing a total of 18,000 feet, were seized. Nicol's numerous official letters were of no use. The film was forwarded to the customs office where it could be retrieved. For a fee of 278 rupees, or approximately ninety-three dollars, they managed to regain their prized possession.

A young man who had served as Nicol's assistant when he visited three years earlier greeted them at the bus station. He guided Nicol and Loren to their rented houseboat on one of the canals near the city. The houseboat, which Nicol christened the "Ritz," cost five dollars a day for the servants, lodging and food. Rajah, who owned the houseboat, proved invaluable during the next month while they were shooting a movie about native life in Kashmir and began preparations for their cross-country trip to Lake Pangong.

The stay in Srinagar, an ancient city located in the Vale of Kashmir, Nicol compared to vacationing in paradise. Lakes fringed the city that rested on both banks of the Jhelum River. Canals ran between the bodies of water with boats as the major mode of transportation. Hundreds of flowers were in bloom and always in the distance the encircling wall of mountains could be seen. They met Colonel Reginald C.F. Schomberg, the famous British consular intelligence officer and the author of several travel books. Schomberg suggested modifications to their route.

Their destination was to be Lake Pangong, a 130 mile-long lake at an elevation of 14,000 feet, which ran for about a hundred miles into Western Tibet, crossing the boundary between Ladakh or "Little Tibet" and Tibet proper. The journey by horseback and by yak would cover nearly 200 miles over terrain with an average elevation of 11,000 feet and passes to 17,000 feet.

Assistants had to be hired. Pack animals, food and supplies were purchased for everyone. Hiring adequate help proved to be the most difficult task of all. Before leaving the houseboat, Nicol had already fired one young man, who proceeded to do less each day and then went on strike, demanding double wages. Their cook went on a holiday before the expedition ever got underway and they were left with a man, whose cooking was done in less than sanitary conditions and spoke no English. At the last minute, the houseboat owner, Rajah, decided to accompany them to act as their interpreter.

They started off on August 14, the day before Partition Day, the date of India's independence from British rule. Nicol made the first of two payments of 1,500 rupees to the man they commissioned to organize the hired help, for the guide, the cook and the pack animals. Unfortunately this man gave the cook, whom he disliked more every day, the responsibility of handling the rupees needed for purchasing supplies during the trip. The 1,300 pounds of supplies were roped onto the backs of the pack animals at Sonamarg.

The first day they covered nearly nine miles and the second day out took them over an 11,000 foot pass which would officially close on October 15, not to be reopened until the following June. They would have to return well before that date. They had plenty of time.

On the third day, Nicol fired one assistant, who refused to carry more than twenty pounds and did that in a sullen and surly manner. The cook, who was a friend of this man, retaliated by making dinner two hours late. The next morning a volunteer appeared hoping for work. Nicol hired him since he appeared strong and willing. Nicol nicknamed him "Puss in Boots." The smiling man strapped on sixty pounds with no complaints or superlatives as he stepped out with the rest of the caravan.

Repeatedly, Nicol and Loren were exposed to the spiritual beliefs of their companions, Rajah and the assistants. Rajah believed an evil spirit, the djinn, lived in the mountain tops. The djinn in Moslem legend was a spirit capable of assuming human or animal form and exercising supernatural influences over men. Rajah predicted problems would arise if the djinn was angry. The caravan's problems began in earnest within a few days of their departure.

First Loren's stirrup broke and he spilled from his pony. If it had happened only a few steps earlier, he would have plunged to his death as he crossed a narrow bridge over a gorge. Then Rajah's pony shied at seemingly nothing, throwing him over it's head. The djinn was with them.

Turning in their ponies at Kargil in central Kashmir, eighty miles northeast of Srinagar, Rajah rented fresh animals. Unfortunately the saddles came with the beasts and there were no leather ones available. Wooden ones would have to suffice. Adapting to the unforgiving saddles proved difficult for Nicol and Loren.

Twice in the following days, as Loren, Nicol and Rajah ventured on side trips, the cook, oblivious to his instructions, continued on. Famished, the three men overtook him each evening at the day's stopping point.

To their surprise one afternoon they rode around an out-cropping in the trail and there lay the cook, Gulam, moaning. The pony designated for carrying the cooking supplies had bolted and dumped their cook. Gulam had broken his hip when he fell from the pony. Since he preferred to ride rather than walk as had been the arrangement when he was hired, he had spread the pony's load among the other pack animals. A messenger was sent to the next village and four men came bearing a stretcher. "Puss in Boots" lifted Gulam onto the stretcher. The fall from the pony solved Nicol's major problem of the expedition. They no longer would have to tolerate Gulam.

Nicol soon discovered the money Gulam had been commissioned to spend for firewood and fresh food along the way was already two-thirds gone. Only five hundred rupees remained after a few days of travel. Nicol feared the expedition would have to turn back. Neither he nor Loren carried a significant amount of money with them since there would not be anywhere to spend it. Fortunately, Rajah was willing to obtain credit on his name at the next village. Rajah, who had accompanied them at the last minute to serve as interpreter, now also became the guide, the banker and the cook.

The making of a motion picture continued at every step of the trip. Loren filmed the Ladakhi, or Tibetans, wearing their bright-colored, knee-length coats, the two British missions they stopped at overnight, the king and queen of Ladakh, two lama-series of Western Tibet and the Chang-pas, Tibetan nomads who had never before been captured on film.

Everywhere they heard of the fear of Russian agents. The alarm raised by communism was heard much as it was in the United States. Unknown travelers were considered possible agents and more than once Nicol had to defend their purpose, which was making travel movies for educational purposes. Occasionally he was not believed. The people of the remote regions of Kashmir and Western Tibet rarely saw travelers, let alone a movie being made about their country.

Arriving in Leh, the ancient capital of Western Tibet, Nicol picked up his mail. There was one letter, which had taken three months to arrive. Nicol realized, as never before, how far he was from home. They traveled east over the Chang La Pass at 18,400 feet toward their destination. The land now was almost uninhabited except for the nomad herdsmen, the Chang-pas.

The day before departing for the last leg of the trip, Nicol caught one of their assistants giving them canteen water that had not been boiled. Appalled, he learned the procedures set up for purifying the water had been disregarded for several days. The very next afternoon Nicol went to stand up and felt indescribably weak. During the night he awoke in a cold sweat and writhing from cramps. He diagnosed his trouble as dysenteric fever brought on no doubt from drinking the unboiled water. So far Loren had not suffered. Nicol began taking sulfa tablets, four every four hours. The next day he tried to go on but after a few miles he felt too weak and slid from his horse to the ground. Knowing he must make it to the next favorable camping spot, which would be the last night before reaching their destination, he climbed back on his horse with the help of "Puss in Boots." He remembered little of the remaining miles covered that day.

Nicol's illness prevented him from traveling on to Lake Pangong which he longed to see. The immense mountain lake piqued his interest and he desired to view the terrain of the area. Nicol insisted that Loren and Rajah continue without him. They needed the pictures for their movie. As Nicol watched them depart, bitter disappointment swept over him. To come so close to his goal and be unable to reach it drained his remaining resolve. Lying in his tent for the next three days he reflected on previous experiences. His disappointment was especially poignant as he recalled the German doctor in Dutch Guiana who deserted and left him in the jungle waiting for his return. On Hainan Island he became desperately ill and had to abandon the remaining trip into the interior. His mission to France had been thwarted by the blown cover.

Nicol was dissatisfied. He was on a self-appointed mission. He had been nursing a pet idea. During World War II, he had often flown in a C-47 over the Hump, the section of the Himalayas separating India from the China-Burma theater. He thought there was not one spot suitable for landing in the thousands of square miles of mountains. Was Lake Pangong equally as unsuited

272

for landing? This is what he wanted to know. Now illness was going to prevent him from seeing for himself. Viewing the lake himself would answer the question.

Prior to his departure, Nicol visited the State Department and the Central Intelligence Agency, which was established only that year and charged with evaluating data about other countries. He wanted to know what they thought about this section of the world, if they had any operatives in it and if they would be interested in financing his trip. He found that any expenditure of more than one thousand dollars spent in the field by an agent had to be referred to Washington.[5] This was vastly different from the position Nicol had with the OSS in Asia. Given initially half a million dollars and later another half a million, he was able to have his own personal check cashed at any Finance Office in Asia up to fifty thousand dollars a day.

Nicol felt the money would have been well spent towards the self-protection of his country. But he found the people of Washington who were doing this sort of job were needed in places where the news was occurring. Kashmir and Tibet were currently peaceful. Nicol suspected that the situation could quickly change in Kashmir. Nothing was happening yet but could at any time. His Washington contacts promised to assist in any way with letters of introduction, appointments at embassies, whatever Nicol needed for making his film of the country.

Nicol sent Loren off to film what he had traveled for months to see. He was unable to write letters or in his diary as he was so fond of doing. He repeatedly opened his notebook and simply stared at the blank pages. Finally summoning the strength to move from his sleeping bag to a camp stool at the door of his tent was all the energy he possessed.

Loren and Rajah returned safely from the shores of Lake Pangong. Nicol was relieved when their little caravan came into sight across the desolate plateau. He had repeatedly sighted a strange man near his encampment during the past three days. For more than a week before someone appeared to be following them and Nicol feared for Loren and Rajah. When he inquired upon their return, they had not sighted anybody at the lake. The unusual man suddenly disappeared. They feared he was a communist agent.

Prying observations of Lake Pangong from Loren, Nicol was satisfied to learn the lake shore supported room for runways between the mountains and the water. Loren had taken five hundred feet of moving pictures and four dozen stills. Nicol could hardly wait until they were developed.

Nicol feared, as many people in the U.S. did at that time, the potential spread of communism. His viewpoint is particularly interesting as it was a complete departure from his beliefs while in Vichy, France. At the time he served in the OSS in 1942, Nicol recognized that the French were often more afraid of the Russians than of the Germans who occupied their country. Nicol had repeatedly reassured his contacts and acquaintances that the Russians were on the side of the Allies. Now he appeared as worried about the spread of communism as the French people had been afraid of the Russians five years earlier. Nicol looked at everybody they encountered on the trail as a potential Russian spy. Paranoia gripped him, especially as he lay helplessly ill in the tent for three days.

The return trip was made with great haste. The weather was unseasonably cool and several high mountain passes needed to be crossed before the first snowfall. Then Loren became ill with dysentery fever. Three days were spent waiting for him to regain enough strength to travel.

It began to snow after they crossed the Chang La Pass. The weather held up for two days and they still must cross the Zogi La Pass, a major crossing of the Himalayas, otherwise they would be spending the winter there. Nicol wore two shirts, two sweaters, a fur coat and a rain coat. Even with all the layers of clothing he was miserably cold most of the time. Finally on October 7, they reached Srinagar more dead than alive. Nicol had lost thirty-seven pounds and Loren had lost forty.

They had allowed plenty of time, but winter came earlier than expected. After experiencing the months of political unrest in India and all the areas they traveled, Nicol concluded a letter to his mother-in-law with, "the weather had gone mad like everything else in India."[6]

21

THE AGE OF MOVIES

The final days in Kashmir were full of anxiety and consternation. Crossing the Zogi La Pass in the central Himalayas only forty miles from Srinigar, they beat an early snowstorm by less than twenty-four hours.

The next two weeks were spent in a hospital recovering from their illnesses. Since they did not need to be in Bombay for the return trip to the U.S. until mid-November, they allowed adequate time to recover their health. The remaining time was spent on the "Ritz" houseboat. As they prepared to leave Srinigar by bus for India, Loren thought it may be wiser to try to obtain seats on the daily plane through Nicol's connections. Convincing Nicol that the safety of their films were at stake, they decided to forego the bus trip. It was fortunate for them since the bus was detained in India by a group of Pathans[1] who robbed the passengers. One white man was shot and died a couple of days later.

Nicol realized during his years of experience as an expedition leader that frequently situations turned out quite differently from what he anticipated. Never had he found that to be more true than in India in 1947. He always hoped and planned to be in that part of the world where current events would draw the crowds to his lectures that winter. This expedition brought his plan closer to success than he thought possible and also closer to disaster than ever before.

The summer of 1947, with Partition Day moved forward by Viceroy Mountbatten, was a tense and momentous time in India.

Nicol found apprehension everywhere. Business dragged and respect for Europeans decreased. While he was far off in Ladakh, the easternmost province of Kashmir,[2] the storm broke. Moslem refugees in India migrated to Pakistan and the Hindu minorities in Pakistan to India. Although the leaders of the new states had promised protection to minorities, neither community felt safe. Amid sporadic rioting some ten and a half million people fled from one state to another. The refugees, nearly dead from exhaustion, precipitated the violence that boiled over. After British colonial rule withdrew on August 15, 1947, nearly half a million people perished during the rioting. Nicol's moving picture footage of India and Tibet was soon to be a lecture-circuit sensation.

Nicol and Loren filmed so much footage with such success they decided to create two new feature movies when they arrived home. The first covered only India, while the second focused on the travels through Kashmir to Lake Pangong. With the movie on India completed first, Nicol left to begin his circuit while Loren applied finishing touches to the second movie.

Nicol's India lecture circuit was a stunning success. Capitalizing on the "red scare" theme that became the anti communism plague that swept over America during the 1950s, Nicol made his first presentation at the Curran Theatre in San Francisco.[3] Nicol shared his emotional fervor with his audience. He explained that he expected the "great Russian bear on the far side of the Himalayas to start to work"[4] in the fertile field of internal strife in India.

Nicol reported that in Kashmir alone, so many Communist agents had been arrested and put in jail that finally they were let go because there was not enough room to keep them incarcerated. He told of Tibet's plan to close its frontiers to keep out the Russians who were coming there to prospect for gold and of European Russian families being relocated along the borders of Sinkiang,[5] the largest province of northwestern China. Nicol's consolation to the audience was that Washington had changed its earlier position. As events occurred in the Far East, Washington was becoming interested in the pattern, unlike the State Department and the CIA prior to his expedition.

Nicol's travels in the turmoil of India drew tremendous audiences. Six weeks later he returned to each location and presented the Kashmir film.

Nicol's career returned to its prewar schedule. He now planned that every two years he and a professional photographer would travel to make a new motion picture. He then would return to create and show the picture to hundreds of people at geographic societies, town halls, universities and clubs. He tried to travel to a country which he thought would be in the news in the months to come. On repeated occasions, Nicol was very successful determining where the news would be next. The advent of air travel was conducive to more people traveling. To some degree this caused a change in his audiences. Previously the lectures attracted those who never ventured far from their home state, while now people viewed his films to obtain ideas on where to travel. A journey to a remote location was not enough to ensure the packed lecture halls the next season. He needed adventure, sensation and a locale that made the news. India and Kashmir fit all the criteria just as the Burma Road expedition did before the war.

As Loren worked on the movies, Nicol began writing his fifth book. Initially titled *Red Door to Tibet,*[6] Bobbs-Merrill wanted the focus to be a travel book, not a "communist scare" thriller. The title was changed to *Golden Doorway to Tibet* and five thousand copies were printed.

The book received mixed reviews. *The New York Times*[7] concluded their review with "to a certain extent the travel book is a frustrating experience." Nicol was considered one of the most successful lecture-travelers in the business, but a poor writer of travel-adventure stories. Other reviews brushed aside his latest book as a by-product of material needed for the lecture circuit.

Though the book was not a success, Nicol did have a faithful following. The adventure seekers looking for a nearly unknown part of the world raved that this latest effort was a thriller. The book was full of political happenings, important religious people, the mysterious travels through Kashmir and amusing incidents. The West Coast newspapers wrote the most favorable reviews. After all Nicol was their native son.

Nicol dedicated the book to his mother-in-law without asking her permission. He sent an autographed copy to Anne, who had been the first western woman to visit Tibet during her early days of safaris and expeditions. This was her first knowledge of the dedication:

To ANNE ARCHBOLD
One of the great travelers of our time, who has forgotten more
about the far corners of the world than I will ever know.
— NICOL SMITH

Anne was a philanthropic woman to an unprecedented degree.
She always contributed her gifts anonymously, wishing to keep
her life completely private. Nicol clearly knew from experience
about Anne's desire to remain unnamed and he probably felt
apprehension about the dedication. Shortly after his return from
World War II he had been on the Twentieth Century Limited
returning to New York after a presentation to the rotary clubs in
Chicago. In the train's dining car Nicol met a distinguished gentleman from John Hopkins University Hospital who had been an
Army medical official during the war. Before the war he had
been on a team that developed the formula for sulfa drugs. Nicol
was impressed. He had witnessed in China the lives the drugs
saved of those desperately ill with amoebic dysentery. After a
lengthy conversation about the research and the yearly forty thousand dollar grant from a "remarkable little old lady in Georgetown
who raises seeing eye dogs,"[8] Nicol knew he was speaking of none
other than his own mother-in-law. Remarking that he knew the
woman quite well, the doctor requested that Nicol keep their
conversation private as Mrs. Archbold did not want her name
associated with the grant. Unfortunately Nicol repeated the story
at a dinner party a few days later. Within the week Anne heard
of Nicol's story-telling. She quietly admonished him during a
stroll through her Georgetown grounds.

Besides presenting her with each new movie, the dedication
was his only means of thanking her. She acquiesced after her
initial reservations about the dedication. Politely she thanked
Nicol in her humble manner of the public acknowledgment:

> Your book has come. I am very pleased with the dedication,
> although I do not feel it is correct. I am flattered as you can
> imagine. I have read the first part and found it most interesting.
> I appreciate your dedicating the book to me. I will write you
> later about my enjoyment of it. The pictures are excellent.[9]

Nicol was disappointed with the lack of book sales. Discouraged, he was glad she appreciated the dedication, but he doubted he would write another travel book.

Finishing the Tibet picture, Loren returned to his home. Nicol began showing it on the lecture circuit. The film *Kashmir and the Himalayas*, an all color film, did not flow smoothly with Nicol's narration. Aggravated, he discussed the problem with Loren, but the photographer vehemently defended his editing. Nicol wanted to modify the movie, but his schedule required that Loren join him and complete the edits within a day or two as his speaking engagements rarely fell more than two or three days apart.

Finally, after considerable thought, Nicol asked Art Hall for advice. Currently employed by Nicol, he was in charge of running the projection equipment and acted as chauffeur between lecture locations. At every opportunity Art had assisted Nicol. Most recently he planned and organized the supplies for the Kashmir expedition. Maybe Art knew a little about photography.

Art knew very little about editing a moving picture or photography but he was willing to try. Nicol extended their reservation at Winter Park, Colorado, and Art went to work. Art repeatedly proved himself to Nicol, whether in building a house or outfitting an expedition. Nicol had faith in him.

The movie footage taken on the India-Kashmir trip differed from Nicol's previous filming. This expedition propelled Nicol into a new era of movie production. He organized the local people and the settings for the filming. In order to get the scenes he wanted, he paid the people. Writing to Anne from Kashmir he told of his new experience:

> It is the first time I have ever written a story and had the great fun of seeing it put onto film. It is something new for a travel film and yet it is a story based on the life of the people so that we feel it is quite natural. Some of the scenery has been superb and we have been able to work in the arts and crafts of the country as part of the background instead of the usual screen snapshots. We have also employed the services of a number of animals, horses, cows, dogs, etc. They have been excellent and most obliging. The horse always drinks water at the right time and when we tell him he has had enough and to look at the

camera for a moment he does so. At the same moment we are telling the actors not to look at the camera. The horse is heads up most of the time over the two legged participants.[10]

Within days, Art finished editing the movie. He and Nicol quickly ran through his lecture, making changes to the narration to fit the timing of the movie. Leaving Winter Park, Nicol and Art rushed to make the next engagement on the lecture circuit.

Nicol quickly recognized Art's ability along with his willingness to work together. Deciding that Loren was not the photographer for him, he hired his chauffeur-projectionist on the spot. Art, reputedly a jack-of-all-trades, knew nothing about making moving pictures. He had built Nicol's house, supplied his trips, chauffeured him on the lecture circuit and ran the movie equipment. Editing the movie came easily to Art. Photography was his next challenge. In three months Nicol planned to leave for Venezuela on a trip to make the first moving pictures of Angel Falls. Art would be the photographer for the expedition.

Contacting an old high school buddy, Frank Shugrue, who was in the movie industry in Southern California, Art began informal yet intensive training in photography and film editing. He found the trade to his liking. Aware of the changes this new opportunity would bring to his life, Art felt he needed to consult his family. His wife, Virginia and his daughter, Patty, agreed this was a unique opportunity for Art. Inspired by the favorable feedback from Nicol and from his family, Art embarked on his career as a photographer of adventure travel.

Art met Nicol in Chicago several weeks later to continue his training. Nicol contacted a photographer who was taking newsreel pictures while riding in a radio car. Art joined them and learned how to take pictures in a crisis when there wasn't time to set up and plan every shot. Two weeks of filming accidents and fires rounded out his training.

Making motion pictures evolved into a science of photography with the hiring of Art. Nicol, who was an accomplished photographer himself, although much of his experience was with older equipment, marveled at the patience Art displayed when engrossed with a subject. Writing to Anne from one of his expeditions, Nicol shared the miracle of Art's work:

The Indians captured all sorts of rare insects and invariably brought them to us to be photographed. Art enjoys this phase of his work more perhaps than any other. The narrower the field, the greater the magnification of the insect, the more his work appeals to him. This sort of photography is extremely trying. The slightest mistake with the lens and the creature to be photographed is out of focus.[11]

Art and Nicol became a team that served each other well during the next twenty-five years. Art continued to improve on his quickly acquired skills, and all the photography work was delegated to him. In later travels, Art would be sent ahead to begin preliminary work as Nicol completed his lecture circuit which grew to include England.

Art's work with Nicol soon encompassed his wife also. Virginia found herself included in trips where she spent several weeks assisting Art before returning home to care for their daughter, Patty. When it became necessary to stage portions of the filming, Virginia acted as the script girl, insuring the people entered and exited at the correct times, appeared in the same clothing each day and the miscellaneous other details that Art and Nicol disliked.

Art fell quite naturally into the role of photographer. He was organized from the outset and eased some of Nicol's burden. Every time they passed through customs, Art submitted a list of every photography item they carried. Presenting his list to the customs official, it prevented the endless delays caused by searching each trunk, suitcase and supply box.

The itemized customs list included the best in photography equipment. Cine-Special Kodak and Kodak II cameras, a dozen different Ektar lenses, along with tripods, lighting equipment and film chambers able to contain one hundred to two hundred feet of film were carefully packed for each expedition along with film for stills and nearly ten thousand feet of moving picture film.

The experience Art gained while working with Nicol was premium. Nicol owned the best equipment money could buy. Anne became such a fan of his, she contributed each year to Nicol's expeditions. The annual three thousand dollar gift allowed Nicol to purchase the newest equipment and film. Nicol was generous with film as Art convinced him it was a worthy investment. His career depended upon the quality of his movie. Nicol purchased ten times the amount of film required to make a movie and Art shot it all.

Many countries they visited did not have facilities for developing film. Months of travel, taking stills and shooting moving pictures was an investment with no security. Their only insurance was the amount of film they shot, the more exposed footage the better chance of a feature length film.

~~

Anne Archbold provided more than just money to Nicol. She also offered contacts. Frequently she and her son John furnished Nicol with several letters of introduction for his travels. Now Anne persuaded Nicol to spend several weeks in England lecturing on his Kashmir film.

Nicol hadn't previously visited England. His lectures there drew some of the largest crowds he had yet attracted. He spent two weeks constantly on the move lecturing and attending receptions. Eight hundred attended his lecture at the Royal Geographic Society and almost as many were at the Royal Central Asian Society.

The receptions found Nicol among the rich and famous. Anne's lifelong English friend, Gretchen Green, was instrumental in making contacts and escorting Nicol to all the appropriate receptions. Nicol met Lady Astor, the Prince and Princess Zeid of Iraq and the Earl of Huntington. Writing to Anne nearly every day during his stay, the highlight of his trip was a luncheon held for him at Windsor Castle, again arranged by Gretchen.

Landing in New York, just ten days before his scheduled departure to Venezuela, Nicol wrote Anne:

> As I wrote you from London, the English visit was made possible through your generosity. I greatly appreciated it. There is little more that I can say.[12]

The whirlwind trip to England was a spectacular success. Three days later, Art arrived in New York with the modified Willys jeep. Their departure for Venezuela was only days away.

Nicol changed lecture agencies after his return from England. His next series would now be booked by Kamen Film Productions in Glendale, California. Cliff Kamen was an acquaintance of Nicol's who also worked the travel and lecture circuit. Nicol and Cliff worked with the same booking agent and had experienced difficulty with the company. Finally, Cliff decided to form his own company with his wife, Bunny, planning the circuits and bookings for Cliff, Nicol and three other men for their winter tours.

Nicol made new films more frequently than many of his competitors. The monetary assistance he received each year from Anne was a boon to his career. Her support was always a gift and never solicited by Nicol nor did he ever expect her help. Always grateful, he wrote generously, informing Anne of every detail of his travels.

The movie alone was not what kept Nicol popular on the lecture circuit. He had a talent for his chosen profession. None of the other travel lecture presenters was the entertainer that Nicol had become. Nicol was a natural at holding the attention of his audience whether he was in a small group or on the stage in front of an audience of thousands.

With Kamen Film Productions his audiences grew. Booked across Canada, he lectured to some of his largest audiences. The attendance and the number of engagements continued to grow in the states as well. Lectures to private groups were scheduled at a cost of nearly one thousand dollars.

Nicol's talks were always memorized after the first couple of presentations. He was spontaneous and his stories were about people. He knew interesting people around the world. His movies presented the famous and the not so famous with fascinating stories and beautiful scenery. Local customs and art were included along with rare animals and unusual tales of intrigue. Nicol swept his audiences off to the far corners of the world. No one could match his performance.

Unfortunately, during a train trip, Nicol left the film case containing the Kashmir movie in his compartment while he dined. When he returned, the movie was gone. The case was carefully labeled with his name and address. The movie was never returned to Nicol nor was it ever seen on the lecture circuit again.

Needing material for another movie, Art and Nicol departed February 24, 1950 for Venezuela.

The preparations for Venezuela was different from Nicol's previous travels. The country's recent prosperity brought on by the development of oil resources and the mining of diamonds had caused rampant inflation. The American interest in Venezuela was at an all time high and Nicol was determined to make the trip.

To keep expenses at a minimum, he and Art decided to purchase a Willys jeep since gasoline was cheap, costing only twelve cents a gallon. Moira provided the funds to buy the vehicle and Art outfitted it for the expedition in his backyard. Their home for the one thousand mile journey was a Willys four-wheel-drive truck of standard size. It was outfitted with extra gas tanks so they could drive almost six hundred miles without refueling. The compact body contained a portable kitchen with a three-burner gas stove, two folding beds complete with springs, mattresses, bedding and mosquito nets which could be folded up against the side of the truck during the day and lowered, supported by chains, like an upper berth in a Pullman, at night. A rolled-up tarpaulin attached to the roof of the vehicle protected the berths from the tropical downpours. They carried a beach umbrella to cover the kitchen for such occasions. The portable dining room was a folding table with four attached seats. During a storm an extra tarpaulin could be attached from the umbrella to the table to also protect them from bad weather.

There was sufficient room in their traveling home to accommodate 21,000 feet of film, two motion picture cameras, a tripod, two still cameras and an immense amount of assorted canned foods. Two army surplus lockers served as closets for their clothing.

The magnet that drew Nicol to Venezuela was a mountain and a waterfall. The mountain, Auyán-tepuí, or Devil Mountain, was fabled to be haunted by devils. The Taurepan Indians who inhabited the jungle surrounding the mountain believed that it was the home of evil spirits who would punish with death anyone so rash as to venture into their domain. The waterfall was Angel Falls, the highest waterfall in the world at 3,212 feet, which is eighteen times the height of Niagara Falls and more than twice as high as Bridal Veil Falls in Yosemite National Park.

Few people had viewed Angel Falls. For hundreds of years the Taurepan Indians told of a waterfall which descended directly from the clouds of heaven. But the jungle had kept its secret and the world had not heard of the falls until a few years before. An American bush-pilot-explorer and treasure-seeker, Jimmy Angel, flying over Auyán-tepuí in 1935 had glimpsed the waterfall as he passed over the mountain. Two years later he came back for a second look with his wife and a Venezuelan friend. The plane crashed on the slopes of the mountain, but the three were rescued by Indians. Ever since, the fall had been known as Angel Falls.

Twelve years went by before anyone from the outside world again visited the beautiful falls. In 1947, a photographer by the name of Ruth Robertson made a series of color pictures of Angel Falls from an airplane and resolved to complete the set by taking photographs from the base of the falls. Two years later, she returned with a movie cameraman and an engineer to the base of the falls after a forty day journey through the jungle. There they measured the falls but failed to shoot a successful moving picture.

Nicol wanted a complete movie of Angel Falls. He planned to journey through the jungle in his Willys to reach the incredible water fall.

～

The Willys jeep was hoisted aboard the *SS Santa Paula* of the Grace Line on a bitterly cold day in New York. Next, fifty boxes of food, film and cameras were stowed with the jeep. Five days later, they reached La Guaira, Venezuela's main seaport.

Their first hotel cost thirty dollars each night for one room. Nicol decided they should move on and begin the journey that was to cover 4,000 miles of Venezuelan countryside. Art obtained a driver's license and Nicol secured letters of introduction to the governor of each state they planned to visit. A young Belgian was hired to act as their interpreter and assistant. Camping along the road each evening, they supplemented the canned goods larder with eggs, at two dollars a dozen, and fresh fruit.

Visiting the unfinished castle of the late dictator Juan Vincente Gomez, Nicol found the enormous building had been turned into a biological research station. The man in charge was Ernst Schäfer, the famous German explorer. Nicol was delighted to meet the German who had traveled to Tibet ten years before Nicol's expedition. Schäfer had been honored by Hitler and his government and received many prizes for his films and discoveries of unknown animals. Throughout the Nazi era, Schäfer remained apolitical. Then in 1939, he was prohibited from lecturing and writing in Germany when he refused to cooperate with the German Culture Ministry and the propaganda machine.

Schäfer successfully secreted Jewish scientists and two Polish explorers. The Gestapo sent him to a penal colony when his activities were discovered. Rescued by a Swedish explorer and turned over to the American occupation authorities at the end of the war, he was rehabilitated and granted a visa to continue his work. Nicol and Schäfer struck up a friendship as two kindred souls. Sharing stories of their travels and their war experiences, they became lifelong friends.

The next stop was Lake Maracaibo, an immense lake where oil had been discovered, to visit Creole Petroleum, then the world's largest producer of crude oil. Filming included the 1,600 wells in and around the lake, an area that turned out to be one of the world's richest oil deposits.

The trip was unexpectedly shortened when Nicol and Art were offered a plane to fly to a village only two days from the base of Angel Falls. They were prepared to travel the forty days through the jungle to reach the village as Ruth Robertson had done two years earlier but now that would be unnecessary.

Departing from Caracas, the capital city located in the coastal range near the Caribbean, the jeep was left in a hanger with the interpreter making it his home while Nicol and Art continued the expedition by plane. Repacking the supplies, they took nearly all the camera equipment, with canned foods for themselves and presents for the Indians:

> We took off and in a matter of minutes we were flying, at mile height, almost due southward over the green tree tops, the grasslands and the marshes of the high plateau, the Gran Sabana. It was a magnificent panorama, 'the lost world' which Conan Doyle once described in fiction. And suddenly, hardly

more than an hour after we had left the city—and it seemed no more than a few minutes, so marvelous had been the panorama spread out below us—we came in sight of the juncture of the little tributary, the Carrao, with the Coroni, some forty miles north of the precipitous northern cliffs of the magic mountain, Auyán-tepuí, and their incomparable waterfall.[13]

An hour and a half later the pilot, Charlie Baugham of Ransa Airlines, landed at the primitive airstrip cut out of the jungle at Mayupa on the Carrao River. As they landed, the float on the carburetor stuck. One engine refused to function and there was no place from which to summon mechanics. Nicol began to envision a forty-day hike through the jungle to return to civilization. Writing to Anne he shared his thoughts:

> Here I am seated on the ground at the air strip—two days journey from Angel Falls. As we landed, something went wrong with the plane. Art and the pilot are trying to fix it. If you receive this letter—they have been successful—I sure hope you receive it.
> Our trip was on a six-passenger Lockheed this morning. Everything went perfectly until we arrived. Now one of the motors refuses to function and Art and the pilot have to tear it apart.[14]

Their guide to the falls was the same man who had taken Ruth Robertson the previous year. Her trip was the first successful one ever made to the base of the falls. Nicol was the third party to attempt to reach the base of the falls and he hoped to make the first motion picture. The photographer accompanying Ruth Robertson had no luck with making a moving picture.

Hiring Indians for the upstream trip proved to be difficult. The diamond fields located on the banks of the Caroní River, near the British Guiana-Brazil border, enticed the Indians to prospecting, leaving few behind in the jungle.

Angel Falls is located in the Bolívar state of southeast Venezuela on a tributary of the Caroní River. It drops from a plateau in the Guiana Highlands, a thickly forested, mountainous tableland that covers half the area of Venezuela. The highlands contained large resources of minerals and precious stones, but only gold and diamonds were being mined. The inaccessibility of the region retarded exploration and development.

Fortunately for Nicol, a previous party that attempted to reach the falls left an outboard motor that was still usable on the hollowed log canoes. Unable to round up any Indians for the trip upriver except for one family, Nicol used the outboard to power one canoe while the Indian family paddled the other.

The two-day canoe trip was arduous because of the many rapids requiring portages along the jungled shores of the river. Scrambling over rocks, Nicol, stripped to the waist and wearing tennis shoes, carried the contents of the canoes around the rapids. Wading in the cool water seemed a relief after hours in the scorching sun. Reloading the canoe and settling in for the next upstream stretch was a welcome change after each portage.

The third day they glimpsed the magnificent falls, but it was only a glimpse. Almost instantly heavy clouds blanketed the mountain, concealing the view of the falls.

The following morning the guide led them to an opportune position for photographing Angel Falls. They cleared bushes and tree branches with machetes. The clouds remained all morning and afternoon until dusk. The next morning they returned to the position to make their movie but again the clouds hung over the ethereal view. Nicol began to wonder if the clouds would prevent him from filming the highest waterfall in the world. He had been told in Caracas that clouds shrouded the falls 360 days a year. He hoped he would witness one of the remaining five days.

Suddenly, at exactly 10:50 A.M. on the third day, the clouds parted and Art went to work. The cameras began turning. The cloud bank still touched the rim of the stupendous cliff at the very point from which the cataract began its fall. The 5,000 mile journey from California had not been in vain.

Foot after foot of film was shot and stills were taken. Next, they struggled to a lookout rock at the very base of the falls. It was a long, hard climb scrambling over slippery rocks and logs. It took an hour and a half to reach the base, a distance of not more than a mile from their camp in the clearing.

Located almost under the falls, they craned their necks to photograph the lower span of 564 feet. Nicol wrote in his notes:

The upper span drops 2,648 feet, the lower 564—a total of 3,212 feet. But what can cold figures tell? It is like saying that a Rubens masterpiece contains a certain number of square inches. One can only gaze and gaze at the incredible beauty of the spectacle, and silently thank the good fortune that led you there.[15]

Nicol's new film, *Venezuela Venture*, was previewed by the National Geographic Society and the American Museum of Natural History. They were excited about the successful filming of the magnificent falls. Nicol's new movie was a sensation.

∽

22

SVMMERS ALONG THE STANISLAVS

Summer always brought Nicol and Moira back to
Lashio Lodge along the Stanislaus River. It was the only place
that felt like home to them. Every fall as they closed the lodge
they promised each other the next season would find them along
the river for a longer stay. But every year Nicol's profession demanded more and more of his time.

Art and Virginia always resided at the river whenever Nicol
and Moira were in residence. The Halls kept everything running
smoothly from preparing the lodge for guests, organizing horseback rides and hiring additional help. While Nicol spent six
months in India and Kashmir, Art built his family a cabin at the
top of the rise behind the Smith's Lashio Lodge. Board's Crossing seemed like home to Art and his family ever since the summer of 1939 when they lived in a tent along the river. A permanent
roof over their heads clinched that feeling.

Virginia also became good company for Moira during Nicol's
extended absences. Virginia never drove, so Moira willingly chauffeured Virginia and Patty and included them in her activities.
Moira rarely ventured to her home on the river unless she and
Nicol planned a lengthy stay. With Art and Virginia working on
their home, Moira frequented the river, driving her Cadillac down
the steep and windy, rutted road to Lashio Lodge.

Feeling she needed a reason to justify her stay at the river, she
managed the finances for the additional building:

Nicol, I am still terribly pinched and Art and Virginia's house
is costing anywhere from one thousand to two thousand more

because lumber and everything is much more expensive than when he built our house.[1]

Moira continued to become increasingly concerned about her finances. Ever since the days of training with Bex McBride in her Arlington home, Moira insisted on keeping a close accounting of her money. Everywhere she and Nicol traveled, her adding machine was part of the luggage. Determined to maintain her investments, she allowed herself to spend only the interest. Realistically her spending never even reached that figure. Her share of her grandfather's fortune provided her with an annual interest that exceeded many people's yearly incomes.

The months Nicol was in India and Kashmir was the first trip Moira did not accompany him on since their marriage. It was also his first expedition since the end of the war. He had been home, although he had been on his post-war lecture circuit for nearly nineteen months before he left for India.

Occasionally Moira's letters to Nicol reflected her desire for a change in their lifestyle, although she appeared to understand the need for additional material for new movies and lectures. She revealed little about her feelings on his career. Moira's infrequent and few existing letters rarely included her personal thoughts, but simply recorded her plans to visit her mother and when she had last visited Eva, her childhood governess. But once, writing from Hillandale to far away Kashmir, she shared her dreams. This was the sole time after their engagement that her thoughts appeared in her written correspondence:

Wish you were here but you just had to have new material. Nicol this coming summer let's just have a quiet time and always keep this place just for ourselves because when we are alone, we can have lots of fun together and go on rides and different things and I hope you are for it.[2]

The extended absences must have been difficult for Moira. Nicol was not only her husband but her closest friend and confidant.

The summers at their river lodge since World War II involved entertaining Nicol's society friends. Each weekend brought a different but carefully selected group. Guests came from around the world, from Sue Smith's social set, Nicol's childhood society friends and occasional family members.

Several thank you letters were framed and hung on the wall as confirmation of the memorable times guests had. William Saroyan, the Fresno author who drew upon his Armenian culture and personal background for his impressionistic writing, graciously thanked Nicol for the weekend visit in 1950:

> That was a great weekend and party and I couldn't have had a more wonderful time. It was good to be chatting again with people I hadn't seen in a long time, especially your delightful mother. What good fun it is to see you two, and I'm so glad I've met Moira. Thanks again, old boy....[3]

Letters flooded the post office box at Camp Connell after the summer weekends. Gary Cooper, Cyril Bryner and Herb Caen, the quintessential San Francisco columnist, were among the many weekend guests. Herb Caen's popular San Francisco newspaper column included his impressions of a visit to Nicol's river lodge:

> ROUGHING IT: En route from Tahoe to Santa Barbara, we turned off at Dorrington, in Calaveras County, and followed a tortuous one-lane dirt road through the mountains—just to see how Nicol Smith was making out.
>
> Nicol is the socialite explorer-lecturer-author of B'lingame who spends three months each year on the north fork of the Stanislaus River, in the primeval heart of California's last wilderness. Even the ubiquitous phone company hasn't strung a wire into the place. Fish jump confidently in the river, reasonably certain that nobody is about to hook them into a frying pan. What I mean is, cousin, it's rugged.
>
> After bouncing over the rocks for what seemed like hours—in fact, it was hours—we limped into a small clearing, and there was Mr. Smith, looking chesty in shorts, standing in front of his mountain retreat, a handsome stone-and-wood chalet.
>
> 'As long as you're here, why don't you stay for dinner?' he suggested.
>
> If we had visions of bear steaks cooked in boar grease, they soon vanished. We sat down to a handsome continental dinner, complete with imported wines, cognacs and crepes suzette, prepared by his French cook, Marie.
>
> So don't worry about Nicol Smith, up there on the north fork of the Stanislaus River. He'll survive.[4]

An article in the society section of a San Francisco paper most appropriately captured the weekends at the Smith's with the title "Culture in the Wilds:"

> Nicol Smith gives fabulous weekend house parties each summer at his lodge on the upper Stanislaus River....
>
> His stone and timber houses, which have grown and grown even to a tree house guest room, boast a central beautiful Queen Anne drawing room, tapestry rugs, rare jades and a magnificent Queen Anne secretary desk. He recently sold a valuable Van Gogh and owns Whistler's 'Seated Woman.'
>
> Guests do pretty much as they please—fishing, riding horseback, walking, talking and playing bridge or poker. Nicol has only one standing rule: Meals are served on the dot, gourmet food prepared by his cook Millie.[5]

A cook was hired and Virginia Hall made sure supplies were on hand and the guest rooms were prepared. Then she could retreat to her home while the festivities took place over the weekend. The cook, Millie Pusich, a local woman from Angels Camp, prepared gourmet meals and Nicol provided the entertainment. His after dinner storytelling captured everyone's attention and cards and gambling could last long into the night.

↩

Moira felt increasingly annoyed by the weekend activities. She preferred the quiet serenity of the mountains and the river. Horseback riding, swimming in the river, exploring with the camper's children and picnics interested Moira, rather than the lavish dinners, playing cards and entertaining guests. The campers were the people who Moira enjoyed. She liked riding through the back country with Patty Hall and her visiting girlfriends.

Moira's old feelings of inadequacy returned. Her marriage to Nicol had temporarily offered a new self-confidence which now seemed to erode. When a guest displeased or embarrassed her, she reacted with anger. Several friends were driven away during outbursts of temper. She was unable to forgive even her best friend, Ky Bell, who embarrassed Moira during a short weekend visit. The wedge driven between them endured for the remainder of their days.

The following summer on the river was busier than ever. Nicol completed the work on *Golden Doorway to Tibet*, his last published book. The entertaining continued and the guest list grew. Art built an additional lodge for Nicol and Moira, where they could escape the guests and enjoy their privacy. Still more guest rooms were needed. A tree house room was added with its own bath. The lovely addition was secluded in an old oak tree on the steep hillside beyond the two other houses. A path led from the back door of Lashio Lodge, under the sheltering pines to the door of the tree house. The ground supported the back of the room, the entrance and the modern bathroom while the branches of the huge tree supported the bedroom and the deck overlooking the river rippling over the smooth granite boulders.

Additional accommodations included a bath house and a patio on the riverbank. A second generator and a larger propane tank became necessary to provide electricity for the guests. Telephone service never reached the river, although it was now only five miles away. The Dorrington Hotel at the top of the hill, owned by Nicol's friends, Flo and Andy Anderson, graciously accommodated the needs of Nicol and his guests. Their neighborliness was always reciprocated by a dinner invitation at the river lodge.

With Art now employed as a photographer, the two men were always gone simultaneously. Moira and Virginia became good friends and enjoyed each other's company. It was a quiet friendship, built upon honesty and openness. Virginia liked Moira's sweet disposition and defended her when confronted by a critical guest.

The quiet summer that Moira desired never occurred. Following Art and Nicol's return from Venezuela, the movie editing began in the second story of Hall's river house. Nicol spent weekdays working with Art and the weekends entertaining. Two more winters of lecture tours followed by a five-month trip to Patagonia, Chile and Argentina left Moira feeling deserted.

Nicol returned from South America to the apartment at Hampshire House and Moira's announcement: she wanted a divorce. She recalled for Nicol that he had been away for three years during the war, an unavoidable absence which she accepted. Then in 1947 he and Loren spent nearly six months in India and Kashmir. Venezuela was followed by Kurdistan and then another five months in South America on the most recent trip.

Bewildered, Nicol unpacked and took a long bath while he contemplated the news. Hoping to change Moira's mind, the couple discussed their differences.

Moira wanted a quiet, secluded life. Nicol was the life of the party. She had tired of his absences. Nicol couldn't survive on Moira's money alone and besides he thrived on the adventure and lecture circuit. Their positions were irreconcilable.

Moira filed a separation agreement in Reno, Nevada, on May 15, 1952, prior to Nicol's return from Argentina. Their divorce was granted in July of the same year.

⌁

The divorce was devastating to Nicol. Emotionally he was unprepared for this drastic turn of events. The periods of separation had become a way of life but he always wrote regularly and anticipated each reunion with Moira. Informing Art and Virginia was difficult. The four adults often felt as close as family. Nicol spent weeks at their home in Santa Monica while his emotions healed. He accomplished little during this time and did not feel like returning to Lashio Lodge alone.

The river place would only remind him of how much Moira meant to him and how dearly he missed her. Her quiet presence, always needing him for support and his approval when she made a decision, suited Nicol. Each room was decorated in a simple fashion with their collected art, Chinese urns, jade pieces and antique furniture from around the world. Everything reminded him of Moira. She left everything they bought together and took only her personal belongings to Washington.

Why Moira sought the divorce is not entirely clear. Obviously the lengthy separations would be difficult for many. When they married they planned to travel together and Nicol helped Moira find meaning in her travels with the music recordings she completed for the Library of Congress. While she was always proud of her accomplishment, she never contributed any further recordings.

During the fourteen years of marriage, Moira accompanied Nicol only twice. During the trip to China she stayed with Harriet Meyer while Nicol crossed the Burma Road. During the trip to Dutch Guiana she met him after the stop in Martinique and she remained in the Dutch colony while he went on to French Guiana. Both times they took Mary Carter as a companion for Moira.

After Nicol's return from World War II, she never accompanied him on another expedition. No reason has been discovered why this change occurred. A thorough investigation of Moira's keepsakes revealed she kept the two maps that outlined the trips they made together. Her greatest accomplishments and fondest memories were during her years of marriage to Nicol. Perhaps the times together were not enough to quell Moira's loneliness and fear of their separations.

Nicol's emotional fears encompassed the other Archbold family members. His nearly lifelong friendship with Moira's brothers might change, as well as his relationship with her mother, Anne. His fears went unfounded. In a letter to Nicol, Anne shared her appreciation for keeping the news of their divorce quiet:

> Your letter with the clipping has just come. I think you have managed this all very well. Nothing has appeared in the paper here that I have heard of. No 'What has she said, he said.' I hope the future will hold happiness for both of you as the past has.[6]

Anne did not like publicity about her family. She was glad the news of the divorce was kept quiet in Washington, D.C. She kept the San Francisco newspaper clipping among her letters from Nicol.

Moira and Nicol ended the leases on both of their apartments. Nicol was given the deed to the river place and Moira returned to Georgetown to live in a rustic log cabin on her mother's estate. The divorce agreement required Moira to pay her ex-husband four thousand dollars per year until he remarried or died. The payments continued until Moira's death in 1990.

Nicol's relationships with the Archbold family continued unchanged and the divorce was amicable after a period of emotional healing. As the years progressed, Nicol hoped Moira might have a change of heart. Moira occasionally visited the river and she and Nicol dined together when he was in the East. She wrote two or three sentence letters of thanks after each of her visits to

Lashio Lodge. In a letter accompanying an alimony check in 1962 from the Archbold's financial manger at Rockefeller Plaza in New York, Nicol received advice about Moira.

> I received your letter of October 28. Thanks for the news, etc. But there is one thing—don't you be rushing Moira—you keep your mind on your lecturing. Give Moira time, she cares deeply for you.[7]

Apparently Nicol hoped to reunite with Moira. The divorce papers and the thank you notes from Moira remained in the bottom of his briefcase for the next thirty years.

Nicol was the one person among their fashionable social circle who accepted Moira as she was and not as society attempted to define her. Years later Nicol commented to a close friend, "if everyone had left us alone, Moira and I would have done okay and probably we would have stayed together." Nicol's words attested to his genuine feeling of the real problem that arose in their relationship. Obviously he was aware of the remarks made by many about why had he married Moira.

Previously Moira had rarely made decisions of such magnitude entirely on her own. Nicol's absences may have allowed the influence of others, who felt she inhibited her husband's success, to play an important factor in her decision. Why she parted with the man who had given her the happiest years of her life and cared for her more than anyone else is a mystery that stayed with Moira until her death.

23

FROM ADVENTURE TO
TRAVELOGS

The success of the Venezuela movie prompted Nicol to return to South America. Plans began for a trip to Argentina and Ecuador shortly after returning from Kurdistan in the fall of 1951. They hoped to arrange their transportation by outfitting another new Willys jeep.

The previous winter, Art, waiting for Nicol to complete his speaking engagements in Toledo, Ohio, presented himself at the Willys headquarters. He inquired whether any employees might be interested in viewing their new film *Venezuela Venture*. In a small meeting room he initially showed the movie that included scenes of the outfitted Willys jeep to the head executives. The scenes were unlike any they had ever seen. The small room soon filled to overflowing with employees as the movie progressed.

Art and Nicol hoped the showing would allow them to trade in their jeep for a new one for their next expedition. Correspondence between Nicol and Marden Bishop, the director of publicity for Willys, continued during the spring and summer to no avail. No jeep was presented for the upcoming expedition, not even at an 18 percent discount suggested by Nicol in his last letters before departing.

The following spring the two men returned to South America. In Quito, Ecuador, Nicol dined with the cousin of the president and Art photographed old marketplaces with Indians engaged in trading before they continued on to Argentina.

The high Andes entranced Nicol with their beauty. Along the Argentina-Chili border he spent weeks at the Nahuel Huapí

National Park, touring the forty-one mile long lake at the foot of Mount Tronador. The park had been established in 1934. With the lake's many arms, peninsulas and islands, surrounded by forests and snow-covered mountains in a temperate climate, it was the favorite resort area of the Argentinean Andes. They were loaned a station wagon along with an Argentine guide, Victor Funes, who Nicol found knowledgeable and efficient. Among the sights they filmed was a grove of hundreds of young sequoias, transplanted from their native California.

Nicol and Art were the first to film the Marinelli Glacier at Tierra Del Fuego, Argentina. The southern tip of South America was a barren and desolate land. It was separated from the mainland by the Strait of Magellan, bounded on the east by the Atlantic, on the west by the Pacific and on the south by the Antarctic waters. The high winds as well as the chilly temperatures, were uncomfortable for Nicol. The aborigines, called Fuegians, were primitive people and of great interest to Nicol. The lives and customs of the Fuegians were captured on film for the next movie.

Returning to the states after the South America trip, Nicol did little that summer after his divorce from Moira. The letters from John and his ex-mother-in-law, Anne, reassured him the divorce had not estranged their relationships.

With the South American film complete, Nicol began another lecture season. Each year the audiences grew in numbers and more speaking engagements were scheduled. He was now considered among the best, if not the most outstanding, in his profession. The lecture season of 1952-1953 brought record audiences. His circuit included Canada and England. He was asked to consider a seventeen-day engagement with twenty-three shows in Hawaii.

Nicol was ready for a change. It was the hardship and danger of his expeditions that he was prepared to change. Earlier that year, Leonard Clark, who he accompanied sixteen years before to Hainan Island, invited Nicol to search the Andes for the highest mountain in the world. Nicol declined the invitation. Leonard never returned from his trip. He was lost in the wilderness of South America and died alone.

Nicol felt the loss of his comrade was an unspoken warning. The carefree days of his youth were over. He preferred the comfort of hotels and restaurants to the foot travel across Hainan Island. Overland travel in a 1937 Ford rumbling across the Burma Road while sleeping on the ground was no longer appealing. The remodeled Willys offered rugged accommodation. At forty-three he still longed to travel, but wanted to forego the adventure of the unknown.

Each subsequent trip changed for Nicol. Gradually he left behind the daring escapades and the wilderness jungles of mysterious lands. Instead, he traveled to Hawaii, the islands of the Caribbean, Scotland, New Zealand and Australia. He began sending Art and Virginia on short trips to areas he had already filmed to update a movie after showing it for a couple of years.

His lecture circuit did not change. He was constantly in demand. He presented nearly 190 lectures each season with audiences reaching into the thousands. In Grand Rapids, Michigan, he delivered the Chile lecture on three consecutive evenings, drawing 12,000. Kamen Film Productions was doing an outstanding job of promoting his films. Nicol was a travel sensation.

Unsure of his next trip, Nicol sent his Christmas cards in December of 1952 without mentioning any travel plans. His mother-in-law wrote back to inform him she would not be sending her customary gift:

> I am not sending my Christmas present this year. Should you leave on another expedition I would then consider being of help.[1]

Nicol and Anne wrote each other weekly. Nicol sent gifts and flowers from wherever he was in the world. Anne was seventy-nine that winter and her letters were wistful, with wishes she was traveling with Nicol. As Nicol planned his trip and filming of Hawaii, Anne again expressed her desire to travel:

> I have just enough time to send you three thousand dollars before the Hawaiian venture. That will be great fun to do. I wish I could be there. I think of Hawaii as the "Crossroads" of the Pacific. I'm sure you will find material for another book. Next year bring the film down for me to see.[2]

With Nicol's letters and films, Anne was able to travel vicariously throughout the world. His letters described the details of his travels and recalled distant friends to her from afar. Their relationship remained that of a mother and a son, yet equals in their pursuit of travel and adventure.

Frequently Anne shared in her letters her personal turmoil over the lives of her sons, in particular the eldest, Armar. His partying and drinking caused her despair. She wished they would find meaning in their lives. Nicol was her perfect, surrogate son.

Nicol's relationship with Anne was not unusual. He was thoughtful to the point of devotion with the older women who had helped him during his early quests for adventure. Besides Anne, he corresponded with Miss MacAleer, the retired owner of the San Francisco secretarial school where he had taught during the depression. He frequently sent flowers to Miss Mac, to Anne and to his mother. He loved to please. And please he did, as well as brighten the days of each of these elderly women. He wrote generously to each of them. He also wrote to his mother's maid and nurse in order to keep informed of her deteriorating health. Miss Mac asked him to manage her financial affairs during her last years. He sent books and dresses to Anne. He sent his mother pocket money or bought her a new hat and suit when she despaired over her wardrobe. Occasionally he wrote an article for his mother's society news column. Nicol was the devoted son from afar for many.

ᴌᴐ

The Hawaiian trip went smoothly. On his return Nicol rushed to Columbia for a quick trip to update the South American film. While on tour that winter Nicol had two new experiences. His first was a television presentation of the Angel Falls film "Venezuela Venture." From his parents home in Burlingame at The Crossroads to Anne's winter quarters in Nassau, Bahamas, he received word the show was a success. The following years brought Nicol's movies to television again and again.

During the lecture circuit, Nicol received word his Aunt Myrtle Smith Emrick had passed away in Pennsylvania. Changing his schedule, he went to his cousin Elizabeth's in Thorndale. After attending the service, he continued on his circuit. It was the first funeral Nicol had ever attended.

Unfortunately for Nicol, the next years of his adulthood brought the deaths of several loved ones. Armar Archbold, Moira's oldest brother, died in Scotland while celebrating after announcing his engagement to the Countess of Seafield, reputedly one of the wealthiest women in that country. Armar, only a year older than Nicol, had been the first boy Nicol met when he settled in at Choate in 1925. The death devastated Anne. Only a few years before her home in Bar Harbor had burned to the ground. The two tragedies were more than the eighty-four year old woman could bear. She never seemed to recover from the death of her eldest son. Anne remained quiet and withdrawn for the remainder of her life.

Nicol's travels continued. His next filming venture was to capture the islands of the Caribbean, including Barbados, Dominica, Trinidad and Antigua. The film covered all the islands in the British Caribbean Federation, the first nation to come into being on the doorstep of the U.S. since Panama in 1906.

Incorporating his lecture circuit on the Caribbean with a trip to England, Nicol presented his latest movie to the Royal Geographic Society, which was followed by a trip through Scotland for new material. After three weeks in Scotland in miserable weather, he returned to the states to continue his engagements. He had promised his parents he would be home in time to attend their fiftieth wedding anniversary in June.

Sue retired from her column writing at the *Examiner* on May 1, 1958, and planned to spend lazy days with her husband. Her health was poor and often she had not been able to leave her bed. Instead she had been writing her column with the help of friends and family. Her last column was a tribute to all she had to be thankful for:

> On this day, perhaps as never before, I count my blessings, for it has been a trying year, but, as so often, God's mysterious way has given me time to think over the many things I might otherwise have taken for granted.
>
> On this day I am thankful that I can see the beauty of the world from my window, even though I must see it from my bed. I can hear the music, thanks to the radio, when I am not able to attend the opera or a symphony. I can hear the song of the birds.
>
> I give thanks for returning health after severe and long

illness, and am thankful that I can experience the joy of living.

I am thankful for the many friends who cheered and comforted me during hours of trial, and who have shared my joy and sorrow.

I am grateful for the contentment that abides in my heart today; and for solitude at times when in quiet meditation I can realize what we have to give thanks for: the health of a husband; the safety of a son; a comprehension of the needs of the little people of the world, and a feeling of sympathy and pity for those less fortunate; a desire to assist in any way possible.

A deep sense of gratitude for the goodness that has given me the care and devotion of Ruth Schwab, who for the past eight months has untiringly worked to nurse me back to the health I have gained.

May the Giver of all good gifts bless us, each and every one, and may our thanks strengthen our resolution to recognize the blessings and be worthy of them.[3]

The thoughts of this column caught friends and family members by surprise. The ever suave, society savvy Sue Smith appeared to rarely contemplate life. Her son alone knew of the hardship she suffered as the Smith fortune dwindled and her health began to fail. As a woman of spirit she never allowed the difficult times to dishearten her zest for life nor dampen her vivacious personality.

Sue retired after more than twenty years of gallant reporting about the most colorful and fascinating members of society, whether local or abroad. Not only had her son contributed as a columnist, but also her friends Barbara Hutton, the Woolworth heiress, Elsa Maxwell, her close friend who years before used the Smith home for her parties and Noël Coward, the English playwright, composer and actor.

Writing a personal letter to an associate in San Francisco, Sue shared the news that her doctor had encouraged her to retire for the past year:

Dr. McLaughlin has thought for the past year the tension was injurious to my breathing and I should give up the job.

The paper offered me a job of sending in three articles a week, but after thinking it over I have concluded to retire.

> I have only the greatest feeling of kindness towards all I
> have come in contact with on the paper. They have been more
> than kind and I will miss the contacts.[4]

The golden anniversary celebration was a success. All their friends from more than thirty-eight years in Burlingame joined them at the country club to celebrate with their son.

Sue's retirement was short as she passed away six months later on January 2, 1959. Seventy-three years old, she was renowned as a grande dame of San Francisco and peninsula society. Her career of writing started after a brief stint in moving pictures. In 1930, Douglas Fairbanks, the popular star of silent films who founded the independent studio, United Artists, approached Sue and asked her to consider entering the acting profession. She consented and was cast in her first movie. After a private viewing of that first attempt, she declined a film career.

Sue first attracted Hearst's attention with her amusing and articulate storytelling when she visited his castle at San Simeon. Throughout her life Sue distinguished herself by her rollicking sense of humor and her varied interests.

Herb Caen graciously wrote his condolences to Nicol:

> Please accept my deep sympathy on the loss of your won-
> derful mother, whose friendliness, charm and tremendous spirit
> I will never forget. She will live on in the hearts of all of us
> who had the privilege of knowing her.[5]

Herb Caen and Sue both wrote for the *Examiner* during the fifties. While Herb evoked the history and atmosphere of daily events in San Francisco in his column, Sue had captured the lives and the wit of society.

R.H. was not living at home at the time of Sue's death. He was at a tuberculosis sanitarium. Although it was later discovered that R.H. did not have tuberculosis, his poor health, along with extreme weight loss, led his doctor to believe he was suffering from the disease. It was a number of months before R.H. returned home.

The following August, R.H. finally went back to The Crossroads. The house seemed empty without Sue's vivacious personality to fill the silent rooms. He despaired when it was discovered that many of her personal articles were missing. By contacting Nicol, he learned that several items were in his care, but the remaining jewelry, clothing and perfume had disappeared shortly after Sue's death.

Nicol previously neglected to mention the removal of his mother's belongings to prevent his father from becoming unduly upset. From the cook he learned that his aunt and uncle, Sue's brother and his wife, had come to the house and taken Sue's valuables for supposed safekeeping. Nicol wrote to his uncle requesting all items be returned before R.H. arrived home in late August. Nicol's uncle neglected to return the articles.

R.H. was livid. In a letter to his brother-in-law he expressed his anger:

> I returned from the sanitarium on Wednesday in far better health.... As evidence of my remarkable recovery I now weigh 160 lb. against 136 lb. upon entering the hospital. As far as I know I am home for good....
>
> This letter is to advise you to prepare, at once, a detailed statement or inventory of every article taken from this house, excluding wearing apparel such as dresses, shoes, hats and lingerie. As to these items I wish to know exactly what your wife will be using for her own personal use. Such was not given to your wife except for her own personal use. Any wearing apparel not being used by your wife is not to be given away, traded or bartered. Any disposition of these items will be at my discretion.
>
> You mentioned in your letter to Nicol the reason articles were taken by you is that otherwise they would have fallen into strange hands.
>
> From the looks of things I am going to be around for quite some time; that being the case, I am still in a position to enjoy the treasures that surrounded me prior to my sojourn in the hospital.
>
> After the overwhelming grief I experienced during my early days at the hospital and sanitarium, I would have thought that if either you or your wife had any appreciation of past favors extended you by me, I would have at least received a post card from you.
>
> Lack of appreciation on the part of you both relieves me from any future consideration that would have been given you both.[6]

R.H. not only wanted Sue's possessions returned but also a list of personal items they were using. He disinherited both of them.

Nicol arrived five days later and solicited the retrieval of his mother's jewelry. He had written John Archbold prior to his father's return home to say he planned to dispose of his mother's pieces of jewelry and art objects at reasonable prices. "If father remains ill or returns to home, [from the sanitarium] I will be able to see him through with the sales from mother's belongings." One of the first pieces of jewelry Nicol sold went to Lydia, John's eldest sister, for $4,500. Continued sales of Sue's jewelry allowed R.H. to live in comfort and pursue his financial business endeavors, many of which Nicol had no knowledge.

Nicol worried about his father staying at The Crossroads alone but was unable to convince him to sell and move to a cottage at the Burlingame Country Club. The only solution was to hire a companion for R.H. During the winter lecture circuit Nicol met a man that would stay with R.H. and who later became Nicol's assistant.

Bill Greene was a drifter. Moving from job to job he had difficulty making a living because he lacked a particular skill and he had lost his left hand in an accident. Nicol needed a temporary driver as he crossed Missouri that winter. He met Bill who seemed eager for employment. He even offered to help with R.H. if Nicol could pay his way to California. Nicol consented and Bill began his thirty years of employment with the Smith family.

∽

One previous winter Nicol had been introduced to a lovely lady who lived on Oconomowoc Lake west of Milwaukee. He visited her as frequently as his career allowed. Each winter while in Milwaukee, Wisconsin, he planned to stay several days with Marion A. Tallmadge. She was the heiress to the Schlitz beer fortune.

His last visit had been during a winter circuit when he and his driver, John Timossi, passed through Milwaukee. During dinner, Nicol, Marion and John were interrupted by her son. Demanding to speak to his mother, he claimed he immediately required $80,000 for a business venture. Marion excused him, promising to attend to the matter later.

Marion and Nicol became close during his visits to her home and her occasional visits to Burlingame. She planned to come to the river during the summer, but never made the trip. She died in a fire that consumed a wing of her home. The San Francisco newspapers included a short article about the strange death:

> Mystery continues to baffle Milwaukee officials investigating the death by fire of Mrs. Marion A. Tallmadge, who had many friends in this area. She was a great friend of Nicol Smith and was entertained by the Sheldon Coopers and the Francis Martin Jr's., when she spent some time at the Burlingame Country Club in 1955.
>
> The body of the 49 year old heiress to the Schlitz beer fortune was found in the burning ruins of her 25 room home....
>
> The fire broke out shortly after Mrs. Tallmadge had returned home from an evening with friends that had included a Milwaukee Braves baseball game. Her servants slept through it in their quarters, and so did her son, David, and his wife in a separate house.
>
> Only one wing was left standing in the house and that contained a small arsenal, consisting of 49 machine guns, thousands of rounds of ammunition, 100 pounds of dynamite and two cases of gunpowder.
>
> They belonged to her son David, who told authorities he was licensed as a gun manufacturer.
>
> What the fate of firemen battling the blaze would have been if it had reached the arsenal is awful to imagine. There seems to be no connection between the arms cache and the fire, but the investigation of what started it is still continuing and friends here are following it with interest.[7]

Nicol followed the newspaper accounts of the ensuing investigation. By contacting Marion's friends he was kept abreast of new findings. Nicol was never satisfied with the outcome as the mystery remained unsolved. Writing to his cousin Elizabeth Smith Knauer in Pennsylvania several years later, Nicol confided his true feelings. Marion was the only woman he had considered marrying after his divorce. Prior to her death, they had discussed their future together. Marion's unfortunate passing left Nicol forlorn. He longed for companionship and love:

I am doing 180 shows this year plus the TV, so I keep solvent and enjoy my life. Frankly Elizabeth, if I didn't work, I wouldn't know what to do with myself. If Mrs. Tallmadge had not been killed in the fire a few years ago and we had married, I could have settled down. I guess now that I will go on until I drop.[8]

His gracious friends around the world could not make up for the love he had felt for Moira and later for Marion. Marriage never again entered his plans except for an occasional longing to mend his relationship with Moira.

Women of fame and fortune repeatedly appeared in Nicol's social circle. Nicol's attraction to rich women began early in life. His first female friends included Barbara Hutton, the Woolworth's store heiress who was considered the richest woman in the U.S., his mother's friend, Elsa Maxwell, Marlene Dietrich, the actress he occasionally escorted in San Francisco during the thirties, and many other well-known and often well-to-do women. Then Moira, an heiress to Standard Oil millions, brought not only her wealth to their marriage but also the generosity of her mother to Nicol, which continued even after their divorce. Now Marion Tallmadge, heiress to the Schlitz Beer fortune, had attracted Nicol. Nicol consciously decided to forget the idea of remarrying.

Money was never a topic of discussion that Nicol shared with others. He worked hard and managed his finances with distinct ability. He was exceptionally generous with close women friends but his spending was never lavish. Nicol's earnings during his career never amounted to any great fortune. The money he had he preferred to use to entertain in style at his rustic Lashio Lodge, rather than to accumulate the usual material trappings of the upper class.

But Nicol's career was aided and enhanced through the generosity of the Archbold women. Moira repeatedly financed parts of the trips, mainly the two she accompanied him on, and she purchased the Willys jeep for the Venezuela expedition. Year after year, Anne provided funds for much needed film and photography equipment. Without their help Nicol's travels may not have taken place as often or for such extensive trips. Moira may have felt unhappy about her husband's absences, but lack of finances could have kept him home.

Would Nicol have settled down in marriage to Marion as he mentioned in his letter to his cousin? It is doubtful he really understood the reality of what he confided to cousin Elizabeth. Nicol never knew permanence of location. His life had always been on the move. Although he probably wanted to settle down, it would be safe to assume he would have longed to travel again before much time passed.

The events of the months after his mother's death prevented Nicol from leaving his father's side for more than a short period abroad to New Zealand to make a new film. Now Nicol and Art planned an extensive trip to Australia to complete their next film.

Through the Qantas Airways Limited office in San Francisco, Nicol met Hugh and Margery Birch who provided him with many ideas and introductions for the trip. As the planning progressed, Charles Nichols, an old friend from Choate, contacted Nicol. He hoped to send his daughter abroad to travel and develop her ability with photography. Nicol graciously invited Joan Nichols to accompany him and to work as a still photographer. Joan, twenty-four years old, belonged to a wealthy New York chemical family, was thrilled at the chance to go abroad with a noted traveler and lecturer such as Nicol Smith. Educated at Cambridge, Joan was an intelligent woman and an excellent traveling companion.

Art departed first for Australia to make transportation and tour arrangements. Nicol joined him in April. The new movie would begin in Sydney and feature its Harbour Bridge which spanned 1,650 feet, the world's largest arch bridge. They continued on to Canberra, Melbourne, and the Healesville Sanctuary, the home of kangaroos, emus, koala bears and platypuses. Next they visited the Great Barrier Reef near Green Island and exotic Whitsunday's Brampton Island where coral abounded in fantastic shapes and colors. The largest coral reef in the world, off the east coast of Queensland, provided Art with a sanctuary for photography experimentation.

Art's ingenious ability to visualize and then construct almost anything made it possible for Nicol to produce the first underwater travel movie. Before leaving home, Art created a plexiglas container that could hold his movie camera. Loading the film in the camera, he then placed the camera in the clear, water-tight container, replaced the trap-door and carefully tightened the clo-sure to prevent leakage. With only rudimentary control of the camera's functions he was able to film the Great Barrier Reef from underwater.

Leaving Perth, they traveled to the interior town of Alice Springs in the Northern Territory and on to Ayers Rock, a natu-ral monolith containing an estimated 500 million tons of stone, rising from the plains in lonely majesty. Nicol photographed the superb sunrises and sunsets from their deserted location. Art and Joan climbed to the top of the 2,850 foot rock under the relentless sun with forty pounds of cameras and tripods. Nicol enjoyed the view from halfway up.

Back in Alice Springs they rented a car and drove to Anningie Station in the Outback to visit Tony Chisholm, the godson of the Duke of Windsor, and Judy Chisholm, on their 1,700 square mile ranch. During the drive, the wildlife intrigued Nicol. Wild donkeys, pigs and boars, along with buffalo, kangaroos and walla-bies, abounded. Rolls of film were taken of the animals. At the Healesville Sanctuary more film was shot of emus, koala bears and platypuses. From the northern city of Darwin, Art, Nicol and Joan traveled with an outback hunter, Clem Hill, and the incomparable native tracker of the Northern Territory, Munjunga. There they filmed wild water buffalo. Crossing the remote fron-tier region in a Land Rover, Nicol was entranced by the beauty of the sparsely populated region.

Surfing scenes concluded the chronicle of their five-month journey that covered 12,000 miles by plane and 7,000 by car. Nearly each day Nicol wrote to his friends Hugh and Margery in Sydney to thank them for their many introductions that aided his trip. Several years later, Nicol wrote to Hugh and Margery about the incredible success of his Australian film. "Australia is now out in front as our all time most popular film. It goes right along like a trust fund."[9]

Rome, the Eternal City, beckoned Nicol as the subject for his next film venture. Leaving the states in late March at the con-clusion of the lecture circuit, Art and Nicol planned to spend eight weeks traveling and filming in Rome.

Situated on both banks of the Tiber River was one of the richest cities in the world in history and art. Rome was a great cultural, religious, and intellectual center. Three wide meanders of the Tiber, spanned by many bridges, intersected the city. The smaller part of the city lay on the right bank and contained Vatican City. On the left bank was the "center" of Rome, the Piazza Venezia.

Nicol had not been to Italy since his first travels on the Odyssey Tour in 1929. Rome, except for the suburbs, remained virtually undamaged by World War II. The Germans had occupied the city for nine months before U.S. troops took the city on June 4, 1944. Postwar years witnessed a remarkable economic, artistic, and intellectual revival. Pope Pius XII designated 1950 a holy year and Rome received many thousands of pilgrims.

The new filming progressed without difficulty. Nicol and Art captured the history, the art and modern day Rome in their work. They visited the beautiful Vatican City on Easter Sunday and witnessed the Pope and cardinals venerating a new saint. The most famous fountains of Rome, the Trevi, the Naiads and the Fountain of the Rivers were photographed. They moved on to the Colosseum, the Roman Forum and the Arch of Constantine and the Quirinal Palace.

Reel two of the film included the story of Bulgari, one of the finest jewelers in Europe. Displays of millions of dollars worth of gems were pictured. The audience also saw the secrets of cutting and polishing of priceless jewels. Water sports and soccer were followed by a visit to the home of a Roman family, to a crowded supermarket and the most famous restaurants.

Rome was going to be a difficult movie for the lecture circuit. The following winter Nicol wrote to Anne:

> Rome was a difficult lecture to get in order. There is so much history to cover with dates to remember. I was a little fast with the narration at first but now have weeded out the extra words and have slowed down to the right length.[10]

Not only would the lecture material on Rome later prove to be rigorous, Nicol's departure from Rome was delayed due to an unexpected situation. Eight days before his departure for home in the middle of May, Nicol was stricken with a heart attack. The summer of movie editing and house parties at Lashio Lodge was canceled. A month later he was still in the Salvator Mundi International Hospital recovering from the heart attack when he suffered severe pneumonia followed by phlebitis. Nicol remained in the hospital for a total of nine weeks. It seemed like a lifetime.

During the hospital internment, R.H. passed away at The Crossroads in Burlingame. At the time, Nicol's condition was so critical the Italian doctors did not want to inform him of the news until his condition stabilized.

The situation at the hospital became grimly ludicrous when the Italian doctors insisted Nicol's health could not bear the bad news from California. Art's responsibilities included keeping the news from the patient. As Nicol's closest friends in California planned R.H.'s services, letters began to arrive telling of the arrangements.

Art's insistence on breaking the news did not budge the doctors. Their modern medical practices saved Nicol's life but their medieval beliefs kept his father's death a secret for three weeks. Finally Art's practicality won over the medical staff. He could no longer keep the influx of letters away from the patient. Nicol wanted to read them himself after Art patiently finished each letter, reading aloud while carefully altering the facts to hide R.H.'s death. Nicol had to be told.

Nicol accepted the news of his father's death from Art with anguish. Knowing the gravity of his own situation did not help matters. He slumped back on the pillows with tears in his eyes.

Three weeks after his heart attack, writing from his hospital bed to his cousin Elizabeth in Pennsylvania, Nicol filled her in on the seriousness of his illness and the passing of his father:

> I was stricken with a coronary in the middle of May. This was followed by phlebitis and pneumonia on June 13. I almost passed out of the picture on the night of the 13th. A team of nurses and doctors worked over me all that night. By morning I was better, but not well enough to hear about father. The doctors would not allow me to be told until this past Monday.
>
> That is why you did not hear from me; I did not know it myself.

On June 13, father, who was very worried over my condition, wrote me his last letter. It was dictated as he could no longer see well enough to write. He was to die in his sleep early on the morning of the 15th. Father went in his sleep with a smile on his face and his fifteen pound cat sleeping on the bed. His poodle, Cloud, his faithful companion was nearby.

Father had been to the city with his driver, Bill [Greene], the day before and it was the driver who discovered that he had passed on when he took him his breakfast at 9:00 A.M.

It seems that when trouble comes it arrives in liberal doses.[11]

His letter to Elizabeth continued with his feelings on his father's life:

Father had a long life and in his later years he lived it the way he wanted to with his Bible, his pets and his rose garden to keep him busy. He was active to the end.[12]

Nicol remained in the hospital for ten more days, totaling nine weeks in all. He lost thirty-two pounds and was still suffering from phlebitis in both legs. Art returned home to start working on the movie while Nicol traveled by ship, leaving Italy on July 20. It was a slow and leisurely trip.

By early August Nicol was back at Lashio Lodge after a week visiting various doctors and specialists in Burlingame and looking into the status of R.H.'s estate. The affairs of his father were in disarray since R.H. had never prepared a will. R.H.'s longtime friend, Dave Ratto, and the family lawyer, Sheldon Cooper, were busy straightening out his business interests, investments and inventions. The only immediate inheritance was R.H.'s desire that his chauffeur, cook and companion, Bill Greene, be kept in the employment of the family. Nicol willingly conceded.

BOOK SEVEN:

THE DUSK OF ADVENTURE

We are a kindred soul of an ilk fast
disappearing.... Sometimes I hear a
voice, and packing my gladstone bag,
I try to follow it to the ends of the
earth.

Barnaby Conrad
Letter to Nicol Smith
Written from Thorvale Farm
Williamstown, Massachusetts

24

FROM MOROCCO TO ALASKA

Nicol's ordeal in the hospital in Rome temporarily slowed him down. He spent the summer recovering at Lashio Lodge but fall brought another rigorous lecture season.

Without servants hired for the summer, guests were minimal. Virginia cooked for Art and Nicol as they worked on their new movie *Eternal Rome* and Nicol slept and relaxed in the sun during the remaining hours hoping to recover from the phlebitis before starting back to work.

Moira and a friend were not deterred by the lack of servants and paid Nicol a visit during August. While Nicol was in the hospital in Rome, Moira had an operation for a tumor in her throat. It was benign and she recovered quickly. Worried about Nicol, she spent several days visiting him at Lashio Lodge.

Chile was the destination for the next season. Art departed before Nicol to arrange transportation and to begin filming the countryside. When Nicol arrived, they started filming in the far northern region of Chile. Nicol remained along the Pacific Coast while Art worked in the high country. Nicol's doctor had suggested he avoid the high altitudes of the mountainous areas.

The filmmaking began in the village of Putre at 11,000 feet in northern Chile near the Peruvian and Bolivian borders with scenes of llamas and alpacas. They filmed panoramas of the seaside and port cities, the Nevados de Payachata, the two snow-capped peaks of more than twenty thousand feet on the Bolivian border to the southernmost tip of the country. The two men captured the entire country from north to south.

The newest technique used in their filming was shooting scenes from a helicopter. Art captured breathtaking views from his lofty advantage while Nicol waited, content to remain on the ground. From the Atacama Desert, with regions where rain had never been recorded in the history of man, to Puerto Williams, the world's southernmost town, the people, their stories and their livelihoods were all captured on film.

This trip was one of Nicol's shortest. He originally intended to update his previously made South American films on Argentina and Peru, but he reconsidered and created an entirely new film just on Chile.

Enroute to Chile Nicol visited Anne at her home in Nassau. He was amazed at how well the eighty-nine year-old woman was doing. He spent several days with her fishing from her yacht, always a favorite sport. Before leaving, Nicol agreed she would be the first to see his new film the following season.

Thanksgiving brought Nicol to Hillandale in Georgetown. All of the Archbold family assembled to celebrate Anne's ninetieth birthday. Nicol's gift was a preview of his film *Chile*. Anne's interest in Nicol's profession had not wavered since his lecture, years before in Nassau. when he announced his engagement to Moira. Now twenty-five years and hundreds of lectures later, Anne didn't miss a detail of Nicol's presentation. It was the best birthday gift she ever received.

A few months later Nicol wrote to Anne of his successes with the latest film. More than twelve thousand attended the show in three lectures in Grand Rapids, Michigan alone. He had spent a total of two weeks in Michigan presenting show after show often with multiple lectures in an evening. He was headed to Pittsburgh for seven lectures in three days at the Carnegie Institute and then on to Washington, D.C., for two lectures for National Geographic at Constitution Hall. He was setting records that winter with up to nine shows per week.[1] Next, he completed a week-long filming session for television. Art and Virginia returned to Peru to work on television material for Nicol.

The *Paris of the Sahara*, aptly named by Winston Churchill, attracted Nicol for his next venture. At Marrakech, the Moroccan city at the foot of the Atlas Mountains, Art and Nicol prepared for an adventure that would take them through Morocco and Algeria.

Picking up the new, red Volkswagen Kombe in Casablanca that Nicol ordered, Art outfitted it as Nicol made contacts and planned their trip. Traveling seven thousand kilometers, they went as far south as the frontier military outpost of Goulimine and east to Fort Miribel in Algeria on the trans-Sahara auto route.

Nicol's interest was piqued by the supposed "Blue People" of the little country of Ifai. Traveling across the Sahara in their bright red car, he and Art were welcomed by the unusual tribe. They recorded the songs and music of the blue-robed people. Referred to as the *Blue People of the Sahara*, Nicol and Art discovered their hands and faces were the color of their cotton robes. The dye continuously rubbed off their garb until everyone had a bluish cast to their skin.

From the capital Rabat, where they filmed the king of the country, to the Atlas Mountains and the Sahara, the largest desert on earth, Nicol captured the excitement of another region. Filming the people, their music, costumes and culture, he succeeded in making another record-setting production.

Winter started with twenty-eight shows in Hawaii, including audiences of twenty thousand school children. Writing to his cousin Elizabeth Nicol shared his feelings on Morocco:

> Morocco was one of the best trips ever and we covered it from north to south. It was full of marvels, strange blue people, tree-climbing goats and the camel border patrol in the Sahara.[2]

It had taken Nicol more than a year to feel fully recovered from his illnesses in Rome, although his schedule remained unchanged. The Chile venture may have been prematurely attempted, but in Morocco he thoroughly enjoyed all aspects of his travel.

The plans for the next year were precarious. Nicol had been invited to return to Africa and make a film of Uganda. He had previously planned to return to Kashmir and venture into Nepal. Uganda sounded interesting to Nicol but he had always felt that region of Africa was not novel material for U.S. or British audiences. Nicol did not pursue the opportunity and he never returned to Africa.

He was also never to revisit Kashmir. Planning a trip to the Indian states of Kashmir and Sikkim, the latter close to where he trained in the Naga Hills during World War II, and the country of Nepal, Nicol's farewell lunch just days before his departure went smoothly. Unfortunately, the permissions necessary to enter each country were not finalized. Approval was given for Kashmir, but Sikkim, an independent state of India bordered by Tibet and Nepal, required a detailed list of every movement and filming he had planned.

Nicol stayed at John Archbold's and went to work. He specified distances, locations and film content. A week after turning in his itinerary, he was "uninvited" to Kashmir. Then a week later, approval was given for all areas, except he could not leave before May 15. Nicol gave up in frustration. The late departure date would force him to attempt the Nepal segment of the journey during the monsoon season. He was afraid of arriving in Delhi only to find out permissions had been changed again.

With the change in plans, the next season's sponsors had to be notified. Most of the sponsors accepted the change, while a few dropped his booking. They wanted a remote subject from the East. This became impossible as all professional travelers were having difficulty in obtaining the necessary formal authorizations for that area of the globe. During Nicol's career, this was the only trip he canceled that hurt his lecture bookings.

During the planning of the second trip to Kashmir, Nicol presented a proposal to his publisher, Bobbs-Merrill, to reprint his book *Golden Doorway to Tibet*. The publisher responded that they needed a guarantee for five thousand copies in order to return their expenses for the reprint. Nicol would need to pay for all printing expenses for the second edition. After removing all the pictures from the book, the resulting cost would be eighty cents per copy.

Nicol was basing his plan for a new edition on his experience from earlier lectures. His earlier Kashmir lecture series had facilitated the sale of *Into Siam Underground Kingdom* his currently published book. At that time, he wrote to his editor asking that the production of *Golden Doorway to Tibet* be stepped up. He was selling a book about his previous experiences during a new lecture topic. He wondered how many new books he might sell if it were ready.

Unfortunately *Golden Doorway to Tibet* was not released in

time for his winter circuit. By the next year, the public's interest waned, plus, his film was stolen. Now Nicol did not want to provide the upfront funding for republishing the book. Plans for a new edition were abandoned, as was the trip.

Nicol's writing career ceased with the end of his adventure travels. The limited success of his last books and the new travelog format of his expeditions had not lent itself to his style of a written narrative of unusual events and travels. Now, after ten years devoted only to travel, lecture and television, Nicol attempted to write again.

Desiring to write fiction, Nicol struggled with several unsuccessful attempts. Resorting to nonfiction about his travels in Morocco, he finally mailed a manuscript to Lois Stewart at Bobbs-Merrill. She forwarded it on to the New York editor.

Nicol titled the manuscript *Granny Was No Hellion*. It prompted a return letter from Lois:

> Lack of time prevented my reading *Granny was no Hellion* all the way through, although I did read chapters here and there. And I enjoyed it but, frankly, I can't see a hard bound market large enough to warrant the production cost, and come out even faintly in the black.
>
> You know that I am no critic, however, and of course I sent the book on to our New York editor on November 12th....
>
> You say she is a grandmother? And that it is <u>her</u> picture in the front of the script? Well, I must say that grandmothers are getting younger all the time![3]

The book chronicled the highlights of the Morocco excursion and centered on the story of a Madame Goddilot, a remarkable lady of eighty who appeared to be in her late thirties. She fascinated Nicol and appeared as youthful on film as she had in person. Nicol speculated she had found what Ponce de Leon was unable to locate, the elusive fountain of youth.

A book was not forthcoming and Nicol's copy of the manuscript was misplaced. Unable to locate his last writing effort and with no further letters from Bobbs-Merrill discussing the manuscript, it is impossible to determine what his editor thought of his last writing attempt.

Nicol substituted the proposed trip for the following year in place of the ill-fated preparations for Nepal, Kashmir and Sikkim. Plans were quickly laid and Art and Nicol left for the Mediterranean.

Malta, Sardinia, Corsica and Majorca, the vacation islands of the Mediterranean, provided abundant material. The history, underwater photography, pirate treasures and enchanting scenery enveloped the two men for nearly a month.

In 1966 Nicol again decided to forgo attempting a trip to Kashmir. A discussion with Hugh Birch of Qantas Airways Limited during a visit to Lashio Lodge introduced a new area to Nicol. Qantas featured Nicol's films, particularly on areas they serviced. The airline would willingly exchange their interest in a Kashmir picture for a film featuring Iran. Nicol and Art spent the summer creating *Persian Panorama-Iran Today*.

Eight hours before his return flight from Iran enroute to Australia to visit the Birches, Nicol suffered his first accident abroad. He broke his foot on a Moslem holiday when no doctors were available. He cabled his friends in Australia about his dilemma and managed to get aboard the plane. Margery and Hugh met Nicol at the airport with a wheelchair and whisked him off to a hospital to have the broken bone set.

Arriving home, Nicol learned Art's 1,300 pound horse Slugger had thrown him resulting in several broken ribs and a compound fracture of the left foot. Movie editing was delayed and entertaining canceled as Nicol took two more falls attempting to maneuver on crutches between his houses on the river. Badly shaken, he wrote notes of regret to his fifty-two friends who were planning to spend weekends at Lashio Lodge that summer.

Work on the movie would have to come later. Writing to John Archbold, Nicol shared his plans:

> I hope both you and your sister, Lydia, will come to visit next summer. I have written her as I have fifty-two other friends. I would be a lousy host and I don't think I could get around well enough to make the weekend go.
>
> It is most fortunate that we were a year ahead with the pictures and we will not release Iran until '67-'68.
> Next year, I plan on doing the 'Charm of Old Vienna' which should be much easier than Iran.[4]

Vienna didn't happen the next year and never was a subject for a movie. Instead, Ireland, an area Nicol also considered less rigorous than previous trips, was the topic for a new film, and the following year he returned to the South Seas to film Fiji, Western Samoa and Tonga.

The rigorous schedules of the lecture circuits and the winter weather were beginning to wear on Nicol. Fortunately, Bill Greene remained as his loyal chauffeur and projectionist throughout each winter series and Art was able to spend the winters with his family. Writing to Anne, Nicol's letters began to focus on the difficulties of winter travel:

> It has been a most difficult lecture season. We were in Chicago for the storm of the century. A journey of some three hours turned into 300 miles due to a detour caused by the adverse weather.... In St. Louis we experienced a tornado. Minnesota and Wisconsin gave us thirty-one degrees below zero and Michigan was paralyzed with three blizzards during our sojourn. Even Richmond, Virginia had a severe ice storm on the evening of our second performance.[5]

Nicol's thoughts began to turn toward retirement. But what would he do? His mountain home was not suitable for year-round occupancy, yet he had no place else to live. He usually spent the holidays with his closest friends in Burlingame and San Francisco. Many of them anticipated traveling as an exciting pastime to pursue following retirement. Nicol couldn't fathom extensive traveling after retiring.

ᴗᴈ

Anne Archbold, the foremost supporter of Nicol's career, passed away at her home in Nassau in April of 1968. The previous Thanksgiving Nicol presented her with *Persian Panorama-Iran Today* in the music room at Hillandale in Georgetown. He felt tremendous grief when informed of her death. He would miss the ardent enthusiasm she always expressed for his profession.

Ninety-five years old, she had been fishing on her yacht two days before her death. Nicol and her three remaining children, Lydia, John and Moira, gathered from around the world to wish a farewell at a private luncheon and memorial service at Hillandale. Nicol had lost his favorite comrade of adventure.

With reluctance Nicol planned another trip. Tonga interested Nicol. He learned that the paradise island had witnessed its last act of cannibalism in 1905. Filming began with a sequence on the King of Tonga and closed with scenes of eight thousand children marching past the winter palace of the same king. In Western Samoa Nicol was the guest of the head of state, Malietoa Tanumal II, who lived in the mansion, Vailima, that had once belonged to Robert Louis Stevenson.

The movie was spellbinding. It captured the firewalkers of Mbengga, a volcanic island of six by four miles belonging to Fiji. Next came a huge fish drive on the island of Serva, where the fish are driven into a pool closed off by a chain of braided palm leaves.

Nicol and Art lived on a yacht, spending each night in a sheltered bay and swimming during the day from beaches of fine white sand. The Yasawa Islands, a forty-five mile long string of sixteen islands, intrigued Nicol. A New Zealander and captain of the yacht, Trevor Withers, shared the secrets of the islands with Art's cameras. The largest of the islands was ten miles long and one mile wide. The men stayed in native huts perched at the edge of the Pacific and fished among the inlets. Nicol enjoyed the South Pacific immensely and began to plan his next excursion. The trip to Bali was postponed at the last moment when Art, walking to the beach from his home in Santa Monica, California, was hit by a motorist. A fractured vertebrae and foot delayed the trip.

The following year was uneventful and Nicol and Art reached their destination of Bali, Java, Sumatra and Komodo Islands in the Indian Ocean. The highlight of the trip was to take place on Komodo Island. Flying from Bali to Bima on the island of Sumbawa in the lesser Sunda Islands, they traveled fifty miles by jeep across primitive country to the jumping off place for Komodo Island. The twelve-hour sailing trip, aboard a primitive vessel that resembled a pirate ship, turned into sixty-four hours of drifting in the Indian Ocean because of the lack of a breeze. Finally the destination was reached and camp was set on a crescent-shaped, desolate beach.

The Oras, as the Komodo dragon is called by the natives, could be found on the island. The world's largest lizards, the ten-foot-long, 250 pound Komodo were creatures of awe and considerable mystery. They existed on only four remote Indonesian islands, which had been so difficult to reach that few people and even fewer biologists had seen the monitors in the wild, thus the mystery that surrounded the name Komodo.

A dead goat was placed in a gully as bait in hopes of attracting the mysterious Komodo. Barely half an hour later the first of the lizards appeared. Art and Nicol were only thirty-nine feet from the largest of their actors, who were eight feet in length and nearly three hundred pounds in weight, as they captured the Komodo on film:

> We saw five lizards in all in two different areas. They crawl on squat, powerful legs that propel these extraordinary reptiles with remarkable speed. With their python shaped heads and long, yellow-orange tongues I watched them tearing the meat from the dead goats. It was easy to believe that the very large ones can consume a dear [sic] or wild boar....[6]

Writing to John Archbold later that fall, Nicol told him the Bali film was complete. The two most impressive Komodo dragons were in the final film:

> The new Bali film is cut and in order. This was one of the most fascinating trips I have ever had and the visit to Komodo, the dragon island, a high spot of my life.[7]

The next spring Nicol rented an apartment in London. Art and Virginia accompanied him, spending more than two months making a feature movie of the city, its history and social life. The blustery weather delayed filming and made it necessary for Nicol to extend his stay until July. The film featured personalities from the Earl of Sandwich, Princess Margaret, Prince Charles, to Gregory Peck and even Frank Sinatra.

Following the completion of *Swinging Old London*, Nicol planned only one more movie. Art left for Alaska while Nicol completed the lecture circuit. Late in the spring of 1973, Nicol joined Art in the last American wilderness.

From Dawson Creek and the Gold Rush country they traveled Alaska witnessing the events of a region with long winters and short summers. They waited for the breaking up of the ice at the village of Nenana on the Tanana River. Each year thousands of dollars comprised the kitty of the "Ice Classic," the wager placed on the date and time the ice would break each spring. Bored with the seemingly endless vista of ice and snow and tired of shivering through their parkas, a railroad construction crew in 1917 took over the previously unofficial guessing game of when the ice would break. Nicol recorded the event that had become so popular that over 200,000 tickets were sold at a dollar each.

Art followed the Iditarod Trail Race from beginning to end, while Nicol met the local people and listened to the story about the race. It honored the memory of Leonard Seppala, a famous dog team driver, who in 1920 with his Siberians took part in a highly publicized dog team relay carrying antitoxin to diphtheria-stricken Nome. Flying over the dog sleds, Art captured scenes from every stage of the 1,063-mile race.

Living in a sod house built around the jaw bone from a whale, they spent three days at Point Hope on the Chuckchi Sea. The annual whale hunt was an event worth the adverse conditions they endured. Snow, driven by the wind, pelted Art and Nicol that blustery June day. Nicol's clothing was inadequate for the snowy June weather. He received warm clothes from the local missionaries in return for a twenty dollar contribution. For their simple abode with no running water he was paying forty dollars a night.

Alaska Journey was made over a five month period, requiring two separate visits to the great land of ice and snow. That summer Lashio Lodge and the sunshine never looked better to Nicol.

25

MEXICO WINTERS

The Alaska expedition concluded Nicol and Art's filming of adventure and travel. They edited their last movie as Nicol began to think about easing into retirement. The previous two winters found Nicol on the coast of Mexico relaxing for a month during the strenuous lecture circuit. He rented a large bungalow a few miles from Manzanillo on the Pacific Ocean between Puerto Vallarta and Acapulco. Accompanied by his chauffeur Bill and his Lashio Lodge cook's younger sister, Bernice, they drove together from Burlingame to the Mexican retreat each January.

In a letter to the Birches in Australia, Nicol described his paradise:

> I have a large and lovely bungalow right above the beach. It is a tropical region with a lawn to the beach and a row of palm trees between us and the sea. The area is reminiscent of Fiji, with jungle covered peninsulas on both sides of the cove. The swimming is superb. There are no rocks or coral on the beach. It is all pure sand and within a few feet shelves off into deep water. The weather is perfect. We have warm days yet it is cold enough at night to enjoy a blanket.[1]

He concluded his letter by informing his friends this break was the first holiday he had taken in years. Nicol never took a vacation from his profession. Since his first tour abroad with the Odyssey Tour, he viewed travel as a means to procure an income. Initially he bought items on his trips to sell. Then the lectures started in 1931. Now, forty-four years later, he prepared to end his lucrative career.

There is no indication among Nicol's papers and correspondence that he came to a definite decision to discontinue his extensive travels. But the frequency of comments in his letters about needing additional rest, complaints about the weather and looking forward to quiet time at Lashio Lodge began to increase.

In another letter written to John Archbold, Nicol again shared his contentment with the month in Mexico:

> We are in Mexico for January, some seven miles north of Manzanillo on the Pacific Ocean. There is superb swimming only a few feet away. Azure skies and brilliant sunshine may be expected daily. Unlike Hawaii with its coral studded coast, here there are miles of untrammeled, pristine beach with large waves and water of a pleasant temperature; I spend hours daily in the sea.[2]

The following two winters, 1974-75 and 1975-76, were the last lecture circuits for Nicol. Unlike other lecturers who generally made new movies every other year, Nicol had produced a new film each year. Although he retired from the expedition portion of his career after the Alaska trip in 1973, he was able to continue with the lectures for an additional two years from the frequency of his previous travel films.

Retirement income concerned Nicol. The financial difficulties of his parents and their later years at The Crossroads carried an important message to their son. The mansion had been in such a state of disrepair when his father died that Nicol sold the place. The once opulent home, The Crossroads, where his parents had lived since he was nine years old, was flattened by a bulldozer. Nicol placed the money in savings. He wanted to be financially prepared for his future.

Lecturing was a lucrative career except for large expenses incurred when developing new material. The cost of expeditions, transportation between lecture locations, lodging, and numerous incidental items turned a fair lecture fee into a mediocre income. For a series of fifteen shows in Canada during January 1974, Nicol grossed $6,265. Over the nine-day booking period he traveled from Winnipeg, where he did four shows for $426 each, to Victoria where he presented two shows for $220 apiece. A show lasted from eighty to ninety minutes. During his busiest season, he had 180 engagements. Although a good income, it did not place him among the wealthy.

If wealth was Nicol's desire, he was in the wrong profession. Through experience, first from his parents insolvency and later from Moira's determined frugality, Nicol learned to economize and save. When he retired in 1976, his finances were in order.

The greatest boon to his income unexpectedly occurred after his father's death. Nicol had supported his father by the sale of his mother's jewels. Necklaces, rings and diamond bracelets brought upwards of four thousand dollars with each sale. During the three years between Sue's death and R.H.'s, his father appeared to spend every remaining penny provided by Nicol on an invention he and a friend were working on in the garage at The Crossroads.

R.H. worked on a series of supposedly worthwhile inventions over a period of fifteen years. Partnerships were formed and private stock sales were made among friends and family, including John and the late Armar Archbold, the family in Pennsylvania and anyone else R.H. could persuade. Unfortunately the invention remained unfinished when he died in 1962.

Unknown to Nicol, R.H.'s greatest assets were various properties he acquired during the late fifties and early sixties. With the assistance of R.H.'s previous associates, land documents, deeds, shares of stock and miscellaneous business papers were rescued from the old safe in the study at The Crossroads. Nicol immediately began to sell the land, the most valuable of which was a recent purchase located along the coast of California in Santa Cruz County and at the proposed site of the Auburn Dam east of Sacramento, California. The money Nicol set aside for retirement began to accumulate.

Selling his feature films also began to generate additional income for Nicol. His first sale occurred unexpectedly when the U.S. Navy contacted him in the spring of 1970. They were interested in purchasing his film of Morocco. Not only did they want the 3,000 feet of sixteen-millimeter motion picture, they also requested his lecture be taped and the four to six thousand feet of outs or raw footage that Nicol and Art cut during the editing. The Navy was prepared to pay $5,000.[3]

Nicol agreed. He planned to use the movie for one more lecture season, but it was nearly six years old and the number of engagements it would bring was negligible. It had seen its best years.

A Navy official traveled from Quantico, Virginia, to California to meet with Nicol and Art. The film sale was finalized. They were never privy to the Navy's reason for wanting the entire Morocco footage.

Film sales continued to provide an income. The films on Ireland and Iran sold for $1,500[4] apiece for a television syndication series titled "Ports of Call." The Scotland and Australia films brought $3,000 apiece from Ralph Windoes Travelogues, Inc., another travel-lecture business. The remainder of the sales went to other lecturers, while only a few were used for television. Much of the remaining footage was lost when Art and Virginia's river house burned to the ground after a stray ember from a campfire blew onto the shake roof. For years Nicol and Art had edited in the upstairs of the Hall's modest cabin between the weekends of guests and entertaining. All the outs, the unused footage, and unsold feature films fell victim to the flames.

Nicol ventured on one more trip after his retirement. With friends from Burlingame and Choate, he traveled aboard the Royal Viking, cruising through the Baltic Sea to Stockholm, Copenhagen and Leningrad. Leningrad was the only city he had visited previously. With only a few countries in the world that Nicol had not traveled to, Denmark and Sweden were two more he could now mark off of his short list. The remaining nations he would never see.

He had traveled around the world many times. He belonged to the Circumnavigators Club, the Explorers Club and the Adventurers Club. He met the requirements for membership in most travel clubs. He was among the first to explore Hainan Island, drive across the Burma Road, photograph Angel Falls and many, many more adventuresome firsts. Few individuals could claim such feats. Nicol, a great traveler and adventurer, had explored the crossroads of the world.

His insatiable curiosity and persistent nature were fodder for his adventuresome spirit. Even after Nicol gave up expeditions filled with travel firsts, he often found himself drawn to the little-known attractions of a well-traveled country. He had to find the "blue men" in the Sahara, experience a whaling expedition, or search for the Komodo dragon. To many in his audiences, his adventures were as thrilling as ever.

Nicol's focus on people did become more apparent. A wandering social register, he knew people around the world. Everyone graciously welcomed Nicol, inviting him to every social occasion, providing introductions and letters of recommendation. Nicol never forgot anyone. He remembered names, addresses and phone numbers of his fondest friends forever. A polite, charming and unassuming man, Nicol thanked every host and hostess, each interviewee and any brief acquaintance for their hospitality. As a result, Nicol was always invited to return and his name graced social registers around the world.

Nicol was a keen observer. He sought the unusual, the adventure and the people of a place whether he was the first American visitor or merely another traveler among many. Nicol received recognition and awards from numerous travel organizations and societies where he lectured over the years. They all spoke highly of his career and offered him well-deserved recognition. Among the dozens of awards he was granted, the Geographic Society of Chicago summed up Nicol's career most aptly when they presented him with their Special Merit Award:

> The Geographic Society of Chicago presents to Nicol Smith its Special Merit Award for his consistent reliability in the production of travel and documentary films that for more than 30 years have helped stimulate public interest in the global scene, and for his prominent role in the film-lecture series of the Geographic Society of Chicago specifically, and in the profession generally.
>
> Especially notable is his enthusiasm for the documentation of remote areas of the earth. He has traveled the highways and the byways to bring the far corners of a wide world to the doorstep of Chicagoans—always presented with integrity and impeccable taste, and in a spirit of congenial cooperation.[5]

The awards gratified Nicol. Weary of travel, he could now enjoy the many rewards of his occupation. Each award was framed and hung on the wall of Lashio Lodge.

Among the idiosyncrasies of Nicol's travel, he never returned to the locations of his service during World War II. Although in France on numerous occasions, he never ventured to Vichy where he had spent the four tense months of service for the OSS. He also never returned to Burma, Thailand, China or Ceylon where nearly two and a half years of his life was spent and resulted in the successful conclusion of an important OSS mission.

An additional important characteristic of Nicol's career was his favored modes of travel. Not a rugged individual, he preferred the minimal luxury of a jeep or a car for touring remote country. When wheels were not practical, he opted for water travel. Nicol also was not fond of air travel. Helicopters and small airplanes were only tools to aid in capturing scenes on film. Generally they were left to Art, while Nicol remained on the ground and made new acquaintances and adopted unusual pets.

Friends were an ever-important part of Nicol's life. A prolific letter writer, he graced friends around the world with pages of his scrawled longhand. He remained forever close to his best friends. In 1970, Barbara Hutton, a childhood friend, lay extremely ill at the Mark Hopkins Hotel in San Francisco with a suite of twenty-three rooms for her entourage. She requested Nicol's company. Informed he could remain with her for only ten minutes, she weakly demanded he stay indefinitely. Holding her hand, Nicol bent close to hear her low voice. She offered Nicol her home in Mexico with its fifteen servants for his winter retreats. He declined, but remained with her for several hours. Writing to a friend, he shared his hopes that his visit had alleviated her loneliness. He felt profoundly sad that Barbara, a woman whose wealth he understood to be near a hundred million dollars,[6] was so alone. He found her as beautiful as he had during their childhood.

He remained as loyal and close to Anne, his mother-in-law, to Miss MacAleer, his employer at the San Francisco school, and even to Moira, his ex-wife. He graced all of them with letters, which were generously written. Never attempting a manuscript for another book, he wrote volumes in letters to his dear friends around the world.

The career of a remarkable man ended. The travel to Mexico each winter continued for the next ten years, along with delightful summers at Lashio Lodge on the Stanislaus River. Among his many guests were childhood friends, travel contacts from around the world and new friends. From one friend, Barnaby Conrad, came a letter thanking Nicol:

> Just a note to thank you again for your incredibly kind interest in me and my life. It was a tremendous piece of luck bumping into you.... We are kindred souls of an ilk fast disappearing it seems to me. Sometimes I hear a voice, and packing my gladstone bag I try to follow it to the ends of the earth.
>
> I hope you are thinking of writing some fiction; I want to read it when you do.
>
> Will be up in San Francisco on the tenth. Hope you get down from the frog-jumping county sometime.
>
> Otra vez, mil gracias!!![7]

Barnaby visited Nicol's river home and completed a portrait of Nicol that captured his lifelong career far better than the finest prose. Seated with his dog at his side, Nicol held a travel book about Argentina on his lap while a map of South America adorned the table beside him. The portrait of the "Traveler of The Crossroads" still silently bedecks the wall of the retired adventurer's room.

EPILOGUE

Nicol Smith still spends his summers at Lashio Lodge along the Stanislaus River. In February of 1986 he was stricken by a debilitating stroke which left him an invalid. He has required constant care since that time and the succeeding eight years have brought little change in his condition.

He has become a quiet man, his stories of adventure locked within his mind. With a prodding question he will share his travels and adventures with a good friend. Nicol's health remains constant. He leads a quiet life while his sleep often brings dreams of times gone by.

NOTES

Abbreviations used in the Notes are as follows:

NS for Nicol Smith
RHS for Robert Hays Smith
JDA for John D. Archbold

1: Settling in Uncle Sam's Western Possession

1. Letter from RHS to the Dickinson Class of 1898 Alumni, Third
    Annual Circular Letter of the Class of 1898, Dickinson College,
    Carlisle, Pennsylvania, 1901.
2. Author interview with NS, Dorrington, California, 1991-1993.
3. "The Law and the Lawyer's Sphere," THE FORUM, June 1900,
    pp. 194-197.
4. THE FORUM, p 1.
5. History of Cumberland and Adams Counties, Pennsylvania.
    Chicago, by F. W. Beers, Warner, Beers & Co. 1886, p. 524.
6. Author interview with Elizabeth Knauer and Helen Little,
    Thorndale, Pennsylvania, July 24, 1992.
7. Author interview with Elizabeth Knauer and Helen Little,
    July 24, 1992.
8. Author interview with NS, Dorrington, California, 1991-1993.
9. "Our Debt to Science," ORATIONS, Dickinson College, Student
    Orations, 1898.
10. Pan-Pacific Who's Who, An International Reference Work;
    Biographical encyclopedia of men and women of substantial
    achievement. Honolulu Star-Bulletin, Ltd. 1940-1941 edition,
    p. 646.
11. Letter from RHS, Third Annual Circular Letter.
12. Letter from RHS, Third Annual Circular Letter.
13. Pan-Pacific Who's Who, p. 96.

14. RHS passed the bar exam on November 23, 1903. Telephone interview with Paula Bankett, Librarian Archivist for the State Bar of California, San Francisco, California.
15 Letter from RHS to Dr. J.H. Morgan, President, Dickinson College, May 23, 1919.
16. Telephone interview with Andrew Jameson, Bohemian Club Histographer, November 1991.
17. *Pan-Pacific Who's Who*, p. 646.
18. *A Companion to California*, by James D. Hart, University of California Press, Berkeley, 1987, p. 441.
19. The major train passenger station, the Oakland Mole, was built on piers off Oakland's western shore. The East Bay, Oakland, Berkeley and Alameda had light damage from the 1906 earthquake and remained fully functioning communities.
20. Letter from Elizabeth Knauer to author, February 7, 1992.

2: Saved at Santa Cruz

1. Letter from RHS to the Dickinson Class of 1898 Alumni, Tenth Annual Circular Letter of the Class of 1898, Dickinson College, Carlisle, Pennsylvania, 1908.
2. *Inventing the Dream, California through the Progressive Era*, by Kevin Starr, Oxford University Press, 1985, pp. 199-207.
3. *Inventing the Dream*, p. 204.
4. Letter from RHS, Tenth Annual Circular Letter, 1908.
5. Sue entered the name as Robert Hayes Smith in the *Chap Record*, spelling the middle name incorrectly. It should have been Hays.
6. *Chap Record*, Frederick A. Stokes Company, Publishers, New York. Entries are made by the hand of Susan Alice Nicol.
7. Letter from RHS to Doctor J.H. Morgan, President, Dickinson College, Carlisle, Pennsylvania, May 23, 1919.
8. Letter from RHS to Dr. J.H. Morgan, May 23, 1919.
9. *Inventing the Dream*, p. 244.
10. *A Companion to California*, by James D. Hart, University of California Press, Berkeley, 1987, p. 492.
11. *Who's Who in California, A Biographical Directory*, Who's Who Publishing Company, San Francisco, 1928-1929, p. 293.
12. "Masers, Beggars write to Millionaire Miner in Vain; He Doesn't Read the Letters," *San Francisco Chronicle*, October 20, 1925.
13. "Men You Should Know About," *Engineering and Mining Journal-Press*, April 10, 1926.

14. *Carson Inv. Co., et al. v. Calumet & Arizona Mining Company; Same v. Phelps Dodge Corporation.* 29 Federal Reporter 2d., November 19, 1928, pp. 300-305.
15. *Carson Inv. Co.,* p. 304.
16. *Carson Inv. Co.,* pp. 302-303.
17. *Carson Inv. Co.,* p. 303.
18. *Carson Inv. Co.,* p. 304.
19. *Carson Inv. Co.,* pp. 304-305.
20. "Panic Sequel of Inventor's Big Windfall," *San Francisco Chronicle,* February 18, 1923.
21. "Carson Copper Suit Settled for 20 Million," *San Francisco Chronicle,* May 11, 1929, p. 3.

3: Two Journeys to Columbia

1. *Sonora Banner,* Sonora California, November 29, 1892.
2. Letter from Mrs. Suzanne Pehkoff to Irene and Lawrence Nicol, October 2, 1967. Lyle is believed to have been the maiden name of Margaret Nicol.
3. United States Census of 1860, Tuolumne County.
4. Letter from Mrs. Suzanne Pehkoff, October 2, 1967.
5. James was born in 1852. Columbia Cemetery Archives, Columbia, California, December 1991.
6. U.S. Census of 1860. Census records spell the family name as Nichol.
7. Columbia Cemetery Archives, December 1991.
8. U.S. Census of 1860, Tuolumne County.
9. Based on known dates and places derived from census and birth records, the journey west and then east must have been made when son, Colin, and then daughter, Margaret, respectively were very young.
10. According to the 1860 census, Alice did not attend school in Columbia, only Susan attended.
11. Columbia Cemetery Archives, December 1991.
12. "In the Court of Sessions of The County of Tuolumne," January term 1860, and "Tuolumne County Jail Book," 1859 and 1860. Provided by the Tuolumne County Archives.
13. The court documents spell Colin Nicol as Colin McNichol. This is the only reference found during research that includes the "Mc." Often Nicol is mistakenly spelled Nichol.
14. Since Susan had lived at home prior to her marriage during the year of 1860, she was recorded as a family member for the 1860 census.

15. *Index to Deeds, Grantors & Grantees*, book A, vol. 13, James Nicol (M. A. Lewis et al) October 14, 1864, p. 503.
16. Columbia Cemetery Archives.
17. Columbia Cemetery Archives. Information provided to the CCA by George Nicol and Julia Nicol's nephew, Benjamin Mock Joseph.
18. "Jamestown-1854, A Bride's Letter From Jamestown, 1854," *CHISPA, The Quarterly of the Tuolumne County Historical Society*, vol. 15, no. 1, Sonora, California, July-September 1975, pp. 501-502. Thanks acknowledged to Mrs. Jean Nicol.
19. "In Memorandum," *Union Democrat*, by E.W. Holland. March 12, 1910.
20. *CHISPA*, p. 501.
21. Adelaide was baptized in 1867. Records of marriages, births, baptisms and deaths from the St. James Church, Sonora, California.
22. To this day, a law degree is not a requirement for entering the legal profession in California.
23. "Mrs. Clark's New Palace," *Union Democrat*, Sonora, California, September 17, 1887. The regal home of George and Julia Clark Nicol still stands in Sonora at the corner of Stewart and Gold Streets.
24. "Hon. G. W. Nicol," *The Banner*, Sonora, California, December 8, 1922.

4: Sonora to San Francisco

1. Stockton City Directory, 1891.
2. *Dodge Genealogy*, 1902, p. 37. The exact date was June 30, 1892.
3. "The Dodge-Shepherd Wedding," *San Francisco Call*, February 16, 1991, p. 6.
4. "Remember Your Classmates? Everybody Knew Susie, Seen in Top Row," *Stockton Daily Evening Record*, March 25, 1927, p. 15.
5. "Society and the Cuisine," *San Francisco Call*, Sept. 30, 1906, p. 24.
6. Columbia Cemetery Archives, December 1991.
7. Columbia Cemetery Archives, December 1991.
8. "The Smith-Nicol Wedding," *Stockton Daily Evening Record*, June 27, 1908.
9. *San Francisco Chronicle*, June 28, 1908.
10. *San Francisco Chronicle*, June 28, 1908.
11. "Dr. Washington Dodge, City and County Assessor," *San Francisco and its Municipal Administration - 1902-4*, pp. 54-56.

NOTES

12. "Dr. Washington Dodge," p. 56.
13. "Dr. Washington Dodge," p. 56.
14. "Comment & Opinion," by Phil Francis, *San Francisco Call*, July 25, 1912, p. 6.

5: The Fairmont Baby

1. *THE FAIRMONT*, an advertising brochure, 1907.
2. "Magnificent Hotel Is Formally Opened," *San Francisco Call*, April 19, 1907.
3. Smith, Robert Hays, Tenth Annual Circular Letter of the Class of 1898, Dickinson College, Carlisle, Pennsylvania, 1908.
4. *Chap Record*, by Susan Nicol, 1907-1908.
5. *Five Handkerchiefs in Haiti*, private writings by Nicol Smith, 1933, p. 4.
6. *A Companion to California* p. 377.

6: Education: California to Connecticut to California

1. Nicol's notes on Belmont Boarding School, p. 22.
2. Nicol's notes, p. 23.
3. James D. Phelan, 1861-1930, was elected to the U.S. Senate in 1915 as a Democrat. The tutor, Mr. John Moran was born in the 1840s which made him a young man in his thirties when he tutored James Phelan and eighty when he tutored Nicol.
4. Smith, Robert Hays, Twenty-seventh Annual Circular Letter of the Class of 1898, Dickinson College, Carlisle, Pennsylvania, 1925.
5. Application for admission, Choate School, July 2, 1925.
6. "The Calcutta Sweepstakes," by Francis Nicol Smith, *The Choate Literary Magazine*, May 1928, pp. 7-8.
7. *The Choate Literary Magazine*, p. 8.
8. "The Black Baron," by F. Nicol Smith. *The Choate Literary Magazine*, May 1929, pp. 35-38.
9. *The Choate Literary Magazine*, p. 37.
10. *The Choate Literary Magazine*, p. 38.
11. Application to Stanford from the Choate School for Francis Nicol Smith, June 1929.

7: The Odyssey

1. Nicol Smith's diary from June 27, 1929 through September 10, 1929, p. 1.

2. Nicol Smith's diary, p. 2.
3. Nicol Smith's diary, p. 13.
4. Nicol Smith's diary, p. 15.
5. Nicol Smith's diary, pp. 15-16.
6. Nicol Smith's diary, pp. 21-22.
7. Nicol Smith's diary, pp. 22-23.
8. Nicol Smith's diary, p. 24.
9. Nicol Smith's diary, p. 46.
10. Nicol Smith's diary, p. 3.
11. Nicol Smith's diary, p. 25.
12. Nicol Smith's diary, p. 32.
13. Nicol Smith's diary, p. 36.
14. Nicol Smith's diary, p. 37.
15. Nicol Smith's diary, pp. 96-97.
16. Nicol Smith's diary, p. 128.
17. Nicol Smith's diary, p. 140.
18. Nicol Smith's diary, p. 149.
19. Nicol Smith's diary, p. 151.
20. Nicol Smith's diary, pp. 181-183.
21. An active volcano on the island of Stromboli off the northeastern coast of Sicily.
22. Nicol Smith's diary, pp. 185-186.
23. Nicol Smith's diary, p. 229.

8: The Nudist Colony

1. The Choate School, report of Francis Nicol Smith for the year ending June 1929.
2. Stanford University, application for candidate Francis Nicol Smith, May 16, 1929.
3. Letter from NS to JDA, October 10, 1929.
4. Letter from NS to JDA, February, 1930.
5. Letter from NS to JDA, February, 1930.
6. Letter from NS to JDA, May 9, 1930.
7. "Seven Sinless Days of Sunshine," by Nicol Smith, 1931.
8. Intourist, notes by NS, 1931.
9. Intourist, notes by NS, 1931.
10. Intourist, notes by NS, 1931.
11. Letter from NS to JDA, June 6, 1931.

NOTES

9: Capitola

1. Letter from NS to JDA, April 30, 1931.
2. Now known as Capitola, California. In 1919 it was a seasonal township known as Camp Capitola. Rispin later named the town Capitola-by-the-Sea.
3. "Behind the Wall & Across the Road," by Mary Bryand, *The Mid-County Post,* September 10, 1991, pp. 5 & 7.
4. August 16, 1929 was the exact date. Dates provided by Lewis S. Deasy, Capitola Historian, Capitola, California, in an interview with the author.
5. RHS had previously purchased two real estate holdings in Santa Cruz County. At this point he formed Nicol and Smith to hold his earlier purchases.
6. Letter from RHS to Dr. J.H. Morgan, President of Dickinson College, May 23, 1919.
7. Letter from NS to JDA, November 28, 1931.
8. College Entrance Examination Board, report of Scholastic Aptitude Test, for Smith, Francis Nicol held on June 19, 1929. Records provided by Stanford University.
9. Letter from Dr. Karl M. Cowdery, Assistant Registrar, Stanford University, to Charles T. Vandervort, Dean, Menlo Junior College, September 30, 1930.
10. Return letter from Dean Vandervort to Dr. Cowdery, October 3, 1930.

10: Letter from Nickerie

1. *Tiger-Man, An Odyssey of Freedom,* by Julian Duguid, New York: The Century Co., 1932.
2. Mato Grosso is the current spelling of the Brazilian state.
3. *East of the Sun?--Or West of the Moon,* private writings by Nicol Smith upon his return from Haiti and French Guiana in 1933, pp. 5-6.
4. *Five Handkerchiefs in Haiti,* private writings by Nicol Smith upon his return from Haiti and French Guiana in 1933, pp. 15-16.
5. *Au Bagne,* by Albert Londres, published in 1923, supposedly brought about modifications to the penal system resulting from the author's investigations.
6. *Cayenne,* by Alexis Danan, published in 1933, closely paralleled *Au Bagne* despite allegations of changes brought about because of the book.

7.   The Duez story is related here as it was originally recorded by
      Nicol during his sessions with Madame Duez, prior to any
      publication of the story.
8.   The name "black book" became Nicol's name for the small,
      black notebook. He continued to use this name for the
      notebook in conversation with the author when referring to the
      Madame Duez story. The name has endured the years.
9.   "Strange Love Tragedy of the Rich Widow of Devil's Isle." *The
      Saturday Home Magazine, New York Evening Journal.* The article
      was headlined on the front cover as "Revelations of the 'Widow
      of Devil's Isle," April 18, 1936, pp. 4-5.
10.   Letter from NS to Mr. David Lewis of Warner Brothers Studios,
      January 24, 1938. All information regarding the potential
      movie of the Duez story was provided by interviews between NS
      and the author and archived files at USC Archives of
      Performing Arts, School of Cinema-Television, University of
      Southern California, University Park, Los Angeles, California.
11.   Copyright Agreement, provided by USC Archives,
      January 20, 1941.
12.   Inter-Office Communication, from Bryan Foy to Mr. MacEwen,
      Warner Bros. Pictures, Inc. April 23, 1941.
13.   Letter from NS to JDA, c/o Archbold Estate, Standard Oil
      Building, 26 Broadway Street, New York City, New York,
      January 7, 1935.
14.   *Bush Master,* by Nicol Smith, Bobbs-Merrill Company,
      Indianapolis, Indiana, 1941, p. 1.
15.   Letter from NS to JDA, addressed from Nickerie, Dutch Guiana,
      no date provided on the letter.
16.   This is the Dutch spelling of the name, also spelled Courantyne
      or Corantyne River.

11: Expedition to Hainan

1.   "An Adventure in Dutch Guiana (Illustrated)," Alice Seckels-
      Elsie Cross presents Nicol Smith in a Travel Talk, printed by the
      publicity agency, circa 1935.
2.   Author interview with Lois Ferguson Clauhsen, Murphys,
      California, June 1992.
3.   "Among the Big Knot Lois of Hainan," *The National Geographic
      Magazine,* 74:3, September 1938, pp. 399-418.
4.   Malignant malaria is the most severe form of malaria. In many
      cases the symptoms recur every three days.

5. "Hainan, New Japanese Conquest, Where They Pay Cash for Wives," *The Boston Herald,* March 19, 1939, p. 3.
6. Nicol Smith's diary from August 13, 1937 to September 19, 1937, p. 55.

12: Moira

1. *The Descendants of John Dustin Archbold and Ann Mills Archbold,* by Beatrice Fessenden Moore, 1973, p. 181.
2. *The Prize, The Epic Quest for Oil, Money & Power,* by Daniel Yergin, Simon & Schuster, 1992, pp. 98-99.
3. *The Prize,* by Daniel Yergin, p. 98.
4. *The Descendants of John Dustin Archbold,* by Moore, p. 177.
5. The uncle's given name was John Foster Archbold. He was Anne's only brother.
6. Story provided from author interview with John Dana Archbold, who was nine years old when his mother moved the children to the United States. Interview conducted at Fox Lease Farm, Upperville Virginia, July 18, 1992.
7. Letter from Moira Archbold to NS, December 6, 1937.
8. Telegram from Moira Archbold to NS, March 3, 1937.
9. Fifty-five years later, the author repeated this story to NS as Rebecca McBride had told it to the author. Nicol laughed zestfully. It was a story he had remembered fondly over the years.
10. Letter from Moira Archbold to NS, February 28, 1938.
11. Letter from Moira Archbold to NS, March 3, 1938.
12. Letter from NS to JDA, March 16, 1938.
13. Letter from NS to JDA, March 16, 1938.
14. Author interview with NS, Dorrington, California, September 1991-June 1993.

13: Burma Road

1. Letter from NS to JDA, July 1938.
2. Letter from Joe Mulholland at Rockefeller Plaza to NS, December 1, 1948.
3. "Shipping News—Round the World Trip," *South China Morning Post,* December 27, 1939.
4. Many names have changed since pre-World War II when Nicol visited this area. Names used are those known at the time of his travel. New names are footnoted. Pakhoi is now Beihai.

5. Laokai, French Indo-China is now Lao Cai, Vietnam.
6. *Burma Road*, by Nicol Smith, Bobbs-Merrill Company, 1940, p. 188.
7. *Burma Road*, p. 227.
8. *Burma Road*, p. 290.

14: The Guianas

1. Agreement between Nicol Smith of Burlingame, California and the Bobbs-Merrill Company, April 6, 1937.
2. Letter from the Bobbs-Merrill Company written by D.L. Chambers to NS, December 11, 1939.
3. Letter from the Bobbs-Merrill Company to NS, December 11, 1939.
4. "New York Times Book Review," *New York Times*, March 3, 1940, p. 4,
5. Letter from the Bobbs-Merrill Company written by D.L. Chambers to NS, December 19, 1940.
6. Letter from NS to Anne Archbold, Paramaribo, Dutch Guiana, May 30, 1941.
7. "Color Glows in the Guianas, French and Dutch," *The National Geographic Magazine*, 83:4, April 1943, pp. 459-480.

15: Lashio Lodge on the Stanislaus

1. "Frank D. Nicol Laid to Rest," *Stockton Daily Independent*, March 23, 1910, p. 8.
2. Calaveras County Historical Archives, 1910 Land Deed Book.

16: The OSS

1. *The Unfinished Century, America Since 1900*, general editor William E. Leuchtenburg, Columbia University, Little, Brown and Company, Boston, 1973, p. 513.
2. *OSS, The Secret History of America's First Central Intelligence Agency*, by R. Harris Smith, University of California Press, Berkeley and Los Angeles, California, 1972, p. 2.
3. *OSS, The Secret History*, p. 2.
4. *Donovan of OSS*, by Corey Ford, Little, Brown & Company, Toronto Canada, p. 337.
5. *Donovan of OSS*, p. 134.

6. Curriculum Vitae of John Dana Archbold, dated
    November 27, 1941.
7. Letter from Joseph A. Rogers, Colonel, U.S. Army to General
    Raymond E. Lee, G. S. C., War Department, U. S. Army,
    Assistant Chief of Staff, G-2, December 29, 1941.
8. Letter from R. P. McCullough, Naval Intelligence Office, San
    Francisco, California to Rear Admiral T.S. Wilkinson, USN,
    Director of Naval Intelligence, Office of the Chief of Naval
    Operations, Navy Department, Washington, D. C.,
    December 31, 1941.
9. *War Report of the OSS, Volume I*, an official history of the OSS
    prepared by the SSU History Project, Introduction by Kermit
    Roosevelt, 1976, p. 74.
10. "Nicol Smith," resume prepared by or for the Assistant
    Secretary of State, stamped for approval by Mr. Shaw,
    April 23, 1942.
11. Memorandum from William H. Vanderbilt to Colonel
    Goodfellow, May 20, 1942, Folder 2653, Box 19/8, Entry 139,
    Register 226, U.S. National Archives, Washington, D. C.

17: Mission to Vichy

1. Chronological Cross-Index of SO Undertakings, October 1-31,
    1942, Register, Entry 99, Box 81, Folder 74, National Archives,
    Washington, D.C.
2. Soldiers of the Night, The Story of the French Resistance, by
    David Schoenbrun, Published by E. P. Dutton, 1980, New York,
    p. 35.
3. Soldiers of the Night, p. 63.
4. Soldiers of the Night, p. 54.
5. Soldiers of the Night, p. 65.
6. Letter from William J. Donovan, OSS, to G. Howland Shaw,
    State Department, May 9th, 1942, National Archives,
    Washington, D.C.
7. Letter from William J. Donovan, OSS, to G. Howland Shaw,
    State Department.
8. Nicol Smith's diary, August 8, 1942 to November 1, 1942, p. 4.
9. Nicol Smith's diary, p. 6.
10. War Report of the OSS, Volume I, p.139.
11. War Report of the OSS, Volume I, p.139.
12. Message Center, Communications, London, Vol. 1, 1 January
    1945, National Archives, Washington, D.C., pp. 53-60.

13. State Department Telegram files, 123 Smith, Nicol/5, National Archives, Washington, D.C.
14. Nicol Smith's diary, p. 8.
15. Nicol Smith's diary, p. 24.
16. Today her medal and picture stands in a frame in Nicol's home. He and Laura remained life-long friends. Nicol received her medals when she passed away.
17. Chronological Cross-Index of SO Undertakings, National Archives, p.8.
18. Nicol still tells this story and he still owns the painting.
19. Letter from NS to Anne Archbold, October 15, 1942.
20. Soldiers of the Night, pp.200-201.
21. Chronological Cross-Index of SO Undertakings, National Archives, p. 8.

18: Mission to Thailand

1. "Origin of proposed Hainan Mission," Secret memo from Captain Carl O. Hoffman to Ensign Putzel, March 17, 1943, National Archives.
2. Author interview with Joseph Lazarsky, July 19, 1992, Middleburg, Virginia.
3. Each of the young men had American code names. Cary's name was Karawek Srivicharn.
4. Sal's name was Sompongse Salyabongse.
5. Ian's name was Ian Khambanonda.
6. Ken's name was Karoon Kengradomying.
7. Paul's name was Phon Indradat.
8. Details about the men on their education and personalities was provided during the author's interviews with NS, Dorrington, California, 1991-1993.
9. Charles' name was Chok na Ranong.
10. Pow's name was Pow Khamourai. Pete's name was Pisoot Sudasna. Bunny's name was Bunyen Sasiratna. Sam's name was Savasti Cheo-sakul.
11. Author interview with NS, 1991-1993.
12. Letter and report from NS to Colonel John Coughlin, July 22, 1944, Folder 3424, Box 202, Entry 154, Register 226, National Archives, Washington, D.C.
13. Letter and report from NS to Colonel John Coughlin, July 22, 1944.
14. Ben's name was Boonrod Binson.

15. Letter and report from NS to Colonel John Coughlin, August 12, 1944. Cover letter was prepared by Colonel Robert Hall to General Donovan at headquarters in Washington, D.C. on August 18, 1944. Folder 3424, Box 202, Entry 154, Register 226, National Archives, Washington, D.C.
16. Letter and report from NS to Colonel John Coughlin, p. 2.
17. Letter and report from NS to Colonel John Coughlin, p. 2.
18. Cover letter from Colonel Robert Hall to General Donovan on NS report.
19. Nick's name was Nithipatna Jalichandra.
20. Jim's name was Chintamye Amatayakul.
21. Letter from Colonel John Coughlin to Lt. Colonel Carl O. Hoffman, in Washington, D.C., March 30, 1945, Folder 2220, Box 126, Entry 154, Register 226, National Archives, Washington, D.C.
22. Letter from Lt. Col. O.C. Doering, Jr. to Col. John G. Coughlin, OSS Headquarters IBT, June 6, 1945. From NS' private collection.

19: The Public Image

1. Letter from NS to Anne Archbold , June 2, 1944.
2. Letter from NS to Susan Smith, January 21, 1943.
3. The collection of NS's letters to his mother-in-law was shared with the author by the late John D. Archbold, her son and Nicol's lifelong friend.
4. Letter from NS to Susan Smith, August 22, 1944.
5. Letter from NS to Susan Smith, August 30, 1944.
6. Letter from NS to Susan Smith, August 30, 1944.
7. Letter from NS to Susan Smith, August 30, 1944.
8. Letter from NS to RHS and Sue Smith, mid-1943.
9. Agreement between NS and Lloyd George, signed at Kandy, Ceylon on August 17, 1945, and witnessed by William C. Williamson, Jr. and Esther Lee Pierson.
10. Blake Clark had written three books before his association with NS. The other two were *Paradise Limited* and *Robinson Crusoe, USN*.
11. "Siam's Frustrated Underground," *New York Times*, by John Bicknell, Sept. 8, 1946, book review of *Into Siam Underground Kingdom*.
12. Coughlin to Major General Robert B. McClure, June 30 1945, Folder 228, Box 20, Entry 110, Register 226, National Archives,

Washington, D.C.
13. Coughlin to Major General Robert B. McClure, June 30 1945.
14. Smith, Nicol, 0914632, Major, AUS, AUS, found in Nicol's personal papers at Lashio Lodge.
15. Interview with returned Men, S & T Branch, OSS, April 28, 1945. National Archives.
16. Official Citation, WASH-OSS-PERS, Freedom of Information Act, Central Intelligence Agency, Washington, D.C.
17. Theater Service Record, August 17, 1945, Freedom of Information Act, Central Intelligence Agency, Washington, D.C.
18. Author's interview with Leopold Karwaski, Scranton, Pennsylvania, July 1992.
19. Letter from Chok na Ranong to NS, February 26, 1994.

20: Trip to Tibet

1. Letter from NS to Anne Archbold, August 3, 1943.
2. Now known as Shache, a city of China in the southwestern Sinkiang-Uigur Autonomous Region.
3. Letter from NS to Anne Archbold, November 20, 1944.
4. Recorded by NS on June 30, 1947. This story has not been verified by the author, but instead is used to symbolize the type of story and investigation Nicol liked to use to make his lectures and movies interesting.
5. "India - Fact & Fancy," lecture by Nicol Smith, Curran Theatre, October 26, 1948, p. 4. This statement was taken from the speech as Nicol wrote it. The information stands on his word only. It has not been verified.
6. Letter from NS to Anne Archbold, October 8, 1947.

21: The Age of Movies

1. An Afghan especially one of Indo-Iranian stock and Moslem religion.
2. Ladakh was the easternmost province of Kashmir when Nicol traveled there. Up to 100 years previously it was the westernmost province of Tibet and was still often called West Tibet when he made his trip. Ladakh bordered on Soviet-controlled Sinkiang as well as on Tibet.
3. "India—Fact & Fancy," a lecture by Nicol Smith, a Town Hall presentation with Paul Speegle as moderator, October 26, 1948. The program cover has the word peace in large letters and

underneath it says "World Confidence, World Citizenship, World Understanding."

4. "India—Fact & Fancy," a lecture by Nicol Smith.
5. A division of China occupying 636,000 miles in the northwest.
6. Agreement between NS of Burlingame, California, and the Bobbs-Merrill Company, August 20, 1948.
7. "Books," The New York Times, June 29, 1949.
8. Writings from NS to Austin S. Moore on Anne Archbold, January 28, 1971. Mr. Moore was commissioned by John D. Archbold to write a biography, not for publication, about Anne Archbold. Nicol contributed a number of stories to Mr. Moore. The biography was never completed.
9. Letter from Anne Archbold to NS, date unknown.
10. Letter from NS to Anne Archbold, August 6, 1947.
11. Letter from NS to Anne Archbold, April 23, 1950.
12. Letter from NS to Anne Archbold, February 15, 1950.
13. Explorer's Holiday, by Nicol Smith, circa 1950 lecture circuit.
14. Letter from NS to Anne Archbold, April 8, 1950.
15. Notes from the private collection of NS written about Venezuela, 1950, p. 22.

22: Summers Along the Stanislaus

1. Letter from Moira Archbold Smith to NS, August 17, 1947.
2. Letter from Moira Archbold Smith to NS, August 25, 1947.
3. Letter from William Saroyan to NS, December 17, 1950.
4. "Herb Caen Classic," *San Francisco Sunday Chronicle*, September 12, 1993. Column originally appeared in the *San Francisco Examiner* on August 30, 1953.
5. "Culture in the Wilds," "Society Sketchbook," *San Francisco News Call Bulletin*, August 11, 1964, p. 13.
6. Letter from Anne Archbold to NS, June 3, 1952.
7. Letter from Joe Mulholland to NS, November 7, 1962.

23: From Adventure to Travelogs

1. Letter from Anne Archbold to NS, November 17, 1952.
2. Letter from Anne Archbold to NS, February 2, 1953.
3. "Susan Smith Says," *San Francisco Examiner*. April 27, 1958.
4. Letter from Sue Smith to Berens Nelson, April 11, 1958.
5. Letter from Herb Caen to NS, January, 1959.
6. Letter from RHS to Mr. and Mrs. Nicol, August 26, 1959.

7. San Francisco newspaper, circa September 4, 1958.
8. Letter from NS to Elizabeth Smith Knauer, January 13, 1965.
9. Letter from NS to Margery and Hugh Birch,
   November 16, 1965.
10. Letter from NS to Anne Archbold, January 24, 1964.
11. Letter from NS to Elizabeth Smith Knauer, July 7, 1962.
12. Letter from NS to Elizabeth Smith Knauer, July 7, 1962.

24: From Morocco to Alaska

1. Letter from NS to Anne Archbold, March 22, 1964.
2. Letter from NS to Elizabeth Smith Knauer, January 13, 1965.
3. Letter from Lois Stewart to NS, December 2, 1964.
4. Letter from NS to JDA, July 28, 1966.
5. Letter from NS to Anne Archbold, March 11, 1967.
6. Letter from NS to Margery and Hugh Birch, June 13, 1971.
7. Letter from NS to JDA, October 13, 1971.

25: Mexico Winters

1. Letter from NS to Margery and Hugh Birch, January 10, 1970.
2. Letter from NS to JDA, January 18, 1973.
3. Public Voucher For Purchases and Services, Department of the Navy, Voucher No. 43166, MCDEC, Quantico, VA. 22134, June 9, 1970.
4. Letter from Hunter Productions, Inc., to Mrs. Bunny Longe of Kamen Film Productions, June 28, 1974.
5. The Geographic Society of Chicago presented the Special Merit Award to Nicol Smith, April 14, 1973.
6. This is Nicol's estimate of Barbara Hutton's monetary worth.
7. Letter from Barnaby Conrad to NS, date unknown.

INDEX

Traveler of the Crossroads
The Life of Adventurer Nicol Smith
by Sharon E. Karr

To Order:
Return with payment to:

Log Cabin Manuscripts
P.O. Box 4341
Dorrington, CA 95223

Traveler of the Crossroads	$19.95	x ___ copies	=$____
Sales Tax (none for Oregon)	$1.45	x ___ copies	=$____
Shipping & handling $2.20 (foreign please add $2.00)			=$____
Total (U.S. currency only)			=$____

From:

Name _____

Address _____

City _____ State_____

Country & Zip Code _____